Changing Places

Changing Places

Britain's Demographic, Economic and Social Complexion

A.G. Champion, A.E. Green,
D.W. Owen, D.J. Ellin and
M.G. Coombes

Edward Arnold

© A.G. Champion, A.E. Green, D.W. Owen, D.J. Ellin and M.G. Coombes 1987

First published in Great Britain 1987 by
Edward Arnold (Publishers) Ltd, 41 Bedford Square, London WC1B 3DQ

Edward Arnold (Australia) Pty Ltd, 80 Waverley Road, Caulfield East,
Victoria 3145, Australia

Edward Arnold, 3 East Read Street, Baltimore, Maryland 21202, USA

British Library Cataloguing in Publication Data

Changing places: Britain's demographic, economic and social complexion.
  1. Labor supply——Great Britain——History
  ——20th century 2. Great Britain—— Population
  I. Champion, A.G.
  331.12′5′0941   HD5765.A5

  ISBN 0–7131–6498–0

Text set in 10/11pt Times Compugraphic
by Colset Private Limited, Singapore
Printed and bound
in Great Britain at the Alden Press, Oxford

Contents

List of tables

List of figures

Preface

The 1970s and 1980s have wrought massive changes in the nature and characteristics of places in Britain. Many of these changes represent the continuation of trends already well established in the first 25 years of the postwar period, but some were different in nature or in degree and, above all, these changes were now taking place in a very different context. Whereas the earlier decades witnessed significant growth – with relatively strong national economic growth in the 1950s and an upsurge in the birth rate in the early 1960s – developments in more recent years have taken place against the background of virtually zero population growth and deepening economic recession. Somewhat paradoxically, it is in fact this relative stagnation that has brought significant change to many places, because in a situation of static or even falling population and employment levels growth in one place must be associated with decline somewhere else – the so-called 'zero sum game' in the jargon of the American scenario-writers. In the prevailing attitudes of depression and despondency hanging over Britain in the 1980s, it is important to emphasize that many places *have* shown impressive growth in size and prosperity in recent years; so that the fact that their growth can be seen as being at the 'expense' of decline elsewhere brings the issues more sharply into focus.

The factors which are primarily responsible for bringing change to Britain's cities and towns can be considered under two headings. The first comprises those broad structural changes which are currently affecting all the advanced countries of the world as they move towards the 'post-industrial society', while at the same time having to cope with major changes in the world economic order. National statistics bear witness to general improvements in living standards, higher incomes, more women in work, higher levels of car ownership, more owner-occupied housing, more people working in non-manual occupations, and so on. Yet they also point to the emergence of issues which call for government action, such as the increase in the elderly population and ethnic minority groups, the fall in numbers of manufacturing jobs, and the rise in unemployment. The key feature of these national and often international trends is that they have different effects on different places, with the extent and particular kind of impact depending on the nature of individual cities and towns. For example, the worldwide decline in new shipbuilding orders and the problems of surplus capacity in the steel industry affect most severely places which are heavily dependent on those particular industries, while the growth in banking, finance and related services brings jobs to those places with an established reputation in this sector or with special advantages for this type of work – not usually the same places as those noted for their heavy engineering skills and very rarely employing the same type of staff, though the growth of low-level jobs in high street branches has been quite widely spread across the country.

The second main group of factors which help to explain why places are changing in their complexion relates to residential mobility, or – put rather more simply – to the fact that people 'change places'. To a large extent, this is literally the case, as people move into a house that some other people have recently moved out of, but the pattern is rarely one of simple exchange. Indeed the newcomers may well differ significantly in their number and characteristics from those moving out, while the distribution of the housing stock is continually being altered by the processes of construction, conversion and demolition. To a certain extent, the changing pattern of population distribution which results from this residential mobility reflects trends in the local availability of jobs and therefore is intimately related to the first group of factors which cause places to change, but a major development in recent years is the increase in the proportion of people moving for reasons not directly connected with work. There has been a substantial increase in the number of retired people for whom by definition access to a job is not a consideration, as there have been, too, in the number of people who work at or from their home and the proportion of households with two or more people working in different places. Taken along with the growing numbers of unemployed and self-employed and the greater ease of commuting over long distances, an increasing number of people do not have their choice of a town of residence determined by the location of an employer, while employers themselves have become increasingly conscious of the residential preferences of their staff and other labour force considerations in making decisions about where to open or relocate their businesses. Through their availability for work as well as through the jobs they generate because of their need for local services, people are increasingly affecting the location of jobs rather than responding to a set pattern of employment opportunities and therefore personal preferences concerning a place to live are exercising a growing influence on the changing character of Britain's cities and towns at less than broad regional scale.

The basic task which we set ourselves in this book is the description of the impacts which these two sources of change – the major changes in employment structure and the highly dynamic processes of residential mobility – have been having on the size and character of places in Britain. What are the principal geographical dimensions of change? Have recent trends been widening the differentials which exist between places or are they helping to produce greater similarities by narrowing the gap between the 'haves' and 'have-nots'? Which places, and which types of places, have been involved most in these changes? Previous studies give us a reasonably good indication of the main dimensions that we can expect to find. The first is the basic divide between North and South which is often popularly equated with the 'drift to the South' though it is rooted in some fundamental differences in economic history and industrial structure. Secondly, these studies draw attention to the differential performance of the conurbations and larger cities, on the one hand, and the smaller towns and more rural areas, on the other, sometimes rather imprecisely termed the 'urban–rural shift'. Thirdly, at more local scale, is the increasing polarization of socio-economic groups and 'life chances' between the older declining inner city areas and the prosperous and dynamic 'outer city' comprising the newer suburbs and the dormitory settlements of wealthy commuters beyond.

This task is by no means as straightforward as it might sound. The fortunes of any particular place are likely to be affected in different ways by each of these three main dimensions and will also reflect individual peculiarities of history and local circumstance. In addition, there is the whole question of place definition to wrestle with; cities and towns cannot be compared satisfactorily unless they are defined on a consistent basis, particularly given the internal contrasts between inner and outer areas. For instance, if a place is defined on the basis of only its main settlement, it is likely to appear less well off than when the definition is extended to include the wealthy dormitory settlements around it. One of the chief drawbacks in the readily available statistics on population in Britain is that the most common geographical unit used for their presentation is the local authority District. For reasons outlined more fully in Chapter 1, the local government framework provides an extremely poor representation of the British urban system, with the districts of larger cities frequently failing to include their commuting hinterland and in some cases including little more than their inner city areas.

A major part of the rationale behind this book is therefore to present statistical data for places defined in such a way as to have meaning in people's daily lives and to have relevance for businesses and others concerned with various forms of strategic planning for places as operational entities. Individual people living in and around a particular settlement tend to trace out a pattern of journeys for work, shopping and leisure which – for the whole area – builds up into composite 'daily urban systems' which are normally quite tightly knit and relatively separate from those focusing on other urban centres.

This study uses a framework of geographical areas which was designed specifically for use with the latest data on population and employment. Produced by staff at the Centre for Urban and Regional Development Studies in the University of Newcastle upon Tyne, it employs functional criteria related to commuting patterns round identified employment and shopping centres and divides Britain up into some 280 relatively self-contained 'Local Labour Market Areas' (LLMAs). Each of these places can be classified according to its regional location and to its size and position in the urban hierarchy in order to examine differentials and trends along the main dimensions of variability in Britain. For the majority of LLMAs it is also possible to get some measure of their internal heterogeneity by drawing comparisons between their central cores and surrounding commuting hinterlands. Most important, however, is the fact that, since the LLMA framework is defined on a logical and consistent basis, real places can be compared with each other with a degree of confidence that is just not possible with most alternative approaches to data presentation such as Districts or Counties.

The structure of the book is relatively straightforward and self-explanatory. Chapter 1 introduces the principal dimensions of socio-economic change which this study will be measuring, describes the basis of the Functional Regions perspective, and outlines the main features and applications of this approach which we will be using. The next six chapters examine in turn the most important demographic, economic and social characteristics which give places their distinctive complexion. Changing patterns of population distribution form an obvious starting point, with Chapter 3 following on with some of the main changes taking place in the structure of the population, particularly the increasing size of the elderly population and ethnic minority groups and the fall in average household size. Chapter 4 shows how the size and composition of the labour force (in terms of those offering themselves for work) have been changing in different places and examines trends in labour force participation rates and in the ratio between economically active people and the rest of the population. Chapter 5 focuses on the changing location of employment and documents the spatial pattern of growth of employment in the newer service industries and the shift to part-time working. Given its prominence as a phenomenon in recent urban and regional change and its high profile as a social issue, unemployment is given separate treatment in Chapter 6, with particular attention being given to North/South differences and to its most severe expressions in the form of long-term and youth unemployment, while Chapter 7 presents data on three other commonly used indicators of socio-economic well-being, namely social class composition, car availability and housing tenure. Finally, Chapter 8 draws on a small selection of key criteria to construct an Index of Local Economic Prosperity which measures the recent dynamism of cities and towns in Britain and provides a simple summary of the way in which the events of the last 15 years have been treating individual places and the people living in them.

The stimulus for a book along these lines came from two different, though related, sources. First was the great deal of interest generated in academic and government circles by the Functional Regions Factsheets which were produced at the Centre for Urban and Regional Development Studies in 1983/84, outlining the preliminary results of analyses using this special geographical framework. Criticisms that the limited circulation of the Factsheets severely restricted their use, particularly for teaching purposes, were a powerful factor in prompting our decision to write up the results in a more formal way. Secondly and more immediately has been the considerable amount of attention given by the private sector and the media to a spin-off from the Functional Regions research which involved a search for 'booming towns'. In response to a request for information by Philip Beresford of *The Sunday Times*, we produced a ranking of Local Labour Market Areas in Britain by using an index of key statistics which reflected the buoyancy of their economic base and the prosperity of their population. The results, which form the basis of the final chapter of this book, were first featured in *The Sunday Times* Business News Section on 29 September 1985 and have subsequently been much in demand from market researchers and economic commentators. To these two groups of interested parties we owe a substantial debt for prompting us into action.

Acknowledgements are also due to a large number of other people and organizations. First and foremost, none of this work would have been possible without the foundation work put in by the team who originally defined the Functional Regions framework and also by the other members of the analytical team who helped to process the statistics and undertake some of the earlier analyses. The former included John Dixon, John Goddard, Stan Openshaw and Peter Taylor, as well as Mike Coombes, while, besides ourselves, Martin Charlton, Andy Gillespie, John Goddard and Stan Openshaw have also been involved in the subsequent substantive analyses. Secondly, we are indebted to the Office of Population Censuses and Surveys and the Department of Employment, which have allowed us to draw upon their data sources; it should be noted, however, that these data retain Crown Copyright. The data on employment growth and unemployment were derived directly from the Manpower Services Commission National Online Manpower Information System (NOMIS), programmed by Robert Nelson and Peter Dodds, of the Geography Department, Durham University. Finally, the majority of the illustrations have been prepared by computer with the help of the GIMMS graphics package.

It should, however, be stressed, as is conventional practice, that full responsibility for the calculations and interpretations presented in this book rests with the authors themselves. David Owen was primarily responsible for Chapter 5 and Anne Green for Chapter 6, while Tony Champion wrote the first drafts of the other chapters and handled general editing matters. The book also draws on Mike Coombes's work on the definition of the Functional Regions framework and on unemployment; on David Ellin's analyses of the New Commonwealth population and car availability, as well as his assistance with much of the computing work; and on the work of Anne Green and Tony Champion on 'booming towns'. David Owen and Anne Green took on the major part of the work required for the illustrations drawn by automated cartography, while Eric Quenet prepared the maps drawn manually, Doreen Morrison prepared the bromides for the illustrations, and a special debt is owed to the Newcastle University computer operators who struggled manfully to keep the India Ink pens flowing smoothly on the computer plotter during the heatwave at the end of June 1986. Finally, the greater part of the typing was carried out by Lynda Clark and Denise Rainford; their perceptiveness in the face of our variable handwriting and forbearance in dealing with an ever-changing manuscript were an endless source of admiration.

Newcastle upon Tyne
June 1986

A.G. Champion
A.E. Green
D.W. Owen
D.J. Ellin
M.G. Coombes

1
The Functional Regions perspective

This book is about the places which make up Great Britain, about the ways in which they have been changing in recent years and about the extent to which these changes affect their nature and the quality of life and opportunities available to the people who live in them. Above all, this study attempts to quantify the differences which exist between places in the characteristics of their populations and in their living conditions both in order to assess the significance of the changes which have been occurring and also so as to allow the principal geographical dimensions underlying these changes to be measured and compared. In so doing, we are seeking the answers to a variety of seemingly straightforward questions which are frequently raised by politicians, planners, businessmen and laymen alike, such as: Is the divide between North and South widening and, if so, is this true for all aspects of inequality? Which are the fastest growing places in Britain and do they share any common characteristics? What does it take for a place in the North to be a 'booming town'? Are Britain's largest cities universally in decline?

It is easier – in this context, at least – to ask these kinds of questions than to answer them. We have two particular difficulties to wrestle with; first, the problem of finding a suitable definition of 'places' and, secondly, the challenge of obtaining satisfactory statistics for describing them. In brief, as outlined in the Preface, we have examined the conventionally used methods of dividing up British territory for the presentation of local statistics and found them lacking in consistency and indeed in basic geographical reality. Instead, we have adopted a framework of functionally defined areas which was designed specifically for the analysis of results from the 1981 Population Census. Because these areas do not conform closely to the pattern of local government Districts, we are limited in the range of data sources which we can use, but a wealth of information is available from the Population Censuses of 1971 and 1981, the Census of Employment which was carried out annually up to 1978 and repeated in 1981 and 1984 (though the local results of the 1984 Census were not available at the time of writing) and the monthly records of unemployment kept by the Department of Employment.

The geographical patterns of differentiation and change which these data indicate are the subject of the other seven chapters. The role of the present chapter is to introduce the principal features of Britain's changing space-economy and to describe more fully the background to the framework of geographical areas or 'places' which we use to study it. In the final section we describe the various ways in which these 'places' can be classified in order to assess the relative importance of the different dimensions of change and, in so doing, we provide an introduction to the structure of Britain's urban and regional system by reference to the distribution of population between its various elements.

Facets of change in Britain

Britain in the 1980s comprises a wide variety of different places and some major changes have affected them in recent years. On the other hand, the present complexion of places is as much a reflection of their longer-term history of development as an outcome of the events of the past 10 or 15 years. Many of the differences between places which we can find in the 1980s already existed at the beginning of the 1970s and are a legacy handed down from previous decades. It is therefore not safe to assume that the differences observed now result only from processes which are still operating. Herein lies the importance of studying *change* between specific points in time and of being able to relate recent trends recorded for individual places to broader dimensions which can be studied in more detail and perhaps be forecast into the future. The aim of this section is to describe the nature of these broader dimensions so that we know fairly precisely what we are looking for and therefore can devise a sensible basis for assembling the available data that can allow us to test for the existence of these trends and gauge their relative magnitudes.

The most persistent dimension of variability in Britain is the basic distinction between *northern and southern parts of the country*. Ten years ago many people reckoned that this contrast was quickly becoming a thing of the past; regional policy had been reinvigorated to stem the 'drift to the South East' and to remove the last vestiges of worn-out urban fabric in the North, while major new industrial investment was targeted to the Assisted Areas by a range of national and multinational corporations. Such optimism, however, has more recently proved to be unfounded, as the recession which began in 1976 and bit more deeply from 1979 onwards led to massive contractions in the newer branch plants as well as further undermining the viability of the traditional industries. The monthly unemployment figures, for instance, suggest that the North–South divide is back with a vengeance, the only major geographical differences being that the dividing line is now much sharper and lies much further south than previously.

A second dimension is provided by *industrial structure*. This is of course a major factor underpinning the basic distinction between North and South, but it also provides a powerful explanation of differences in prosperity and dynamism between individual places within the same broad regional context. This relates not only to the overall balance between primary production, manufacturing and services in a place's employment structure, but also to the types of activities represented within each of these broad sectors and often to the particular type of company involved. Within manufacturing industry, for instance, there has been a significant contrast between the fortunes of places specializing in shipbuilding or the steel industry and those with a strong representation of electrical engineering and electronics, irrespective of whether comparisons are made across the North–South boundary or within a single region. Previous research has also shown that the fortunes of state-owned companies have often differed substantially from those in the private sector, while within the latter it has been noted that in the face of recession multinational corporations tend to adopt strategies towards redundancies and closures which are different from those of locally based firms. In other words, de-industrialization may be a feature of Britain as a whole, when seen from an international perspective, but at the same time there are some types of places where manufacturing has adapted and prospered.

Size of place also helps to explain differences between places within the same broad regional context, as well as across the nation as a whole. Along with de-industrialization this is one of the newest of the currently operating dimensions of spatial change and is still not fully understood. It has become known by a variety of terms including 'counterurbanization' and the 'urban–rural shift' and has been viewed by some as a complete reversal of the geographical trends associated with the urbanization process. Traditionally a strong positive relationship has been observed between growth rate and size of place, with the largest places attracting more than their proportionate share of national growth as a result of various forms of scale economy including their extensive and varied facilities, labour supply and markets. In Britain this relationship appears to have grown gradually weaker since the end of the nineteenth century, but it is only since the late 1960s that city size has become such a significant negative factor in growth that it appears to be affecting the whole settlement system and has turned many of the more remote and rural parts of Britain from net losers to gainers of migrants.

Going down to a more local scale, there is no doubt about the over-whelming importance of centrifugal forces. The process of *suburbanization* was well established in Britain before the end of the nineteenth century. In its initial form it was closely related to urbanization in that it represented the outward physical extension of a growing settlement as the capacity of the original nucleus became saturated, but the term also carries connotations of functional specialization as the new areas took on a rather limited residential or dormitory role and the old core became more specialized as a provider of jobs, shops and other services. Pushed on by greater personal mobility and by the search for a better quality of residential environment, this process leads to a reduction in overall population density within the older inner parts of the growing settlement and to progressively further extensions of its outer limits. Since the advent of rail commuting and particularly of the motor car, much of this new development has been taking place in 'ex-urban' locations which are physically separate from the built-up area of the main settlement and are either grafted on to smaller existing villages in the surrounding area or take the form of a rash of speculative land subdivisions. The resulting form of urban complex has become known variously as the Metropolitan Area, the Functional Region and the Regional City. Because of the importance of this more far-flung pattern of urban development, it has become common in America to distinguish between the 'central city' and the other surrounding municipalities which are functionally dependent on it even though they may be separate in purely physical terms. In Britain the same distinction is recognized, though in the academic literature in this country the two parts are more usually referred to as 'urban core' and 'commuting ring'.

It is important to stress that, in conceptual terms, a clear distinction is drawn between suburbanization and metropolitan development on the one hand and counterurbanization on the other, with the former referring to decentralization taking place *within* the commuting field of a single urban centre and with the latter denoting a broader scale process involving shifts of people and jobs *between* relatively independent city regions. In practice, however, it is very difficult to disentangle the two elements and indeed in some respects they seem to lead to similar overall outcomes in terms of the distribution of population and economic opportunity. This is certainly true in terms of their impact on the hearts of Britain's larger cities because these have been acting as the main source of net migration for both local decentrali-zation and longer-distance deconcentration. Not so long ago the reduction of population densities in these older urban areas was welcomed and actively

promoted by government through the New and Expanded Towns programmes , but since the mid 1960s the state of the inner city areas has become
an increasing cause for concern. Due to the greater residential mobility of the
better off, the apparent attractiveness of inner urban areas for overseas
immigrants and other minority groups, the political geography of council
house building, the problems of renewing worn-out urban infrastructure
and, above all, the large-scale collapse of their industrial base and particularly job opportunities for less skilled manual workers, the inner city areas
have increasingly become the repository of people with the least economic
'clout' in our society – thereby undermining further the quality of life
available there by creating a situation of multiple deprivation.

These, then, are the main dimensions of spatial change which previous
studies have shown to be affecting the complexion of places in Britain in
recent years. The North–South divide, differences in industrial structure, the
urban–rural shift and local decentralization, all these elements have been
acting simultaneously during the 1970s and early 1980s to produce major
changes in the distribution of people and prosperity. They have contributed
to the continued strong growth of medium-sized cities and towns in the South
East round London, to the resilience of what are traditionally thought of as
cathedral cities and market towns, to the revival of flagging fortunes in many
of the more remote rural zones, and to the emergence of new industrial
growth areas particularly in the 'sun belt' focused on the M4 corridor but also
in a number of other more localized sites such as Cambridge and Central
Scotland, dubbed by the media as 'Silicon Fen' and 'Silicon Glen' respectively. The other side of the coin, made worse by the limited scale of overall
national growth, has been the increasing deprivation visited upon once pros-
erous areas. These comprise not just the seedbeds of Britain's nineteenth-
century industrial wealth in the inner parts of the largest cities and across the
major Northern conurbations, but also include places which benefited
greatly from the main twentieth-century growth industries such as motor
vehicles, petrochemicals and a restructured iron and steel industry and indeed
those which were the focus of the wave of international investment which
brought welcome jobs to the Assisted Areas and New Towns in the 1960s.

There remains, however, considerable uncertainty and debate over the
evolving shape of Britain's space economy. There is much statistical evidence
which showed for the 1970s a massive shift in population from the largest
cities and most heavily built-up regions towards smaller settlements and more
rural areas (Champion, 1983a; Fothergill and Vincent, 1985), but this movement appears to have abated somewhat in recent years (Champion, 1983b).
The trend in employment, particularly manufacturing, also exhibited a
marked urban–rural gradient during the 1960s and early 1970s (Fothergill
and Gudgin, 1982; Keeble, 1976), but this was less clear in 1978–81 (Owen *et
al.*, 1986). Attention continues to be given to the North–South divide in
Britain, particularly since the later 1970s when the gap between these 'Two
Nations' seems to have widened substantially (Green and Owen, 1984;
Coombes, 1987; Townsend, 1983).Alternatively, it has been suggested that,
with the development of North Sea oil and entry into the European Community, Britain has been 'tilted on its side' with the east–west dichotomy starting
to emerge as the principal regional differentiator (White, 1985). Yet,
admittedly at a more local level, concern has been growing amongst policy
makers in the South East of England that the pattern of development there
has been unduly favouring the areas west of London at the expense of the
eastern half (Martin, T. 1985).

The main purpose of this book is to describe the geographical patterns that constitute the outcome of these developments and to gauge the relative importance of the separate dimensions in fashioning them. Its primary emphasis is on putting quantitative values on the differences between places which are well known in qualitative and subjective terms and have frequently been alluded to (but rarely defined) in the academic literature and the media. It is, however, concerned not so much with the disparities existing across the country at one point in time in the mid 1980s as with the manner and scale of changes in those differentials over time, specifically since the early 1970s. In this way it is possible to distinguish between those disparities which have been inherited from previous decades and those which are the result of recent events and may be likely to develop further in future years. Our attempts at explanation will, in the main, be confined to assigning relative importance to each of the main spatial dimensions of change which we have just outlined, particularly trying to separate out the role of the broader regional or 'North–South' factor from that of the city size or 'urban–rural' factor. We do this by dividing Britain up into a set of 'places' and by classifying each of these places according to its position with respect to these dimensions.

The functional approach to defining places

The most important ingredient affecting the success with which we can carry out this task is a satisfactory method of defining 'places'. It is essential that we should organize the available statistics in such a way as to reflect the geographical realities of each place, and it is even more important, since our main purpose is to compare one place with another, that any definition should be applied in a consistent manner across the entire country. How else can one expect to answer with any degree of confidence even such simple questions as: What is the population of Britain's largest city? How much larger is this than the population of the second largest city? Which place is growing the fastest?

In such an advanced country as Britain – the first nation to become highly urbanized, one of the first to adopt a regular Population Census for national stocktaking (the first being held in 1801), and the pioneer of so many innovations in urban planning – one would be forgiven for assuming that the official authorities would have produced these sorts of statistics as a matter of course, but this is just not the case. The standard geographical unit for the presentation of demographic, economic and social statistics in Britain is the local authority District, or aggregations of these to the level of the County or Region, because it is through this framework that the machinery of government primarily operates; and the problems arise because the Districts do not faithfully represent Britain's towns and cities, either because their boundaries are out of date or because they were originally defined on the basis of other criteria such as administrative efficiency or political convenience. Since it forms the main methodological contribution of this book, we need to explain and justify our choice of definition and to introduce the range of terms which we will be using in subsequent chapters to describe elements of Britain's urban and regional system.

In wanting to describe and compare places in relation mainly to population and employment characteristics and trends, we seek a definition which, on the one hand, will not split up places which are functionally interdependent and, on the other, will not group together two or more places which have few links with each other; in other words, they should form individual and relatively self-contained local labour market areas. The task has become far more complex with the passage of time. In the pre-industrial era towns were generally tightly knit, were in many cases demarcated physically by a defensive wall, and were relatively few and far between. Things became more complicated with the Industrial Revolution, because new settlements sprouting up close to each other began to coalesce into wider conurbations even though at first they tended to maintain their separate identities which were built around the local mines or factories. Far greater problems, however, have arisen with the stimulus given to suburban spread by bus, tram, train and motor car, with the resultant erosion of the distinction between town and country and with the intertwining of the outer parts of one place with those of another. We have now moved substantially through the era of the 'city region', where the main settlement acts as a market and administrative centre for the people in the surrounding region who visit it on a *weekly* basis and have their groceries and newspapers delivered from it, towards the day of the 'regional city', in which the outer settlements serve the same function as the older suburbs of the main centre used to perform (and continue to do) and are equally tied to the main centre by *daily* commuting and shopping journeys.

The concept of functionally defined areas is not an easy one to grasp, because most people have strong attachments only to a very localized area such as a particular neighbourhood or even a single street. Possibly the best way of appreciating these ideas on the meaning of 'places' is in terms of being asked where one lives by people who live a long way away. If someone from the North East goes on holiday or a business trip to the South of England and is asked where he comes from, he is not likely to venture 'Osborne Avenue' or even 'Jesmond' but is much more likely to reply 'Newcastle upon Tyne', of which that locality is a part. Similarly, a sixth-form student being interviewed for a place in the geography department at Newcastle University is much more likely to say that he comes from 'London' rather than from 'Islington' or even 'Bexley'. The same applies to a person who comes from a dormitory settlement on the outskirts of a city, in that such an individual will probably volunteer the name of that city. This is the scale of the 'places' with which this book largely deals.

The CURDS Functional Regions framework

The framework developed by the Centre for Urban and Regional Development Studies (CURDS) at Newcastle University specifically for the 1981 Census represents the latest in a series of studies initiated by the academic community for producing a set of urban-centred regions for the analysis of urban and regional change (Hall, 1971; Drewett *et al.*, 1976; Hall and Hay, 1980; Berg *et al.*, 1982). Its central feature is the way in which it defines places as far as possible as self-contained entities – something which the local government areas singularly fail to do, particularly at the two extremes of the urban hierarchy. For the larger cities, it was found necessary to add all or parts of surrounding local authorities because their own Districts fail to embrace the wider area which depends on them for jobs and services, while at the other extreme some of the extensive Districts in more rural areas contain more than one town that should each be considered an urban centre in its own right or contain parts which look outwards to more than one other centre. Even the East Midlands, which has a fairly straightforward urban structure, can provide examples of each of these problems: the city of Leicester needs to be grouped with surrounding Districts; South Kesteven contains both Grantham and Stamford within the same District; and Charnwood District needs to be apportioned between Leicester and Loughborough.

The CURDS approach gets round these problems in the following way. It takes 1971 data on employment and journey to work for the pre-1974 local government areas in order to establish a set of urban centres and delineate their commuting fields. The procedure begins with the identification of urban centres, defined in terms of a minimum degree of concentration of employment and retail activities, followed by their translation into a set of urban *Cores* by extending their boundaries outwards to embrace the whole of the main settlement's continuously built-up-area. A further step is the amalgamation of those adjacent centres which were closely interlinked – a crucial stage in that it determines how many separate 'places' can be identified in each part of the country. The next step is to attach to each Core its primary commuting field, termed a *Ring*, which comprises those areas sending at least 15 percent of their employed residents to jobs in the Core and more to that particular Core than any other. The Core and Ring of any place is termed the *Daily Urban System*, being the main population concentration and the primary area within which the daily patterns of movement take place. Finally, the remaining parts of Britain are then allocated as *Outer Areas* to the urban centres to which they are most closely tied in commuting terms, thus producing a comprehensive regionalization of the whole territory of Great Britain.

The outcome of this procedure is the derivation of a set of 280 urban-centred regions which are relatively self-contained in terms of journey-to-work flows and are therefore known as Local Labour Market Areas (LLMAs). This set provides the definition of 'places' which we use most commonly in this study. They are mapped in Appendix 1, and some key statistics are presented in Appendix 2. They vary widely in geographical extent and population size, depending on the degree of physical urbanization and on the distance between identified urban centres. In a relatively small number of cases – 52 in all – the Daily Urban System of the LLMA (i.e. Core and Ring together) contained in 1971 a population of under 50,000; these are termed *Rural Areas* and in subsequent analyses the distinction between their constituent zones has been dropped. The remaining 228 LLMAs, however, are termed *Urban Regions* and can be subdivided into their component Cores, Rings and Outer Areas, wheresoever appropriate.

The 'places' represented by the LLMAs provide the basic building blocks for higher-order definitions of settlements in Britain's urban and regional structure, which are valuable for certain purposes in their own right as well as for providing further information about the context in which each of the individual places are located. First, the allocation of each Rural Area to the Urban Region to which it sends the largest commuting flow produces a set of 228 *Functional Regions* (FRs), which can be interpreted as the geographical areas over which the majority of private and public-sector services are provided. Of these FRs, many are highly self-contained in terms of journey-to-work patterns and are known as *Freestanding FRs*, but the remainder are located in and around the more heavily populated areas where the urban centres are more interdependent. Where an FR sends over 7.5 per cent of its employed residents to work in one other particular FR, these regions are combined as part of a Metropolitan Region in which the FR which is the main beneficiary of these commuting flows is termed the *Dominant* and the FRs providing the commuters are called *Subdominants* (Fig. 1.1).

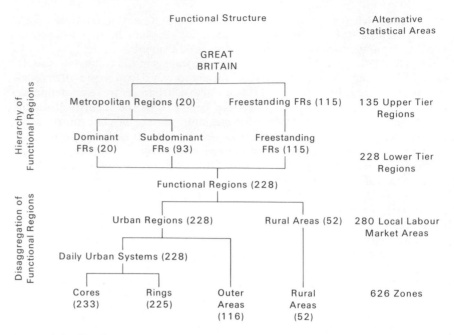

Figure 1.1   The Functional Regions framework

The structure of the Functional Regions and Metropolitan Regions is shown in Fig. 1.2. The bottom half of Fig. 1.1 demonstrates how the zones can be built up into the Urban Regions, how the Urban Regions and Rural Areas together constitute the level of the Local Labour Market Area used as our principal definition of 'place' in this study, and how these two types of LLMAs can be amalgamated to form the 228 FRs shown in Fig. 1.2. At the higher level of regionalization, the procedures identify a total of 20 Metropolitan Regions, ranging in size from the case of London, which contains 30 Subdominant FRs in addition to London itself, to six cases which involve a simple pairing of the adjacent FRs, again with one usually much larger than the Subdominant in population size. In all, the Metropolitan Regions account for 113 FRs, leaving the remaining 115 as Freestanding. As laid out in Fig. 1.1, this sequential process of aggregating smaller areas into progressively larger units provides a set of alternative spatial scales for the presentation and analysis of data, ranging from the 626 zones through the 280 LLMAs and 228 FRs to the 135 upper-tier regions. Each level of the hierarchy is defined consistently on the basis of a set of criteria that aims to reflect one aspect of Britain's urban system. In this way, the different levels are appropriate for different purposes.*

The functional area structure of Britain

We round off this chapter with a description of the way in which Britain is structured in functional area terms. This section serves three useful purposes

*The original Functional Regions framework developed by Coombes *et al.* (1982) comprised 627 zones and 281 LLMAs because the Northallerton and Richmond Rural Area was split into two, giving 53 instead of 52 Rural Areas. Because this split is not possible with the Department of Employment data, we have chosen to treat these two Rural Areas as a single unit throughout this book.

METROPOLITAN
REGIONS

A Blackburn
B Birmingham
C Cardiff
E Edinburgh
F Nottingham
G Glasgow
I London
J Newport
L Liverpool
M Manchester
N Newcastle
P Portsmouth
R Preston
S Sheffield
T Teesside
V Coventry
W Swansea
X Brighton
Y Leeds
Z Bristol

— Metropolitan Region
— Functional Region
[A] Dominant
[ ] Subdominant
[ ] Freestanding

Figure 1.2 Functional Regions and Metropolitan Regions. Note that the Orkneys are combined with Thurso Rural Area (in Inverness Functional Region) and the Shetlands are combined with Aberdeen

at this stage. First, it introduces the way in which the various dimensions of spatial variability are to be measured using the FR framework. Secondly, it presents a clearer picture of the organization of space in Britain, using the 1981 distribution of population as the principal indicator of the relative importance of each element of a particular dimension. Thirdly, in doing this, it gives details of the population base which has given rise to the ratio and percentage values described in subsequent chapters.

As outlined in the previous section, two of the main features of the FR framework are the split downwards into zones and the aggregation upwards into Dominant, Subdominant and Freestanding types (Fig. 1.1). The distribution of population across these two dimensions is shown in Tables 1.1 and

Table 1.1 Population distribution, 1981, by zone

Zone	Population (thousands)	% GB	Area (km^2)	% GB	Density (persons/km^2)
Cores	33,446	61.6	13,442	6.0	2,488
Rings	14,466	26.6	84,430	37.7	171
Outer Areas	3,558	6.6	51,177	22.8	70
Rural Areas	2,802	5.2	75,119	33.5	37
Great Britain	54,273	100.0	224,168	100.0	242

Source: Population Census Small Area Statistics

1.2 respectively. These reveal the high degree of concentration which exists in the British urban system.

Concentration is particularly evident at the localized scale of the *zone* (Table 1.1). In 1981 over 60 per cent of Britain's total population dwelt in the Cores that comprise the continuously built-up areas of the settlements at the hearts of the 228 FRs. Since these areas account for only 6 per cent of national territory, they are characterizd by very high population densities averaging nearly 2,500 persons/km^2 or 10 times the national level, with the densities in the other three types of zone all correspondingly below average. A further 1 in 4 people inhabit these centres' primary commuting Rings, so that some 88 per cent of the British population live in areas which are easily accessible to, and have a considerable dependence upon, the 228 principal urban centres in the country. At the other extreme, only 1 in 20 live in the Rural Areas, the relatively self-contained areas which have no settlement with a Daily Urban system of more than 50,000 people, even though these account for a third of national space (Table 1.1).

A high degree of concentration is also evident in terms of *types of FRs* (Table 1.2). The 1981 Census found only 37 per cent of the population living in the Freestanding FRs despite the fact that the latter account for twice that proportion of Britain's land. By contrast over 3 in every 5 people (34 million in total) were enumerated in Metropolitan Britain, the groupings of FRs which represent the 20 most heavily urbanized and complexly interlinked regions in the country (Fig. 1.2). Well over half of these live at the hearts of these Metropolitan Regions in the 20 Dominant FRs themselves and two-fifths in the six largest Dominants. Most impressive of all, 1 in 7 of Britain's entire population dwell in the national capital even though the latter accounts for only a fraction of the country's total land area. Indeed London is as large

Table 1.2 Population distribution, 1981, by type of Functional Region

Type (and number) of Functional Regions	Population (thousands)	% GB	Area (km^2)	% GB	Density (persons/km^2)
London (1)	7,837	14.4	3,368	1.5	2,327
Conurbation Dominants (5)	5,749	10.6	6,542	2.9	879
Other Dominants (14)	6,589	12.1	17,779	7.9	371
All Dominants (20)	*20,175*	*37.2*	*27,688*	*12.4*	*729*
Subdominants (93)	13,820	25.4	29,238	13.0	473
Metropolitan Britain (113)	*33,995*	*62.6*	*56,926*	*25.4*	*597*
Freestanding (115)	20,278	37.4	167,241	74.6	121
Great Britain (228)	54,273	100.0	224,168	100.0	242

Source: Population Census Small Area Statistics

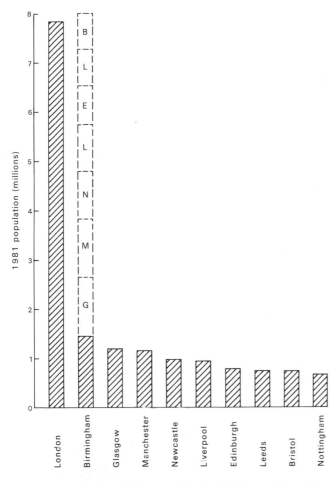

Figure 1.3 Britain's 10 largest cities, by 1981 population size
Source: Population Census

as the eight next largest FRs put together (Fig. 1.3). This represents a degree of concentration and primacy in the settlement system that is rarely matched by other countries in the Developed World.

A valuable aspect of the FR framework is its ability to provide a basis for measuring and comparing the urban–rural and North–South dimensions. The urban–rural continuum is defined in terms of the *size and status of Local Labour Market Areas* and is shown in Table 1.3. Because of its massive size and unique status in Britain, London is distinguished from the five next largest cities which dominate the principal regional conurbations (Birmingham, Glasgow, Manchester, Liverpool and Newcastle upon Tyne) and these, in their turn, are considered separately from the other large provincial centres (Leeds, Bristol, Edinburgh, Nottingham, and Sheffield). The smaller Dominants are grouped in a Cities category with the other LLMAs whose Daily Urban Systems contained over 166,000 people at the 1971 Census, while Towns comprise all other LLMAs with a DUS of over 50,000 people, leaving the Rural LLMAs as the final group. The urban–rural progression is reflected in Table 1.3 in both the average size and the overall population density of places in each category.

Table 1.3   Population distribution, 1981, by LLMA size

Size group (and no of LLMAs)	Population 1981 (thousands)	Average size 1981 (thousands)	% GB population	% GB area	Density (persons/km²)
London (1)	7,836.9	7,836.9	14.4	1.5	2,327
Conurbation Dominants (5)	5,711.9	1,142.4	10.5	2.9	1,309
Provincial Dominants (5)	3,482.4	696.5	6.4	2.6	589
Cities (61)	17,393.9	285.1	32.1	20.4	380
Towns (156)	17,045.5	109.3	31.4	40.0	190
Rural Areas (52)	2,803.0	53.9	5.2	33.5	37
Great Britain (280)	54,273.5	193.8	100.0	100.0	242

Source: Population Census Small Area Statistics

As regards the *regional* dimension, it is technically possible to aggregate the 280 LLMAs to produce groupings that are very similar to the Standard Regions used by the official statistical agencies (such as the South East, South West and East Anglia), but for our purposes a more useful approach is one which fits more closely to the formal and functional structure of Britain. Our primary objective is a satisfactory split between North and South, which according to the analyses presented in the next few chapters runs broadly between the Severn estuary and Lincolnshire, putting the main industrial cities of the Midlands in the North but allocating the southern, less urbanized parts of the East Midlands to the South (Fig. 1.4). For some purposes, however, a further subdivision is made in both parts. Within the North it is useful to draw a distinction between the more peripheral 'regions' of Wales, Scotland and the Northern Region, which form the traditional seat of the regional problem, and the industrial heartland of the Midlands, North West and Yorkshire, which have joined the regional 'have-nots' only within the last two decades or so. The split made in the South recognizes the basic distinction between those parts heavily dominated by the national capital (defined as London's Metropolitan Region) and the remaining zones which, extending out into the South West, East Anglia and the southern margins of the Midlands, comprise mainly freestanding LLMAs along with the smaller Metropolitan Regions based on Bristol, Portsmouth and Brighton. The basic dimensions of these four broad regional divisions are listed in Table 1.4, showing that, on the one hand, the Periphery accounts for almost half the national territory but contains only 1 in 4 of the British population, while, on the other, the South contains somewhat less than half the country's population on a third of its land, with a particularly high concentration in the London Region.

To some extent, the urban–rural and North–South dimensions overlap in practice. This can occur at two different scale levels, both of which can be handled by the aggregations just outlined. The broad regional divisions shown in Fig. 1.4 and Table 1.4 can be used to monitor broader aspects of the urban–rural shift than the size categories of Table 1.3, not just in comparing shifts between the national core region of the South and the remainder of the country but also in looking for signs of regional decentralization within these two halves of Britain and in testing for the existence of centrifugal trends across the four blocks on a general continuum ranging from the London Region through to the Periphery. Secondly, in some of our analyses we look

1 London Metropolitan Region ⎫ South
2 Rest of the South   ⎭
3 Heartland   ⎫ North
4 Periphery   ⎭

Figure 1.4   Broad regional divisions of Britain

at the more specific pattern of urban–rural shift within North and South separately, by distinguishing the constituent LLMAs of Table 1.3 by regional location. Normally, because of their small number of cases, the three largest settlement categories are collapsed into a single category of 'Large Dominants' cases, producing four size categories with the shares of the populations and land areas of North and South shown in Table 1.5.

Table 1.4   Population distribution, 1981, by broad regional division

Regional Division	Population		Area		Density
	(thousands)	% GB	(km²)	% GB	(persons/km²)
London Region	12,372	22.8	14,309	6.4	865
Rest of the South	12,224	22.5	58,169	25.9	210
South	*24,596*	*45.3*	*72,478*	*32.3*	*339*
Industrial Heartland	18,657	34.4	40,980	18.3	455
Periphery	11,020	20.3	110,710	49.4	100
North	*29,677*	*54.7*	*151,690*	*67.7*	*196*
Great Britain	54,274	100.0	224,168	100.0	242

Source: Population Census Small Area Statistics

Table 1.5   Population distribution, 1981, by regional division and LLMA size

Regional division	Large Dominants	Cities	Towns	Rural Areas	Total
Population (%)					
South	34.9	27.6	33.1	4.4	100.0
North	28.5	35.7	30.0	5.8	100.0
Britain	31.4	32.0	31.4	5.2	100.0
Area (%)					
South	6.2	28.2	49.9	15.6	100.0
North	6.0	16.7	35.3	42.0	100.0
Britain	6.1	20.4	40.0	33.5	100.0
Density (persons/km^2)					
South	1,908	332	225	96	339
North	924	419	167	27	196
Britain	1,249	380	190	37	242

Source: Population Census Small Area Statistics

Finally, for some purposes, it is worth going a step beyond the integration of urban–rural and North–South dimensions shown in Table 1.5 in order to try and isolate the role of all the main elements of spatial change outlined at the beginning of the chapter, including place in the Functional Region hierarchy and structure of the economic base. Because of the limited number of LLMAs it is impossible to achieve this objective systematically within a multidimensional matrix, but as a compromise a *19-fold-classification of LLMAs* has been developed, incorporating the various dimensions as far as possible while maintaining reasonably large populations in each grouping (Table 1.6). The principal criteria used in this classification are:

- place in Functional Region hierarchy: Dominant, Subdominant, Freestanding
- urban status: London, Regional Capitals, Town, Rural
- rank of Metropolitan Region : London, Conurbation, Subregional
- regional location : North, South (of a line running roughly between the Severn Estuary and Lincolnshire)
- employment structure : Service, Commercial, Manufacturing.

The constituent members of each of the 19 categories are listed in Appendix 3.

In the chapters which follow, we rarely use all these 19 categories in any one analysis, but the classification serves two more manageable functions. First, we make selective use of categories which indicate extreme performances or which allow the isolation of one particular dimension, such as the role of economic structure in Freestanding towns. Secondly, we can use these categories as building blocks for higher-level groupings of places in Britain, such as for drawing comparisons between North and South for Freestanding Urban Regions alone.

Summary

This chapter has outlined the principal dimensions of differentiation and change that we are likely to find in a study of places in Britain and has described the geographical framework of areas which will be used in the remainder of this book. The dimensions of change which are most commonly

Table 1.6 A classification of Local Labour Market Areas

LLMA class	No. of LLMAs	1981 population (000s)	Example
London	1	7,836.9	London
Conurbation Dominants	5	5,711.9	Manchester
Provincial Dominants	5	3,482.4	Edinburgh
Subregional Dominants	9	2,887.9	Portsmouth
London Subdominant Cities	7	1,740.2	Southend
London Subdominant Towns	23	2,794.9	Maidenhead
Conurbation Subdominant Cities	13	3,303.0	Motherwell
Conurbation Subdominant Towns	22	2,364.4	Northwich
Smaller Northern Subdominants	24	2,875.2	Rugby
Southern Freestanding Cities	12	4,149.5	Norwich
Southern Service Towns	22	2,481.0	Canterbury
Southern Commercial Towns	14	1,829.1	Trowbridge
Southern Manufacturing Towns	13	1,214.0	Wellingborough
Southern Rural Areas	19	1,082.7	Penzance
Northern Freestanding Cities	13	3,893.8	Derby
Northern Service Towns	12	1,162.5	Llandudno
Northern Commercial Towns	19	2,079.6	Hereford
Northern Manufacturing Towns	14	1,664.5	Scunthorpe
Northern Rural Areas	33	1,720.3	Penrith

Note: constituent LLMAs in each class are listed in Appendix 3
Source: data from Population Census Small Area Statistics

highlighted in the existing literature are the drift from North to South and the shift from more heavily urbanized zones to smaller towns and more rural areas, but attention has also been drawn to the role of industrial structure, metropolitan status and local decentralization. Our definition of 'places' is based on functional criteria which group together localities which are linked strongly to each other by commuting flows and thus produce a set of 280 relatively self-contained Local Labour Market Areas (LLMAs) which exhaust the national territory of Great Britain. Because they are defined on a meaningful and consistent basis, these places can be compared directly one with another and can thus be ranked according to their size, growth rate or degree of prosperity. These places can also be classified according to the dimensions just outlined, so as to allow the measurement of variability along each dimension and permit the assessment of the relative importance of each dimension in producing Britain's geographical complexion. In addition, this areal framework has the built-in flexibility of allowing the identification of other settlement forms, particularly through grouping places together to produce Functional Regions and Metropolitan Regions but also through subdivision of Functional Regions into the component zones of Cores, Rings, and Outer and Rural Areas.

Further reading

The most succinct account of the principal dimensions of recent geographical change in Britain is provided by Goddard, J.B. 1983: Structural change in the British space economy, in Goddard, J.B. and Champion, A.G. (eds.), *The urban and regional transformation of Britain* (London: Methuen), 1–26. Further background information can be found in Short, J.R. and Kirby, A. (eds.) 1984: *The human geography of contemporary Britain* (Basingstoke: Macmillan); Johnston, R.J. and Doornkamp, J.C. (eds.) 1982: *The changing geography of the United Kingdom* (London: Methuen); and House, J.W. (ed.) 1982: *The UK Space: resources, environment and the future* (London: Weidenfeld & Nicolson, 3rd ed).

Previous studies which have examined the extent of disparities between places in Britain include Coates, B.E. and Rawstron, E.M. 1971: *Regional variations in Britain* (London: Batsford); Knox, P.L. 1974: Spatial variations in levels of living in England and Wales in 1961, *Transactions, Institute of British Geographers* 62, 1–24; Donnison, D. and Soto, P. 1980: *The good city* (London: Heinemann); and Champion, A.G. 1983: *England and Wales '81: a census atlas* (Sheffield: Geographical Association).

The methodology of the Functional Regions approach is written up more fully in Coombes, M.G. *et al.* 1982: Functional Regions for the Population Census of Great Britain, in Herbert, D. T. and Johnston, R.J. (eds.) *Geography and the urban environment: progress and research applications* 5 (Chichester: Wiley), 63–112. A justification of this approach can also be found in Champion, A. G. *et al.* 1983: A new definition of cities, *Town and Country Planning* 52, 305–7, and earlier arguments in favour of using local labour market areas for urban and regional analysis are presented by Hall, P. 1971: Spatial structure of metropolitan England and Wales, in Chisholm, M. and Manners, G. (eds.) *Spatial policy problems of the British economy* (Cambridge: Cambridge University Press), 96–125, and by Smart, M.W. 1974: Labour market areas: uses and definitions, *Progress in Planning* 2, 239–55.

Examples of applications of earlier functional regionalizations to the study of urban and regional change in Britain are provided by Hall, P. *et al.* 1973: *The containment of urban England: 1 – urban and metropolitan growth processes or Megalopolis denied* (London: Allen & Unwin); Drewett, R., Goddard, J. and Spence, N. 1976: *British cities: urban population and employment trends 1951–71* (London: Department of the Environment); and Spence, N. *et al.* 1982: *British cities: an analysis of urban change* (Oxford: Pergamon).

2
Population change

Changes in population distribution are the most obvious manifestation of more fundamental changes at work in the urban and regional system and contribute an essential ingredient of the changing complexion of the places within that system. This chapter deals with the most basic expression of population change, namely trends in the number of people, whereas subsequent chapters refer to various qualitative aspects such as age composition and socio-economic characteristics. Such is the importance of population change that even with this limited brief, this chapter reveals the impact of all the dimensions of change outlined in Chapter 1 and, because of this, demonstrates the full value of the Functional Region (FR) approach.

The most significant dimension revealed in this chapter is decentralization from Cores to other zones, from Dominants to Subdominants, and from Metropolitan to Freestanding. The same is, however, not true at the broadest spatial scale of the North–South divide, where the continuing growth of the Southern core region at a faster rate than the Northern heartland and periphery constitutes a second notable feature. Thirdly, the analysis shows that the performance of individual places can vary significantly within the broader urban and regional framework according to settlement size and industrial structure, as well as being affected by peculiar local circumstances. Both the general patterns and the particular deviations from them help to pose some of the more specific questions which subsequent chapters try to shed light on.

The national context

One of the most remarkable features of the period under study is the absence of significant overall population growth. Whereas the number of people in Britain grew by some 5 per cent in each of the two intercensal decades 1951–61 and 1961–71, the population enumerated by the 1981 Census was no more than 0.6 per cent higher than the level 10 years before, representing barely one-tenth the earlier rates of growth. The estimates made by the Office of Population Censuses and Surveys and the Registrar General Scotland indicate that the annual rate of increase had peaked in the first half of the 1960s, coinciding with a rise in the birth rate and a peaking in the influx of people born in the New Commonwealth. Subsequently, following a progressive fall, the rate of overall population change reached virtually zero in 1974–75 and even became negative in some years during the later 1970s and early 1980s – a development which had been expected by no one 20 years ago when the emphasis was on earmarking major new sites for further development to accommodate massive anticipated increases in population. This move towards zero growth by the national population has, however, by no means led to a drying up of internal shifts, though the residential mobility levels recorded by the 1981 Census were somewhat lower than at 1971, being affected by the major nationwide reduction in job opportunities in the two years immediately following the onset of deep recession in 1979 (see Chapter 5).

Population change at individual places

The variability of population change rates round Britain is immediately obvious from Fig. 2.1, which indicates the percentage change between 1971 and 1981 in the populations of each of the 280 Local Labour Market Areas (LLMAs). The key shows a very wide range of individual performance from an upper extreme of a 61 per cent increase to a 12.5 per cent decline; in other words, one relatively self-contained settlement in Britain had, by 1981, 8 people for every 5 that it had in 1971, while at the other extreme another place lost 1 in 8 of its 1971 population over the 10 year period. Altogether, 62 places saw their populations grow by more than 10 per cent – a very rapid rate of increase compared with the national figure of barely 0.6 per cent – while almost half (134) of the 280 places in Britain recorded growth rates in excess of 5 per cent. Meanwhile, 66 places – over 1 in 5 – registered population decline during the decade. Clearly the period since 1971 had brought substantial change to many places despite the context of the virtually static national population level.

The geographical patterns of population change produced by the sum of the experiences of the individual places convey an overwhelming impression of the exodus from the larger cities and most heavily urbanized parts of Britain. In Fig. 2.1 the conurbations appear as 'windows' of population decline surrounded by areas of growth. The distinction between major city and surrounding places is particularly clear in south-east England, where the national capital is almost completely encircled by fast growing LLMAs, many of which register growth rates of over 10 per cent. It is also quite evident in the West Midlands, while the South Wales coalfield area stands out in stark contrast with the rest of Wales. Faster growing satellites can also be identified round the conurbations of northern England and Scotland, though here fewer have experienced very high rates of growth (Fig. 2.1).

Equally impressive is the fact that high rates of population growth are not confined to the LLMAs immediately fringing the major cities. Indeed, in some cases the innermost rings of satellite towns have shared the declining fortunes of their nearby major city since 1971, as is illustrated by the experiences of Reigate and Redhill, Slough, Watford and Welwyn round London. Round the northern and western sides of London, in particular, the rate of population growth rises progressively with increasing distance from London itself, reaching a peak at a distance of some 70–100 km in an arc stretching from Horsham and Haywards Heath in the south through Basingstoke and Newbury in the west to places like Banbury, Northampton, Peterborough and Bury St Edmunds in the north. In northern England a zone of more rapidly growing LLMAs including Kendal, Harrogate, Northallerton and York separates the poorly performing industrial areas of old Lancashire and Yorkshire from the also generally declining cities of Tyne and Wear, Teesside and Humberside (Fig. 2.1).

The most notable aspect of the decentralization tendencies, however, is the extensive part of more remote rural Britain which experienced high rates of growth in the 10 years up to 1981, of which the North Pennine growth zone is merely a minor part. East Anglia and the South West peninsula are composed very largely of places which recorded growth rates of over 5 per cent, while

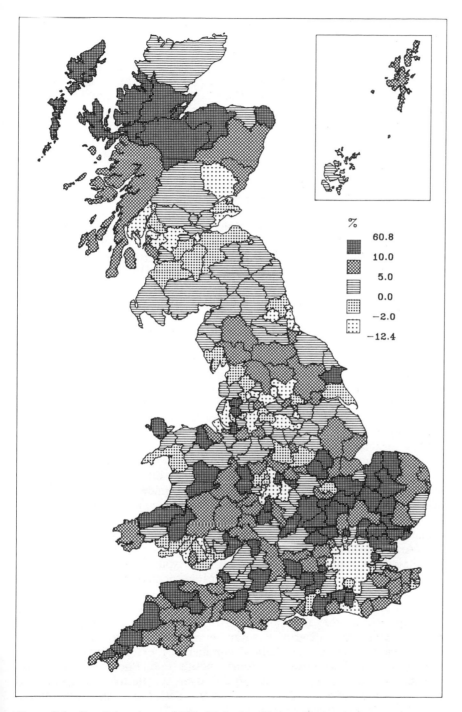

Figure 2.1 Population change 1971–81, by Local Labour Market Areas
Source: Population Census. Note that the Orkneys are combined with Thurso and the
Shetlands with Aberdeen

these vigorous rates of growth can be seen to extend well into the more rural parts of the East Midlands, particularly Lincolnshire, and into central and western Wales – all areas which in the not so distant past have tended to be associated with depopulation as a result of labour shedding by agriculture and other primary production activities and because of the dying out of local crafts and farm-support industries. Rapid growth also characterizes most of the LLMAs in northern Scotland, particularly those centred on the Moray Firth and the Aberdeen–Peterhead areas, chiefly the result of the North Sea oil development which grew rapidly in the early 1970s (Fig. 2.1).

Alongside the pervasive effects of decentralization, however, a second dimension of population change appears reasonably clear – the contrast between the fast-growing South and less dynamic North. Indeed, if it was not for the rather special developments in northern Scotland, the North–South divide would show up more strongly in Fig. 2.1 than it actually does. Otherwise, generally speaking, the proportion of fast-growing places declines with increasing distance from the South East. In population growth terms, the clearest demarcation between North and South constitutes a line running broadly between the Dee estuary in the west to the Humber in the east but extending southwards to loop round the West Midlands conurbation and the larger industrial cities of the East Midlands. Indeed, even if the line is drawn further south to run between the Severn estuary and Lincolnshire – the definition of North adopted in Chapter 1 – the only major areas of rapid growth included in the North, besides northern Scotland, are rural Wales and the North Pennines/Vale of York zone, both sizeable in areal coverage perhaps but characterized by relatively low population densities. The 'drift to the South' thus appears to remain a potent force despite the recent emergence of counterurbanization tendencies.

This much is, of course, well known as a result of previous analyses which have studied the broad geographical patterns of population change on the basis of local authority districts and other types of areal framework, though we would claim that the details of these patterns are more faithfully recorded by the CURDS approach than others which pay little attention to the geography of individual places. Where the FR framework does hold a real advantage, however, is in allowing us to identify with a high degree of confidence the geographical entities which have seen the fastest rates of population change and to rank them in various ways. As shown in Table 2.1, the list of LLMAs registering the highest relative growth is dominated by the officially designated overspill schemes of the New and Expanded Towns programme, with Milton Keynes being the place recording the highest growth rate of 61 per cent, Redditch's population up by 50 per cent over the 10-year period, and with Tamworth, Thetford, Bracknell and Basingstoke all growing by at least a quarter. At the same time, while this accounts for several of the places with the fastest absolute growth, a number of unofficial growth centres have also been catering for substantial numbers of extra people, including Aldershot and Farnborough, Bournemouth and Poole, Norwich and Chelmsford, all up by at least 30,000 over the decade. Dingwall and Invergordon LLMA achieved the fastest relative increase in Scotland, Aberdeen the largest absolute increase (Table 2.1).

Most notable in the list of fastest declining places is the fact that some of Britain's largest cities predominate in the rankings, and not only for absolute losses but also for relative decline (Table 2.1). It is impressive that there is not even one example of a smaller LLMA facing special circumstances that can outstrip the relative declines of Liverpool, Glasgow and Manchester, which

Table 2.1   Population change 1971–81, extreme LLMAs

Highest LLMAs		Lowest LLMAs	
Percentage change			
Milton Keynes	+60.8	Liverpool	−12.5
Redditch	+49.9	Glasgow	−12.1
Tamworth	+37.4	Manchester	−11.1
Dingwall & Invergordon	+34.0	South Shields	−9.4
Thetford	+30.4	Sunderland	−8.8
Bracknell	+28.1	London	−8.6
Basingstoke	+25.7	Greenock	−7.2
Huntingdon	+24.7	Peterlee	−6.5
Widnes & Runcorn	+23.6	West Bromwich	−5.4
Peterborough	+23.4	Consett	−5.1
Telford	+22.5	Dundee	−4.6
Horsham	+19.2	Hartlepool	−4.6
Newmarket & Ely	+18.0	Birmingham	−4.2
Northampton	+18.0	Bradford	−4.1
Banbury	+18.0	Birkenhead & Wallasey	−4.0
Absolute change			
Milton Keynes	+60,995	London	−740,781
Peterborough	+37,752	Glasgow	−166,193
Aldershot & Farnborough	+37,487	Manchester	−145,375
Northampton	+36,910	Liverpool	−134,371
Bournemouth	+36,461	Birmingham	−63,799
Norwich	+34,377	Leeds	−27,374
Chelmsford	+31,792	Sunderland	−26,532
Luton & Dunstable	+30,795	Sheffield	−18,047
Telford	+30,106	South Shields	−16,694
Wigan	+28,658	Coventry	−16,509
Aberdeen	+27,687	Bradford	−15,193
Redditch	+27,361	Birkenhead & Wallasey	−14,760
Widnes	+26,615	Dundee	−11,850
Colchester	+25,772	Brighton	−10,739
Tamworth	+25,749	Greenock	−9,689

Source: calculated from data extracted from the Population Census

had lost 1 in every 8 or 9 of their 1971 populations by 1981, and also that there are few LLMAs in Britain that have done worse in population performance than that of the national capital, with its loss of 1 in 12 of its original size. These losses tend to overshadow the albeit significant levels of loss registered by some smaller places which have suffered particular economic difficulties in recent years, such as South Shields, Sunderland, Greenock and Birkenhead reeling from the decline of ship building and port industries, the former steel towns of Consett and Hartlepool, the coalmining area of Peterlee (despite the New Town status of its main settlement) and the textile city of Bradford.

The North–South divide also comes through in Table 2.1 as strongly as the effect of size of place. Amongst the two lists of fastest declining places, only three of the 30 mentions relate to places lying south of the Severn–Lincolnshire line, two for London and one for Brighton. Meanwhile, the few Northern entries into the list of most rapidly growing places are readily explained in terms of either planned overspill schemes (Redditch, Tamworth, Widnes and Runcorn, Telford and Wigan) or North Sea oil development (Aberdeen, Dingwall and Invergordon). It is, of course, true that the effect of size and regional location overlap, in the sense that the majority of Britain's largest cities lie north of the Severn–Lincolnshire line and smaller cities and towns account for a larger proportion of the places in the South, but the regional contrasts revealed by Table 2.1 are considerably larger than can be explained in terms of size of place alone.

This preliminary examination of population redistribution has highlighted the predominance of decentralization tendencies in the British urban system, but has also revealed the continuing significance of broad regional location for the performance of individual places. In the next section we take advantage of the flexibility of the Functional Regions approach to study decentralization patterns in more detail, while the following section uses alternative groupings of places to gauge the relative importance of North–South, urban–rural and other factors in contributing to the variability in population change rates across Britain.

Decentralization in the urban system

Centrifugal tendencies appear to constitute a major component of the geographical patterns of population change recorded between 1971 and 1981. In Chapter 1 it was stressed that decentralization is neither a single process nor is it clearly understood, with distinctions being drawn between suburbanization, local decentralization, and wider-scale decentralization. The Functional Regions framework allows decentralization to be measured in three different ways in the urban system: first, shifts between the main settlements (Cores) and the other zones of the Functional Regions (Ring, Outer Area and Rural Area); secondly, the exodus from the major cities of the most heavily urbanized regions (Metropolitan Dominants) to their collar of satellite cities and towns (Metropolitan Subdominants); and thirdly, losses from Metropolitan Britain to those Freestanding LLMAs which are relatively independent of the country's largest centres on a day-to-day basis. We look at each of these three scales in turn. There is of course a fourth, even higher-order component of decentralization that distinguishes between the national core region and the more peripheral regions of the country (the North–South divide in our framework), but we leave that until the following section.

Table 2.2　Population change 1971–81, by type of Functional Region and Zone

Type of Functional Region		Zone				
		Core	Ring	Outer	Rural	All Zones
Dominant	000s	−1,693	+314	+27	+15	−1,337
	%	−9.7	+8.9	+8.5	+6.2	−6.2
Subdominant	000s	+111	+320	+79	+6	+515
	%	+1.4	+7.4	+10.6	+4.3	+3.9
Freestanding	000s	+116	+575	+220	+207	+1,118
	%	+1.2	+10.6	+10.2	+9.4	+5.8
All Regions	000s	−1,466	+1,208	+327	+228	+296
	%	−4.2	+9.1	+10.1	+8.8	+0.6

Source: calculated from data extracted from the Population Census

Cores to Rings and beyond

A massive redistribution of population took place between 1971 and 1981 between the Cores of the national urban system and the rest of the country (Table 2.2, bottom row, and Fig. 2.2). In aggregate, the Cores lost nearly one and a half million people, representing a fall of over 4 per cent from their 1971 population level. The major proportion of this loss was captured by the Rings, which accommodated an extra 1.2 million over the decade. This is perhaps unsurprising, because the Rings constitute the type of zone that is most closely related to the Cores in everyday life. Nevertheless, it is significant that the 9.1 per cent rate of growth achieved by the Rings is matched very closely by the rates averaged by the Outer and Rural zones, which are far more independent of the Cores. On this aggregate basis at least, the redistribution of population from the Cores appears to be affecting the more remote locations just as much as the primary commuting zones (Fig. 2.2).

Dominants to Subdominants

The experience of the Metropolitan Regions provides further evidence of the pervasiveness of decentralization. Besides the massive shift out of the Cores to other zones which make up the FRs, a major redistribution took place between FRs (Table 2.2, last column). In aggregate, the 20 Dominant FRs – the cities at the hearts of Britain's principal urban concentrations – lost over 1.3 million between 1971 and 1981, an overall reduction of 6.2 per cent. Meanwhile, the Subdominant FRs which make up the remainder of the Metropolitan Regions increased their populations by 3.9 per cent. As particular examples, London's population dropped by 740,000 but that of its Subdominants grew by 303,000, while the principal cities of the Conurbations (Birmingham, Manchester, Glasgow, Liverpool and Newcastle upon Tyne) together lost 517,000 people in contrast to a gain of 116,000 in their Subdominants (Fig. 2.3). In fact, these six cities account for a very large proportion of the overall loss sustained by the Dominants during the 1970s; the fall in their population by over 8 per cent during the 10-year period constitutes one of the most dramatic developments recorded by the 1981 Census.

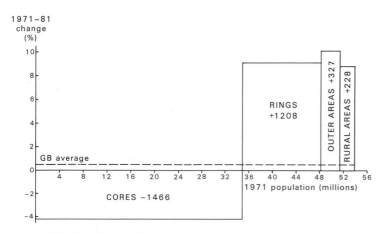

Figure 2.2 Population change 1971–81, by zones
Source: Population Census

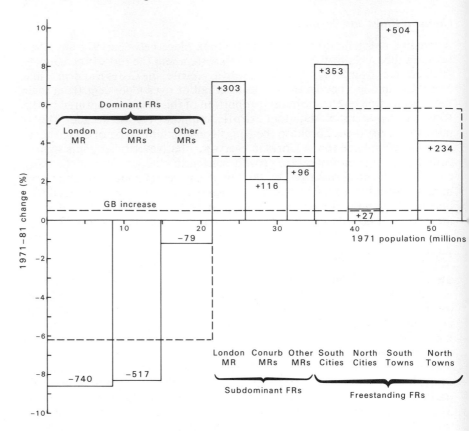

Figure 2.3 Population change 1971–81, by types of Functional Regions
Source: Population Census

Metropolitan Regions to the rest of the country

As Fig. 2.3 shows, the Subdominant city-regions were by no means able to
absorb all the people decentralizing from the Dominant cities between 1971
and 1981. As a result, the 20 Metropolitan Regions lost a total of about
820,000 people during the decade. Over half this loss, amounting to 437,000,
occurred from London's Metropolitan Region, with the MRs of Glasgow
(– 174,000), Manchester (– 115,000) and Liverpool (– 74,000) being the
other main contributors, though in all 12 of the 20 MRs lost population and
the largest absolute gain was the meagre 22,000 added by Bristol's MR.

As a result of this scale of population loss from Metropolitan Britain and
the national population increase of nearly 300,000, the remainder of Britain
comprising the 115 Freestanding FRs accounted for well over 1 million more
people in 1981 than they had 10 years earlier (Table 2.2). This represented a
growth rate of nearly 6 per cent for the decade and increased their share of the
national population total from 35.5 per cent in 1971 to 37.4 per cent in 1981.
These Freestanding FRs, which are relatively independent of Britain's major
cities, therefore grew faster in both absolute and relative terms than the other
two broad types of FRs. Clearly, proximity to the largest cities is no longer a
significant factor in terms of attracting population growth; rather the
reverse.

Zonal changes for the three FR types

In reality, of course, the patterns are not as clear-cut as the aggregate data would suggest. Table 2.2 suggests at least two qualifications, even though this also presents a highly summarized picture. First, not all Cores have recorded absolute decline. The Cores of the Subdominants and Freestanding cities both grew in aggregate even though this represented relative decentralization because the Rings were growing faster than the Cores. Indeed, further analysis shows that 22 out of 93 Subdominants and 28 out of 115 Freestanding cities were experiencing relative or absolute *centralization* with their Cores growing at a faster rate than their Rings.

Table 2.2 also shows that the aggregate picture of redistribution between Cores and other zones presented in Figure 2.2 is by no means entirely a localized phenomenon, but is partly a result of redistribution over much longer distances. By distinguishing the performance of each type of zone within each type of FR, it can be seen clearly that the overall loss of population from Britain's Cores can be attributed entirely to the massive losses sustained by the Cores of the 20 Dominant cities. These contained in 1981 nearly 1.7 million fewer people than in 1971, representing a loss of almost 1 in every 10. Barely one-fifth of this net loss could be absorbed by the remaining parts of the Dominants, with the remainder fuelling the growth of the Cores and other zones of the Subdominant and Freestanding city-regions (Table 2.2 and Fig. 2.4).

A final point to note is that, apart from the Cores, the zones of all three types of FRs shared relatively similar rates of increase, with only the numerically insignificant Rural elements of the Dominants and Subdominants falling outside the range of 7.4–10.6 per cent at this level of aggregation (Table 2.2 and Fig. 2.4). This reflects the effects of two relatively new aspects of population change in Britain that were noted in the previous section, namely the outward extension of population growth into areas which are not so closely bound to the main urban centres as the traditional commuting rings and satellite towns and the strong performance of Rural Areas in Freestanding Britain which have in the past been viewed as having poor prospects. All in all, the overwhelming impression left by these analyses is of a major exodus of people from the cores of a few large cities and the spreading of this overspill very widely over the rest of the urban system.

Principal dimensions of population change

The decentralization process provides a large part of the explanation as to how places in Britain can exhibit such a wide range of growth rates when the size of the national population has hardly changed at all. On the other hand, the degree of variability in performance between individual places is much greater than can be accounted for purely in terms of their general exposure to counterurbanization tendencies. It has been suggested that size of settlement, broad regional location, distance from metropolitan centres and economic structure have all conspired to influence patterns of population change. The FR framework provides an opportunity for attempting to gauge the significance of these factors both by classifying places in Britain on each dimension in turn and by applying a multidimensional classification which can help to isolate the separate effect of each one.

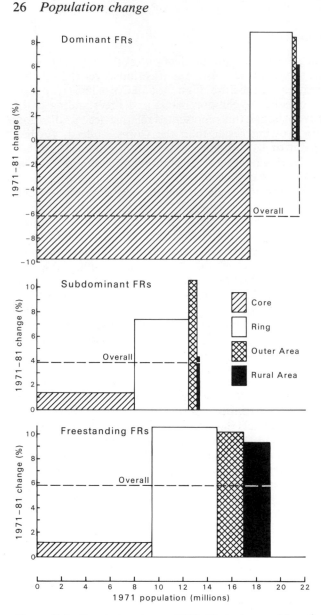

Figure 2.4   Population change 1971–81, by types of Functional Regions and zones
Source: Population Census

Size and regional location

The role of settlement size has featured several times in the discussion so far, particularly the flight from the largest cities and the rapid growth of some smaller places. Table 2.3 confirms that LLMA size is a highly significant dimension, with rates of population change ranging from a decline of over 8 per cent for London and the group of five Conurbation Dominants to an increase of over 8 per cent for the 52 Rural Areas taken together. Moreover, there is a continuous progression across this urban–rural continuum, with smaller size being associated with faster growth – the type of negative rela-

Table 2.3 Population change 1971–81, by LLMA size

Size group (no. of LLMAs)	1971 population 000s	1971–81 change 000s	%
London (1)	8,577.1	−740.3	−8.6
Conurbation Dominants (5)	6,230.0	−518.2	−8.3
Other Large Dominants (5)	3,533.8	−51.4	−1.5
Cities (61)	17,046.3	+347.6	+2.0
Towns (156)	16,014.4	+1,031.0	+6.4
Rural Areas (52)	2,575.3	+227.7	+8.8
Great Britain (280)	53,977.0	+296.5	+0.6

Source: calculated from data extracted from the Population Census

tionship which has received so much attention in the literature on counter-urbanization since it appears to represent a complete reversal of the traditional association between large size, economies of scale, and attractiveness for rapid growth. If there are any breaks in the progression shown in Table 2.3, they relate to the distinctiveness of the six largest cities and to the greater similarity of Towns to Rural Areas than to Cities, but these may relate more to the choice of classes rather than to any substantive aspect of the size factor.

The regional component seems considerably less important than the size factor, at least when examined in the context of broad regional divisions shown in Table 2.4. There is only a relatively small percentage point difference between the 1.8 per cent growth of population in Britain south of the line between the Severn estuary and Lincolnshire and the 0.5 per cent loss of population for the rest of the country. This is a narrower margin than existed in the 1950s and 1960s, but it takes on greater significance in the context of research which has shown that many other Developed World countries witnessed a reversal of periphery-to-core population movements at national scale in the 1970s (Vining and Pallone, 1982). Table 2.4 shows that the North continued to lose population in the 10 years up to 1981 and that the more remote parts of the North comprising Wales, Scotland and the Northern Region of England (the 'Periphery' in Table 2.4) experienced more rapid decline than the more centrally located part of the North (our 'Heartland'). Of course, the main part of Britain's core, as represented by the London Region, was losing population heavily, but the results of such counterurbanization processes were apparently confined to the rest of the South, which benefited more from this source of extra population than from the shift away from the North (Table 2.4).

Table 2.4 Population change 1971–81, by Regional Division

Regional Division	1971 population 000s	1971–81 change 000s	%
London Region	12,809.0	−437.0	−3.4
Rest of the South	11,341.2	+883.0	+7.8
South	*24,150.2*	*+446.0*	*+1.8*
Heartland	18,721.8	−64.6	−0.4
Periphery	11,105.1	−84.9	−0.8
North	*29,826.9*	*−149.5*	*−0.5*
Great Britain	53,977.0	+296.5	+0.6

Source: calculated from data extracted from the Population Census

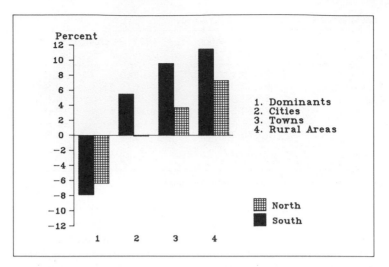

Figure 2.5   Population change 1971–81, by LLMA size and regional location
Source: Population Census

Leading on from this, it has been suggested by previous studies that a very large part of regional differentials in population change can be accounted for by differences in the settlement-size composition; in other words, that the poorer showing of the North is a direct result of its having a larger proportion of its population living in larger places which have been declining because of the general urban–rural shift. We are able to test this hypothesis by classifying the LLMAs according to size and regional location simultaneously, as shown in Fig. 2.5. Both major divisions of Britain show clear evidence of the urban–rural shift, with the range being rather wider in the South, but for three of the four size groups the growth rates are significantly higher in the South, with a similar difference of around 6 percentage points for Cities and Towns but with a somewhat narrower margin for Rural Areas. For the Large Dominants the poorer performance of the South reflects the domination of this group by London (the only other representative here being Bristol); in fact, given its huge size compared with the other Large Dominants, London did well to restrict its losses as much as it did. It would therefore appear from Fig. 2.5 that the regional dimension plays a significant role alongside the urban–rural shift and it is likely that the overall difference between North and South might have been wider had it not been for the depressing effect of the London LLMA on the South's performance.

A multi-dimensional classification

A more systematic attempt at isolating the effect of each dimension is made in Fig. 2.6, which uses the 16 of the 19 LLMA classes (see Chapter 1) that are broadly comparable between North and South. Though it does not therefore include all 280 LLMAs in the way that Fig. 2.5 does, it provides further breakdowns relating to metropolitan status and industrial structure. The role of settlement size is again very clear, with smaller places growing more rapidly than larger places in percentage terms within both Metropolitan and Freestanding Britain and in both halves of the country. The effect of metropolitan status is, however, not so clear-cut. In the South the Subdominant

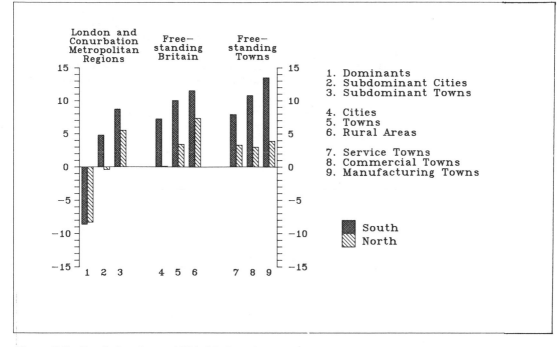

Figure 2.6   Population change 1971–81, for selected LLMA groupings
Source: Population Census

Cities and Towns in London's Metropolitan Region have not been performing as strongly as the places of equivalent size in the rest of the South, but in the North there is very little difference in growth rate between Free-standing Cities and the Subdominant Cities of the five largest Metropolitan Regions, and, more significantly, the Subdominant Towns have been growing faster than their Freestanding equivalents. During this decade, therefore, while our previous analysis in Figure 2.3 has shown that metropolitan status tends to have acted as a depressant on population growth rates, this effect is not consistent across the country, even in terms of the very broad categorization by size and regional location used here.

The part played by industrial structure is also by no means as clear cut as our comments on Britain's de-industrialization in Chapter 1 might have suggested. Admittedly, the decline of employment in manufacturing industry can be considered as partly responsible for the importance of the settlement-size factor, whereas in Fig. 2.6 we explicitly differentiate industrial structure only for Freestanding Towns. At first glance, however, it is surprising that it is places with the largest proportions of manufacturing employment that have grown the most rapidly and that, while there is little variation in performance between the three types of town in the North, there is such a regular direct relationship between growth rate and importance of manufacturing amongst the Freestanding Towns in the South.

The reason for the surprises found in the effect of metropolitan status and industrial structure can be traced to the distinctive history of individual places as well as to broader differences in the underlying processes. The positive association between population growth and manufacturing employment in the Freestanding Towns of southern Britain can be traced, in part, to the larger number of New and Expanded Towns which tend to have well above average proportions of their workforce involved in manufacturing industry, though it is also the case that the types of manufacturing found in these southern towns differ considerably from those in their northern equivalents which tend to be dominated by mass-production branch plants and have poor representations of new high-technology industries. In the North it is the relatively poor performance of the Commercial and Manufacturing Towns compared with their southern counterparts that can be held largely responsible for depressing the average performance of Freestanding Towns below that of the Subdominant Towns. A subsidiary explanation for this difference is that the process of overspill from the major provincial capitals is not as well developed as it is from London. Moreover, in emanating from five centres rather than one and affecting surrounding places which have been experiencing their own economic difficulties rather than having a strong growth momentum of their own, this overspill can more readily be absorbed by the collar of Subdominants rather than having to resort the more distant non-metropolitan areas, except insofar as a proportion of the big city losses in the North has been taking place over the very much greater distances involved in the drift to the South.

Summary

This chapter has shown that, despite the relapse to a situation of virtually zero growth in the national population, relatively few places in Britain have experienced little or no change in their population size. One in five of the Local Labour Market Areas used as our definition of 'place' registered growth rates in excess of 10 per cent for the inter-censal period 1971–81, while a somewhat larger proportion experienced net loss of population. The Functional Regions framework has allowed an examination of the role of various factors in differentiating between the performance of individual places. The most consistent features are that smaller places grew faster than larger ones and that places of comparable size and status grew faster in the South than in the North. The part played by industrial structure is complicated by the diversity of activities subsumed under the label of manufacturing and by the special circumstances of some of the places with high concentrations of manufacturing employment. It seems that the effects of the flight from the big cities on their surrounding regions differ considerably between the case of London and that of the northern conurbations, particularly because of contrasts in their spatial contexts and economic complexion. Perhaps the most conspicuous aspects of population redistribution over this period, however, are the small extent of areas from which the majority of 'net migrants' were drawn – essentially the main built-up areas of half-a-dozen major cities – and the very broad spread of the destination areas, going far beyond the traditionally recognized suburban rings and not only affecting adjacent city regions but also going into relatively remote and rural localities.

The policy implications of these massive shifts are already well known. They are not limited to questions of regional balance and regional policy but also involve issues of strategic land-use planning, ranging along the urban–rural spectrum from inner city decay to pressurized rural areas and in most cases spanning a broader scale than can be encompassed by the statutory local planning authorities. While the British government has responded with a review and cutting back of regional policy during the first half of the 1980s and a simultaneous upgrading of its efforts to deal with the problems of the inner city, it has consistently turned its face against consideration of the broader strategic matters. Yet it is sanguine to note – and this is not so widely recognized – that it takes time for fundamental shifts in population distribution to occur and for their full implications to manifest themselves and, while the absolute volumes of net population shifts between areas since 1971 seem massive, they have not markedly reduced the high degree of concentration in Britain's Cores and Dominants (cf. Tables 1.1 and 1.2). Three in every five persons continue to live in the 20 Metropolitan Regions, while London retains its overwhelming degree of dominance over the nation's next largest cities, still leaving great potential for further decentralization if conditions permit and – given the selective nature of most migration streams – opening up the possibility of a widening of the differentials between places in their shares of the 'haves' and 'have-nots', employed and unemployed, white and coloured, and young and old.

Further reading

Background information on population change in Britain can be found in Compton, P.A. 1982: The changing population, in Johnston, R.J. and Doornkamp, J.C. (eds.) *The changing geography of the United Kingdom* (London: Methuen), 37–73; and in Lawton, R. 1982: People and work, in House, J.W. (ed) *The UK space: resources, environment and the future* (London: Weidenfeld & Nicolson, 3rd ed, 103–203.

The main dimensions of population change in the two decades up to 1971 are analysed by Champion, A.G. 1976: Evolving patterns of population distribution in England and Wales 1951–71, *Transactions, Institute of British Geographers New Series* 1, 401–20. Other accounts of more recent trends are provided by Kennett, S. and Spence, N. 1979: British population trends in the 1970s. *Town and Country Planning* 48, 221–4; and by Champion, A.G. 1983: Population trends in the 1970s, in Goddard, J.B. and Champion, A.G. (eds.) *The urban and regional transformation of Britain* (London: Methuen), 187–214.

Several recent studies have given particular attention to counterurbanization tendencies in Britain, including Champion, A.G. 1981: Population trends in rural Britain, *Population Trends* 26, 20–3; and Robert, S. and Randolph, W.G. 1983: Beyond decentralization: the evolution of population distribution in England and Wales, 1961–81, *Geoforum* 14, 75–102.

3
Demographic restructuring

Just as important as the size of the population living in a particular place are its composition in terms of demographic characteristics such as age structure, household types and ethnic groups and the way in which these are changing over time. In the first place, demographic structures reflect past events in the history of a place and can therefore afford an insight into the factors' responsibility for trends in overall population numbers, whether through the ageing of an established population *in situ* or through the migration behaviour of various population sub-groups. Secondly, changes in demographic structure – along with aspects of socio-economic change examined in Chapter 7 – can have profound effects on the size of the labour force, the range of house types needed, and the demands placed on the service sector.

Moreover, just as we have seen in Chapter 2 that the virtually static size of the national population masks important shifts in its geographic distribution, so too does it fail to convey any sense of the major changes which have been taking place in its demographic structure in recent years. Nationally the number of older people has been increasing as the very large birth cohorts of the early years of the century have moved into pensionable age groups, while the reduction in birth rate since the mid 1960s means fewer pre-school and school children in the early 1980s than a decade before. Average household size is becoming smaller with more people living alone and with the reduction in the number of very large families. The proportion of overseas-born and ethnic minorities in the population has been increasing, as immigration from the New Commonwealth and Pakistan and elsewhere has continued – albeit at a lower rate than in the first half of the 1960s – and as both these newcomers and the earlier arrivals have engaged in family building.

Furthermore, these sub-groups are not distributed evenly across Britain but constitute widely differing proportions of the populations of individual places. Certain parts of the country, especially seaside resorts and spa towns, have long been renowned for their attractiveness to retirement migrants, while particular cities have developed reputations as the home of large Irish, Asian or West Indian communities. It has also been noted that decentralization from the inner parts of the largest cities has principally involved younger, better-off families, tending to cause acceleration in the ageing of the population and in the reduction of average household size in these areas while, at least for a few years, rejuvenating the age structure of the smaller surrounding cities and towns to which they have moved.

This chapter's purpose is to attach some quantities to these trends for individual places and types of places and to look for any features which are not so well known. In particular, it outlines which cities and towns have the highest or lowest representation of the various sub-groups and then assesses whether these patterns are the product of processes operating over the last few years or whether they are inherited from an earlier period. In the context of the importance of decentralization forces noted in Chapter 2, we are seeking to discover whether the combined effect of population redistribution and national trends in demographic structure is leading to the accentuation of pre-existing differences between places or towards their elimination. We are also looking to see whether any new dimensions of differentiation and segregation are emerging. We cannot hope to cover all aspects of demographic restructuring in this chapter, so we choose to focus on age structure with special reference to the elderly, on household change with reference to trends in household size and on ethnic composition with reference to the numbers of British residents born in the New Commonwealth and Pakistan.

Age structure

National context

The main features of Britain's changing age structure are shown in Table 3.1. By 1981 the proportion of Britain's usual residents who were of pensionable age and over (60 and over for women, 65 and over for men) had reached 17.7 per cent. The major part of this increase was due to growth in the number of very elderly (those aged 75 and over). By contrast, the number of children fell by 12 per cent over the 10-year period, with the particularly dramatic fall in 0–4 year olds reflecting the fall in birth rate since 1964. The effects of earlier birth rate trends are also evident in the intermediate age groups. Thus, considerable upheavals have been taking place in national age structure, amounting to upward or downward movements of some 10 per cent in the size of these broad age groups in only 10 years, but the overall impression is of an increasingly aged society.

Age composition in 1981 for individual places

Fig. 3.1 gives an initial impression of the degree of variability in age structure between the 280 Local Labour Market Areas (LLMAs), showing the range between the highest and lowest proportions for each of the five age groups used and the coverage of the top and bottom quintiles of cases within this range. The degree of differentiation between places is particularly wide for the elderly, with Clacton having over 1 in 3 of its population in retirement age, twice the national average share and over three times the proportion recorded by Tamworth. The majority of LLMAs, however, are grouped

Table 3.1   Age structure 1971–81, Great Britain

| Age group | Age composition | | | Change in numbers 1971–81 (%) |
	1971 (%)	1981 (%)	1971–81 (% point)	
0–4	8.1	6.0	−2.1	} −11.9
5–15	17.3	16.2	−1.1	
16–24	13.1	14.2	+1.1	+8.9
25–44	24.1	26.2	+2.1	+9.4
45–PA	21.1	19.5	−1.6	−7.1
PA+	16.3	17.9	+1.6	+10.0
(75+)	4.7	5.8	+1.1	+24.2
Total	100.0	100.0	–	+0.6

Note: PA = Pensionable Age (65 for men, 60 for women)
Source: OPCS *1981 Census Monitor CM57* and *Key Statistics for Urban Areas*, Table 1

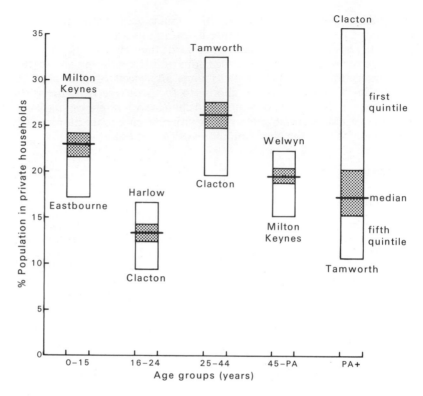

Figure 3.1   Age structure 1981: distribution of proportions for 280 LLMAs
Source: Population Census

quite tightly round the median for each age group, suggesting a dichotomy between a set of places with quite distinctive age structures and a larger group which parallel the national pattern. Amongst the former, there is a clear distinction between the youthful age structures of fast-growing New and Expanded Towns like Milton Keynes, Tamworth and Harlow and the elderly populations of seaside resorts and retirement towns like Clacton and Eastbourne.

Fig. 3.2 puts a spatial perspective on to this distinction between young and older populations. The areas with significantly greater than average shares of 25–44 year olds in 1981 are concentrated in a massive and compact zone to the north and west of London, with the few remaining areas adopting similar locations round the other major English cities (Fig. 3.2A). New and Expanded Towns head this group, with Tamworth, Milton Keynes, Redditch and Huntingdon to the fore, but many other towns such as Chelmsford, Aldershot and Hertford have also grown rapidly. The top quintile of places in relation to the representation of the elderly is dominated by the four clusters of East Anglia, the South Coast, the South West peninsula and western Wales, with the remainder made up largely by other seaside resorts further north (Fig. 3.2B). The two maps give a clear impression of the long-term effects of migration drawing younger working-age people into the more suburban parts of Metropolitan Britain and helping older people escape from the pressures of more urbanized areas and take advantage of the generally lower house prices and better quality environments of smaller and more peripheral places.

Figure 3.2 Age structure 1981, by LLMAs – A: 25–44 year olds; B: pensionable age and over
Source: Population Census

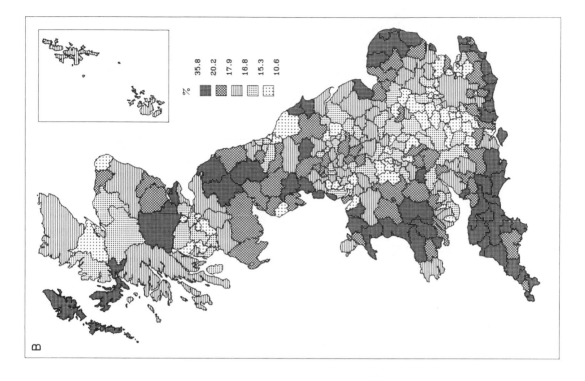

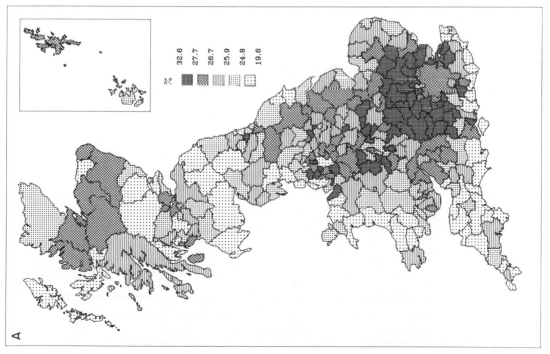

The elderly 1971–81

The increasing number and distinctive distribution of the elderly make this population sub-group particularly important in terms of public policy and indeed also for understanding urban and regional change. The question is whether the present concentrations of older people have been produced by recent migration trends or have been inherited from an earlier period and, in relation to this, whether the spatial polarization of the elderly has been increasing or declining in the last few years. In addition, it is important to look at individual places to see which have experienced the greatest gains not just in the proportions of elderly in their populations but also in the absolute numbers, because these have implications for medical and related services, as well as for housing needs and shopping patterns.

The geographical patterns in Fig. 3.1 suggest the Metropolitan–Free-standing dimension as the most appropriate for measuring the degree of differentiation in the proportion of elderly in 1981 and for examining the extent to which this changed during the preceding 10 years. Table 3.2 confirms the direct relationship between proportion of elderly and distance from the metropolitan heart of the country, but is notable that the Dominants themselves do not fit this pattern, since the Subdominants have by far the lowest proportion owing to their attractiveness for young families moving away from the larger cities. It is equally clear from Table 3.2, however, that this distinctive pattern is not of recent making; it already existed in 1971 and indeed over the subsequent 10 years the growth in the elderly's share of the population has been slowest in the Freestanding Rural LLMAs and fastest in the Dominants.

The large extent to which the 1981 pattern was inherited from before 1971 is confirmed by the experience of individual LLMAs (Table 3.3). The 10 places with the highest proportion of the elderly in the populations in 1981 also had relatively high levels in 1971, with none lower than fourteenth rank then. Similarly, seven of the lowest 10 LLMAs in 1981 had even lower proportions of elderly in 1971; all but Redditch and Milton Keynes were in the bottom 13 then. As in 1981, the 1971 distribution of elderly was focused very clearly on the coastal areas of East Anglia and the South East, an extensive part of the South West peninsula, and central and northern Wales.

In terms of the changing numbers of elderly people, Table 3.4 shows that the largest absolute increases between 1971 and 1981 were generally recorded by the major cities. In terms of the relative increases in numbers of the elderly, by contrast, it is generally the small rapidly growing areas which have

Table 3.2 Age structure, 1971–81, by LLMA type

LLMA type	25–44 years old			Pensionable age & over		
	1971	1981	1971–81	1971	1981	1971–81
Dominant	24.2	26.2	+2.0	15.5	17.3	+1.8
Subdominant	25.2	27.1	+1.9	14.6	16.0	+1.3
Freestanding Urban	23.8	26.1	+2.3	17.3	18.5	+1.2
Freestanding Rural	23.7	25.9	+2.3	18.2	19.2	+1.0
Great Britain	24.3	26.4	+2.1	16.0	17.5	+1.5

Note: Pensionable age = 65 for men, 60 for women
Numbers may not sum to totals because of rounding
Source: calculated from data extracted from the Population Census

Table 3.3 The elderly as a proportion of all people in private households, extreme LLMAs 1981

Highest LLMAs	1981 %	(1971) (%)	Lowest LLMAs	1981 %	(1971) (%)
Clacton	35.8	(33.8)	Tamworth	10.6	(11.1)
Eastbourne	32.8	(32.6)	Harlow	11.1	(7.6)
Worthing	31.9	(34.0)	Basildon	11.2	(9.7)
Hastings	30.2	(31.2)	Redditch	11.6	(12.6)
Llandudno	28.2	(28.3)	Milton Keynes	11.7	(14.0)
Torquay	28.0	(28.0)	Crawley	11.7	(9.0)
Chichester & Bognor	27.9	(25.3)	Stevenage	11.8	(8.0)
Chard	27.7	(25.5)	Ellesmere Port	11.9	(9.8)
Margate & Ramsgate	27.4	(28.0)	Bracknell	12.0	(10.4)
Bournemouth	26.1	(24.8)	Basingstoke	12.4	(11.6)

Source: calculated from data extracted from the Population Census

experienced the greatest growth (Table 3.4). In Stevenage, Thetford, Bracknell, Harlow and Crawley the number of pensionable age or over grew by around 50 per cent or more. Though these numbers were building on only a relatively small base and were accompanied by quite large increases in younger age groups, they indicate the need for a set of age-specific facilities which had probably not been available previously and, in the case of the New Towns particularly, represent harbingers of much larger increases in the numbers of elderly and very elderly in the foreseeable future.

The very elderly

Amongst the elderly, it is the group aged 75 and over which has grown most rapidly in the last few years and poses some of the most challenging problems for public-sector services. In general their spatial occurrence is very similar to that of the whole elderly population, though they constitute less than a third of the latter. Both in 1971 and in 1981 the seaside resorts contained the highest proportions of very elderly in their household populations, with Worthing, Hastings, Eastbourne and Clacton having around 1 person in 10 in this age group in 1971 and with the biggest percentage point increases to 1981 occurring in Clacton (+ 3.3), Eastbourne (+ 2.8), and Chichester and Bognor Regis (+ 2.0). The smallest proportions in 1971 were located in the

Table 3.4 1971–81 change in the number of elderly in private households, LLMAs with largest absolute and relative increases

Largest absolute increases			Largest relative increases		
LLMA	Number	(%)	LLMA	%	(Number)
London	22,826	(1.7)	Stevenage	64.2	(3,839)
Birmingham	22,449	(11.1)	Thetford	59.3	(4,917)
Bournemouth	16,226	(15.7)	Bracknell	52.3	(3,375)
Coventry	14,318	(23.2)	Harlow	48.8	(3,528)
Norwich	12,312	(18.2)	Crawley	48.2	(3,233)
Sheffield	12,303	(11.7)	Huntingdon	43.2	(2,710)
Bristol	12,022	(10.8)	Corby	41.8	(2,263)
Nottingham	11,743	(11.9)	Welwyn	37.5	(3,120)
Stoke	11,730	(15.7)	Basingstoke	35.8	(4,332)
Newcastle	11,451	(7.8)	Milton Keynes	35.6	(4,901)

Source: calculated from data extracted from the Population Census

longer established New Towns like Stevenage, Harlow and Corby with only 1 in 50 aged 75 or over, while between 1971 and 1981 the least change in the proportion occurred in the later New Towns and more recent growth areas particularly in northern Scotland. Indeed, in three LLMAs (Milton Keynes, Redditch and Dingwall) the proportion of the population aged 75 and over actually fell during the 10-year period.

In terms of absolute numbers of the very elderly, the largest increase was recorded by London (+ 50,000), followed by Birmingham, Glasgow, Manchester, Bournemouth and Newcastle (between + 12,700 and + 9,000). The relative rates of growth in this age group for most of these larger cities were close to the national average of 25 per cent, but as with the whole elderly population the rate for London was significantly lower at 14 per cent and that for Bournemouth somewhat higher at 33 per cent. None of the 280 LLMAs saw a reduction in its number of very elderly over the 10-year period, with the lowest rates of increase being for Dover, Accrington, Burnley and Blackburn (10–12 per cent increase). Meanwhile, New and Expanded Towns dominate the list of LLMAs seeing the highest percentage rate of increase in numbers of the very elderly, with Stevenage, Thetford, Clacton, Bracknell, Huntingdon, Corby and Welwyn containing in 1981 at least half as many again as they had in 1971.

Households and household size

Along with age structure, household size and composition are associated with some of the most important changes affecting the population of Britain in the last few years. To a certain extent, the two are linked, because an increase in the proportion of elderly people and a decline in fertility rates both tend to depress average household size, but the number of households in a given size of population is also affected by the extent to which 'single' adults live by themselves or in larger households, this in its turn depending on income, personal preference, and social custom, as well as levels of cohabitation, divorce or separation, and remarriage. If these considerations are borne in mind, it is clear that there is unlikely to be a simple one-to-one relationship between population change and change in number of households. Indeed, as we shall show, the relationship between population and households has altered fundamentally since 1971 at national level, while there are also great variations between places in average household size which have largely maintained themselves during the recent past. Moreover, to some extent, household factors can be seen to be partly responsible for the patterns of population change described in Chapter 2, because changes in household size affect the capacity of a given size of housing stock.

National Context

The 1981 Census enumerated a total of nearly 19.5 million private households in Britain, accommodating around 52.8 million people. This gives an average size of 2.71 persons per household (Table 3.5). A direct comparison with 1971 Census data shows that over the decade the number of households had increased by 1.3 million or around 7 per cent, while the number of people living in private households had grown by 0.8 per cent, barely one-tenth as much. In 1971 the average household size had been 2.88 persons, indicating a fall of 6 per cent or – in other words – an increase of 6 per cent in the

Table 3.5 Household size, 1971–81, Great Britain

Size of household (persons)	1971		1981		1971–81	
	000s	% total	000s	% total	000s	% change
One	3,314	18.2	4,242	21.8	+297	+28.0
Two	5,747	31.6	6,222	31.9	+475	+8.3
Three	3,468	19.1	3,327	17.1	−141	−4.1
Four	3,077	16.9	3,532	18.1	+456	+14.8
Five	1,495	8.2	1,436	7.4	159	−4.0
Six	658	3.6	501	2.6	−157	−23.8
Seven and over	437	2.4	232	1.2	−205	−46.9
All households	18,195	100.0	19,492	100.0	+1,297	+7.1
Household population	52,345	–	52,759	–	+414	+0.8
Average household size	2.88	–	2.71	–	+0.17	−6.0

Note: These figures do not take into account the change between 1971 and 1981 Censuses in the definition of 'household' (see text) or the change in the definition of 'population'.
Source: Population Census

occupied housing stock without allowing for the effect of overall population growth.

These figures, however, do not give a completely accurate indication of the rate of fall in household size and its implications for the housing market. Between the two Censuses a change was made in the definition of a 'household' which had the effect of amalgamating certain households that had previously been considered separate. Moreover, differences in the treatment of students between the two Censuses meant a fall in 140,000 in the numbers recorded outside private households at schools and colleges. Both these changes have the effect or artificially swelling household size in 1981 relative to 1971 and thus of damping down in the Census statistics the extent of the real decline in household size over the decade. Due to lack of information the effects of these changes cannot be included in the analyses here.

Bearing in mind the definitional problem, Table 3.5 shows the main reasons behind the Census-recorded fall in average household size between 1971 and 1981. There were dramatic falls in the number of very large households alongside a very marked increase in the number of households comprising only one person. The latter is particularly remarkable, since it is shown to have risen by well over 900,000 – some three-quarters of the overall increase in household numbers – despite being the group which is likely to have been most severely reduced by the definitional change. The reduction in large households has helped to increase the number of four-person households, while the decline in three-person households may partly be attributable to the growth of one-person households, though the definitional change may also be partly responsible for the irregularity in the change rates in the middle of the size range (Table 3.5).

Change in household numbers, by LLMA

The most important aspects revealed by an examination of the household figures for individual places are, first, the fact that the percentage rates of change for household numbers are higher than for population change in every case and, second, that the difference between the two rates varies considerably from place to place. Both these points are exemplified in Table 3.6.

Table 3.6 LLMAs with the largest and smallest increase in household numbers and comparisons with population change rates, 1971–81 (%)

Highest LLMAs	House-holds	(Population)	Lowest LLMAs	House-holds	(Population)
Milton Keynes	68.9	(62.4)	Manchester	−4.6	(−11.1)
Redditch	53.8	(46.7)	Glasgow	−4.2	(−12.0)
Tamworth	45.1	(38.1)	London	−3.7	(−8.4)
Bracknell	44.8	(31.0)	Liverpool	−2.9	(−12.0)
Thetford	42.5	(32.2)	South Shields	−1.1	(−9.2)
Dingwall	37.5	(35.4)	Bradford	−0.8	(−3.6)
Huntingdon	35.2	(26.8)	Accrington	−0.2	(−2.8)
Basingstoke	33.0	(26.8)	Sunderland	0.2	(−8.6)
Widnes & Runcorn	31.6	(24.0)	Burnley	0.3	(−2.6)
Peterborough	31.0	(24.5)	Peterlee	0.6	(−6.5)

Note: Population change rate relates to persons present in private households.
Source: Calculated from data extracted from the Population Census

Most impressive is the fact that only seven of the 280 LLMAs experienced a decline in number of households over the decade – and even part of this can be attributed to the definitional change, because this particularly affects multiply-occupied dwellings so characteristic of the larger cities in this list. LLMAs like Manchester, Glasgow and Liverpool which saw a 11–12 per cent loss of population registered no more than a 3–4 per cent decline in household numbers, showing how difficult it is in a situation of falling household size for large, highly developed cities to build enough houses to hold on to their previous population levels. In some LLMAs, however, the difference between the two rates amounts to no more than 3 percentage points, indicating a much slower fall in average household size over the decade. In the fastest growing LLMAs differences in the rates of household and population change cover an even wider range from only 2 percentage points at Dingwall to 14 at Bracknell (Table 3.6).

Change in household size

The relationship between rates of change in households and population is shown in Table 3.7 in terms of the change between 1971 and 1981 in persons per 100 households. Some of the smallest falls in household size occur in some traditional retirement areas and in a substantial group of LLMAs in the North West and adjoining parts of Yorkshire, while some of the largest falls

Table 3.7 Change in average household size, 1971–81, extreme LLMAs (persons per household)

Highest LLMAs	1971–81 Change	(1971)	Lowest LLMAs	1971–81 Change	(1971)
Rochdale	−0.03	(2.77)	Stevenage	−0.41	(3.27)
Blackburn	−0.03	(2.79)	Corby	−0.41	(3.32)
Rossendale	−0.04	(2.71)	Harlow	−0.40	(3.28)
Nelson & Colne	−0.05	(2.65)	Crawley	−0.35	(3.23)
Worthing	−0.07	(2.39)	Welwyn	−0.33	(3.10)
Hastings	−0.07	(2.43)	Bracknell	−0.31	(3.12)
Braintree	−0.07	(2.81)	West Bromwich	−0.30	(3.08)
Accrington	−0.07	(2.72)	Bathgate	−0.30	(3.22)
Bury	−0.08	(2.83)	Ellesmere Port	−0.29	(3.25)
Halifax	−0.08	(2.70)	Liverpool	−0.29	(3.15)

Source: Calculated from data extracted from the Population Census

took place in the large conurbation cities and in various smaller places which had previously grown rapidly but were entering a phase of maturity or decline in the 1970s. Among the latter, the earlier New Towns are strongly represented among the places with the largest declines in average household size, along with two industrial 'growth towns' of the 1960s and two conurbation LLMAs, all areas which were characterized by household sizes well above the national average of 2.88 in 1971. All of the 10 LLMAs with the lowest falls had started out in 1971 with below-average levels of household size associated with an older-than-average population and presumably had less scope for further falls or subsequently saw some rejuvenation of their population through an influx of younger people, as suggested earlier in the chapter. Overall, there is a fairly strong correlation (r = − 0.75) between 1971–81 percentage point change in persons per household and the 1971 level for the 280 LLMAs.

As with the distribution of the elderly, therefore, the effect of the changes of household size taking place in the 10 years up to 1981 has been to reduce the range of differences between places. To a large extent, the differences which remain are those inherited from before 1971. Thus by far the smallest household sizes continue to be found in the traditional retirement areas made up of the coastal resorts like Eastbourne, Clacton, Worthing, Hastings, Brighton, Torquay and Thanet, all with 2.45 or fewer persons per household. London also falls into this category, with its growing elderly proportion and its significant attraction for young adults, as also do the main cities and adjoining rural areas of eastern Scotland and the Borders.

At the other extreme comes Coatbridge and Airdrie (3.11 persons per household), along with Ellesmere Port, Motherwell, Widnes and Runcorn, Basingstoke, Stornoway, Basildon and Bathgate, all 2.93 or higher. Large average household size thus appears to be associated with decentralization (particularly in the South East) and high-fertility industrial zones (particularly Merseyside, Teesside and Clydeside), while both high fertility and recent growth have helped to maintain the large average household size in north-west Scotland. Indeed the western half of Scotland in general continues to constitute by far the greatest concentration of the larger households (6 +persons) in Britain, with proportions in some cases higher than the various English cities with large New Commonwealth populations like Bradford, Birmingham and West Bromwich.

New Commonwealth and Pakistan immigrants

National context

A third feature of changing demographic structure is the increasing size of the ethnic minority groups permanently resident in Britain, particularly those hailing originally from the New Commonwealth and Pakistan (NCWP). According to the 1981 Census, 3.36 million of Britain's usual residents had been born outside the UK, of which the largest single national group was from the Irish Republic, involving 607,000 or 18 per cent of the overseas-born. Those born in the NWCP amounted to just over 1.5 million, some 45 per cent of the overseas-born, and their number had increased by a third since 1971, pushing their share of the British population up from 2.12 to 2.83 per cent over the decade. It should be noted that, by definition, these figures do not include the children born to NCWP parents after their move to Britain, but constitutes the surplus of the NCWP-born moving to Britain between the

Figure 3.3   Proportion born in the New Commonwealth and Pakistan – A: 1981;
B: 1971–81 percentage point change
Source: Population Census

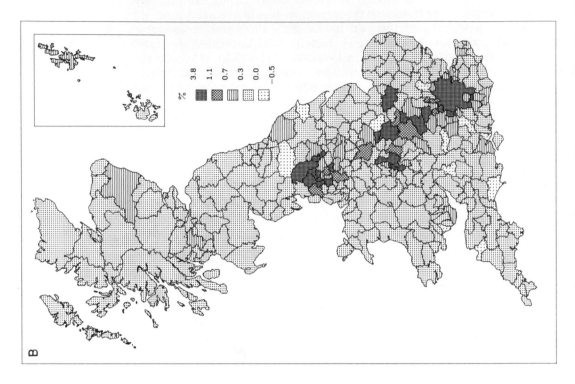

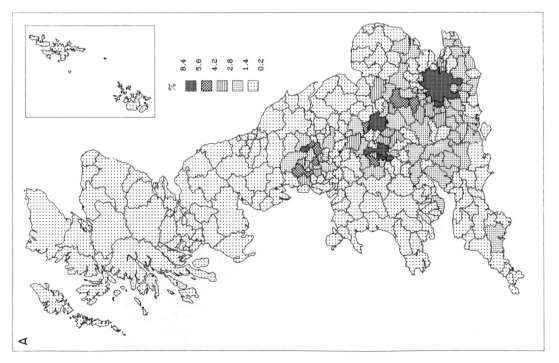

two Censuses over the number who have died or left the country over this period. The only measure of the total number of people of NCWP extraction that can be derived from the 1981 Census – not a very satisfactory one at that, and not readily comparable with the 1971 Census – relates to the private households headed by a person born in the NCWP; 571,000 households containing nearly 2.2 million people or about 4.1 per cent of Britain's household population in 1981. Though even by this extended definition only a relatively small part of Britain's population, it takes on much greater significance because of its distinctive skin colour, its rapid growth and its very special geographical distribution.

Distribution of the NCWP-born population 1981

At the level of the 280 Local Labour Market Areas (LLMAs) NCWP immigrants were highly concentrated in a small number of areas. London and Leicester had almost three times the national average share, while Bradford, Slough, Birmingham and Smethwick had over twice the national average. These six places accounted for 843,000 (55.0 per cent) of all the NCWP-born people enumerated by the 1981 Census.

In all, only 34 LLMAs had more than the national average proportion of 2.83 per cent. As is clear from Fig. 3.3A, these are concentrated in the most urbanized parts of central and southern Britain, including London and its north-western satellites and two parts of England's traditional industrial heartland – the engineering and hosiery areas of the West and East Midlands and the textile areas of east Lancashire and West Yorkshire. Indeed, most of the rest of northern Britain had less than half the national average shares, as did most of East Anglia and the South West peninsula. No Rural LLMA had more than half the national average share.

Concentration is also characteristic within Functional Regions (FRs). In 1981 the NCWP-born made up 4.1 per cent of all residents in the Cores of the 228 FRs compared to only 0.8 per cent in their other zones combined. This contrast is particularly wide in the London Metropolitan Region, where the proportion was as high as 7.6 per cent for the Cores as opposed to 1.5 per cent elsewhere, but it also comes through strongly in relative terms in the Heartland of the industrial Midlands and Northern England, where the levels were 3.3 and 0.6 per cent respectively in 1981.

1971–81 changes in the proportions of NCWP immigrants

The increase of around 400,000 in the number of NCWP-born over the decade largely reinforced the patterns of concentration which had been developing before 1971. Countrywide the proportion of NCWP-born increased by 0.7 percentage points, but the LLMAs which experienced a higher increase than this are relatively few and are concentrated in the urban spine of England running from London through the industrial Midlands to the textile zone of north east Lancashire and West Yorkshire (Fig. 3.3B). Table 3.8 shows that Leicester experienced the most rapid growth in the NCWP-born proportions over the decade, followed by London and Slough, all with increases of over 2.5 percentage points.

While the trends since 1971 have obviously increased the dominance of these places in the distribution of the NCWP-born, it is clear from Table 3.8 that they had already by 1971 proved to be the most attractive places. Only 7 of the 22 LLMAs with percentage point increases of over 1.08 had less than

Table 3.8   Increase in population of NCWP-born, 1971–81, highest 22 LLMAs

LLMA	% point change in NWCP-born 1971–81	% NWCP-born		Location quotient	
		1971	1981	1971	1981
Leicester	3.81	4.62	8.43	2.18	2.98
London	2.66	5.76	8.42	2.72	2.98
Slough	2.56	5.08	7.64	2.40	2.70
Blackburn	2.13	2.92	5.05	1.38	1.78
Bradford	1.98	5.76	7.74	2.72	2.73
Loughborough	1.91	3.19	5.10	1.50	1.80
Luton	1.89	3.22	5.11	1.52	1.81
Nelson & Colne	1.72	2.47	4.19	1.17	1.48
West Bromwich	1.64	3.71	5.35	1.75	1.89
Birmingham	1.56	4.81	6.37	2.27	2.25
Smethwick	1.55	4.60	6.15	2.17	2.17
Oldham	1.39	2.00	3.39	0.94	1.20
Milton Keynes	1.39	1.04	2.43	0.49	0.86
Crawley	1.38	2.19	3.57	1.03	1.26
Dewsbury	1.38	3.41	4.79	1.61	1.69
Peterborough	1.34	1.55	2.89	0.73	1.02
Burnley	1.31	1.09	2.40	0.51	0.85
Keighley	1.18	1.49	2.67	0.70	0.94
Accrington	1.16	1.52	2.68	0.72	0.95
Bolton	1.15	2.88	4.03	1.36	1.42
Wellingborough	1.08	2.09	3.17	0.99	1.12
Watford	1.08	2.11	3.19	1.00	1.13
Great Britain	0.71	2.12	2.83	1.00	1.00

Source: Calculated from data extracted from the Population Census

the national average share of NCWP-born in 1971. Of these, Milton Keynes and Peterborough are both growth towns designated under the New Towns Act and Wellingborough is an Expanded Town under the 1952 Town Development Act, so all of these have attracted high levels of inward movement from the London area since 1971. Oldham, Burnley, Keighley and Accrington, on the other hand, may have gained as a result of their proximity to the established NCWP communities in north-west England. In nearly all these 22 cases (Birmingham and Smethwick being the exceptions) the rate of increase in the NCWP-born has been enough to increase their location quotient, producing greater imbalance compared with the national average.

At the zone level, too, the events of the decade have reinforced a pattern of concentration which already existed. The Cores increased their proportion of NCWP immigrants by 1.2 percentage points between 1971 and 1981, pushing up the 1971 level of 2.9 per cent by a substantial factor. The fraction in the other zones combined, by contrast, remained virtually unchanged at around 0.8 per cent. Thus the margin between Cores and other zones increased from 2.2 to 3.3 percentage points over the decade.

At the same time, it should be pointed out that, particularly at the zone level but also to some extent for LLMAs, the increasing polarization is not due to changes in the distribution of the NCWP-born alone, but is also affected by the decentralization trends of the overall population. In fact, at the zone level the percentage increase in the NCWP-born has been remarkably evenly matched in the Cores and the outer zones, both standing at around 35 per cent for the decade, but this increase only affects concentrations of immigrants in tandem with population change in general. Decentralization from the Cores has markedly increased the degree of concentration of the NCWP-born in these areas and, conversely, in the outer zones the accommodation of large numbers of newcomers has diluted the net increase in NCWP-born. Of course, in partially resisting the decentralization tide, these immigrants are also influenced by other factors, particularly the fact that, for reasons of economic and social disadvantage, they are less likely to be among those who have migrated from Cores since 1971. Additionally, the large established communities of immigrants have proved highly attractive to later newcomers to Britain, even where local job opportunities have been poor, as in the Northern textile towns.

Summary

In spite of the little change in Britain's total population size, some impressive changes have been taking place in recent years in its composition, with the rise in the numbers of the elderly and younger adults, the substantial fall in average household size and the large increase in the proportion born in the New Commonwealth. These trends have affected the geography of the British population in different ways, reflecting not only the impact of the changes occurring in the 10 years up to 1981 but also the differentials inherited from before 1971. The factors affecting age structure and household size during the past decade, in fact, appear to have been operating to reduce the major differentials which existed previously. The more remote coastal and rural areas with the tradition of an older population have thus recently seen the smallest increases in their elderly proportion, while places which had very large average household size in 1971 experienced some of the greatest reductions during the subsequent 10 years. By contrast, the NCWP-born were already heavily concentrated in a few large cities by the beginning of the 1970s and subsequent immigration appears to have been distributed generally in the same pattern, a process which – taken along with the overall loss of population sustained by most of these places – has significantly exacerbated their overrepresentation there.

These patterns of demographic restructuring, particularly when viewed in the context of trends in overall population distribution, have had some far-reaching policy implications and, because of the inexorable momentum of past demographic events, hold plenty of future challenges in store. It is unlikely that the problems caused by the extreme concentration of ethnic minorities in the inner parts of Britain's larger cities will sink far down the political agenda for decades to come, while the needs of the growing number of elderly, and particularly the very elderly, can already be charted out pretty clearly, even though their spatial aspects seem to be somewhat volatile. The implications of past fluctuations in birth rates will be a continuing cause for concern, as the large birth cohorts of the later 1950s and 1960s scramble for jobs and houses and are followed through school by the much smaller cohorts born in the 1970s and 1980s. The general narrowing of differentials between places in age structure and average household size sounds a welcome development in theory, but, taken along with the national trends, is likely to give rise at local level to a range of difficult policy issues as places change in their demographic character in a variety of different ways.

Further reading

A concise introduction to changing demographic structures in Britain is provided by Kelsall, R.K. 1979: *Population* (London: Longman, 4th ed). A range of valuable information is available in Office of Population Censuses and Surveys 1978: *Demographic review 1977: a report on population in Great Britain* (London: HMSO). More up-to-date statistics can be obtained from the quarterly journal *Population Trends* (London: HMSO).

A study which deals comprehensively with both national and regional aspects of population structure, age structure, households and immigration from overseas is Lawton, R. 1982: People and work, in House, J.W. (ed.) *The U K space: resources, environment and the future* (London: Weidenfeld & Nicolson, 3rd ed). Another extremely useful study, which also looks at the implications of demographic trends for housing, pensions, education, health care and other social services, principally at the national level, is Ermisch, J. 1983: *The political economy of demographic change* (London: Heinemann).

An outline of Britain's age structure trends can be found in Davis, N. 1976: Britain's changing age structure 1931–2011, *Population Trends* 3, 14–17, and in Craig, J. 1983: The growth of the elderly population, *Population Trends* 32, 28–33. The fullest accounts of the geography of the elderly are provided by Law, C.M. and Warnes, A.M. 1976: The changing geography of the elderly in England and Wales, *Transactions, Institute of British Geographers New Series* 1, 453–71; Allon-Smith, R.D. 1982: The evolving geography of the elderly in England and Wales, in Warnes, A.M. (ed.) *Geographical perspectives on the elderly* (Chichester: Wiley), 35–52; and Warnes, A.M. and Law, C.M. 1984: The elderly population of Great Britain: locational trends and policy implications, *Transactions, Institute of British Geographers New Series* 9, 37–59.

Trends in the number of people born in the New Commonwealth and Pakistan are examined by the Office of Population Censuses and Surveys 1979: Population of New Commonwealth and Pakistani ethnic origin: new projections, *Population Trends* 16, 22–7. Their geographical patterns are described in a pioneering study by Peach, C. 1968: *West Indian migration to Britain: a social survey* (Oxford: Oxford University Press) and by Lee, T.R. 1977: *Race and residence* (Oxford: Clarendon Press). A useful case study is Woods, R.I. 1977: A note on the future demographic structure of the coloured population of Birmingham, England, *Journal of Biosocial Science* 9, 239–50; while some of the implications of the distinctive geographical concentrations of these minority groups are explored in Runnymede Trust 1980: *Britain's black population* (London: The Runnymede Trust and the Radical Statistics Race Group).

4
Labour force growth

Britain's labour force has grown slowly over the last few years, but – just as for population growth and demographic structure – major changes have taken place in the composition of the labour force and in its geographical distribution. The total number of economically active people grew by 269,000, or not quite 1.1 per cent, between 1971 and 1981, but this represents the balance between a loss of 423,000 men and a gain of 692,000 women. At the level of the Local Labour Market Area (LLMA) the experiences of this decade range from an increase of some 64 per cent at one extreme to a fall of over 12 per cent at the other. The geographical patterns of changing labour supply bear a close resemblance to trends in population distribution, while the shift in the gender composition of the labour force clearly reflects changes in the degree to which people offer themselves on the labour market – something which also differs considerably from place to place.

This chapter looks at selected aspects of the way in which labour force changes have taken place in individual places and different types of places. We begin by describing local differences in the rate of change in overall labour supply, identifying the places which have seen the most rapid growth or the largest decreases and outlining the broad dimensions of national space which account for the greatest part of the variability. We then examine the extent to which labour force participation rates vary between places and the way in which they have changed over time, concentrating principally on married women and on the question as to whether recent trends have accentuated or reduced differences between places. We conclude with an assessment of the implications of local changes in labour force size for the balance between economically active persons and the rest of the population who depend on them for total household income, with the aim of discovering which places have the most and least favourable ratios and how far recent events have altered their position relative to each other and the national situation.

Trends in labour supply

Variation between Local Labour Market Areas

The LLMAs which experienced the greatest changes in the size of their total economically active populations between 1971 and 1981 can be seen from Figure 4.1 and Table 4.1. The places with fastest growth are concentrated south of the Severn–Wash line, particularly in the ring of cities and towns lying 30–100 km to the west and north of central London along the M1, M4 and M11 corridors. In this region well above average growth rates are also found along the South Coast, over most of the South West Peninsula and in the remoter parts of East Anglia. As a result of increasing their numbers of economically active by at least a quarter, New and Expanded Towns feature

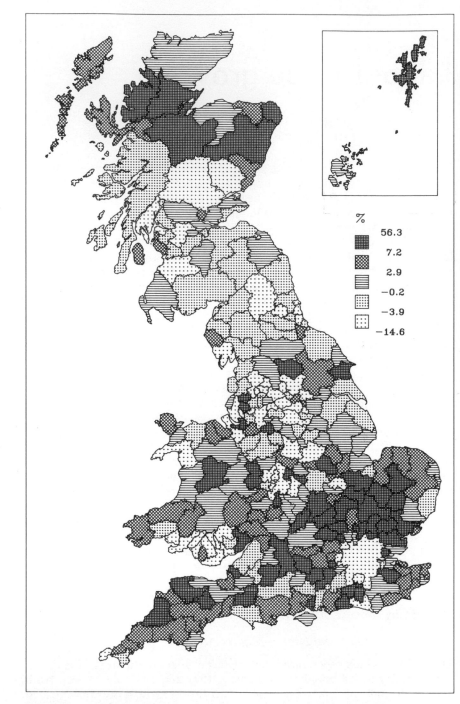

Figure 4.1   1971–81 change in the number of economically active persons, by LLMA
Source: Population Census

Table 4.1 Change in economically active persons, 1971–81, extreme LLMAs

Highest LLMAs	%	(numbers)	Lowest LLMAs	%	(numbers)
Milton Keynes	+64.2	(+29,816)	West Bromwich	−12.7	(−8,898)
Redditch	+44.0	(+12,913)	Manchester	−11.9	(−74,143)
Tamworth	+40.7	(+12,868)	London	−10.6	(−465,621)
Bracknell	+38.4	(+11,838)	Liverpool	−10.4	(−51,836)
Dingwall	+32.4	(+5,039)	Smethwick	−9.0	(−9,916)
Basingstoke	+32.3	(+16,018)	Glasgow	−8.1	(−50,347)
Thetford	+28.7	(+6,887)	Consett	−6.8	(−1,537)
Huntingdon	+28.4	(+7,441)	Accrington	−6.6	(−2,258)
Horsham	+26.5	(+7,500)	Bradford	−6.4	(−11,356)
Peterborough	+23.7	(+17,694)	Birmingham	−6.1	(−45,118)

Source: Population Census Small Area Statistics

most strongly in these areas, together with Horsham, which has been placed under great development pressures by the expansion of nearby Gatwick Airport.

Elsewhere in Britain the main concentration of labour force growth has taken place in northern Scotland around the Moray Firth and in Grampian Region. Dingwall & Invergordon registered the fifth highest percentage rate of labour force growth in Britain, while in terms of absolute numbers gained Aberdeen came third in the country with an extra 24,700 people (compared with 29,800 at Milton Keynes and 26,500 for Aldershot & Farnborough). Otherwise, rapid labour force growth in the North is mainly restricted to certain New and Expanded Towns, with Redditch and Tamworth performing very strongly in relative terms, and a few scattered rural and resort areas (Figure 4.1 and Table 4.1).

As a corollary, places with significant losses in labour force are very largely confined to north of the Severn–Wash line. In the South only seven LLMAs – London, three of its adjacent Subdominants, Brighton, Corby and Penzance – fall in the bottom quintile of places on this criterion, but elsewhere in Britain there are clear concentrations of labour force decline in South Wales and in the industrial areas of the Midlands and northern England (Figure 4.1). The list of most severely affected LLMAs includes some smaller places with local industrial specialisms, but it is dominated by the largest cities which have seen massive contractions in their labour force, particularly in absolute terms (Table 4.1).

Main dimensions of change

Not surprisingly, LLMA size and regional location both emerge as powerful influences upon labour force change, according to the analysis presented in Table 4.2. For Britain as a whole, there is a regular progression through the four size groups shown, with the 9.2 per cent increase in the Rural LLMAs being somewhat greater than for the Towns, which in their turn are separated by a considerably wider margin from the Cities. The biggest distinction, how-ever, is between these three growth categories and the large Dominants, which in aggregate saw their number of economically active persons fall by 672,000. Further analysis reveals that the effect of size also operates within the Large Dominants category, because the contraction can be accounted for entirely by London (– 466,000 or – 10.6 per cent) and the five Conurbation Dominants (– 210,000 or – 7.2 per cent), while the five smallest LLMAs in this category (Bristol, Edinburgh, Leeds, Nottingham and Sheffield) had

Table 4.2   Change in total economically active, 1971–81, by LLMA size and regional location

Size Group	South 000s	%	North 000s	%	Great Britain 000s	%
Large Dominants	−451.6	−9.6	−220.3	−5.2	−671.9	−7.5
Cities	+229.4	+7.8	+51.7	+1.1	+281.1	+3.6
Towns	+379.4	+11.4	+178.2	+4.6	+557.5	+7.7
Rural	+48.0	+11.3	+54.1	+7.9	+102.1	+9.2
Total	+205.2	+1.8	+63.6	+0.5	+268.8	+1.1

Source: Population Census Small Area Statistics

virtually the same combined labour force size in 1981 as in 1971.

The broad regional comparison used in Table 4.2 does not provide such a clear distinction as the size dimension, with labour force growth taking place in both North and South. On the other hand, the overall growth rate in the latter is over three times greater than in the North and the gap widens further if the size groups are compared separately. For the two intermediate categories of Cities and Towns in particular, the differential in performance between the two halves of the country amounts to 6–7 percentage points, while for the Rural LLMAs the difference is about half this. This breakdown gives an indication of the major depressing effect which London has had on the overall performance of the South, for the Large Dominant category there (which comprises only London and Bristol) is totally out of line with the other size groups. Indeed, while the LLMA size factor is important in the North, a relatively small margin separates the growth rates of the three other categories in the South.

Change by gender

Mention has already been made of the major contrast between men and women in labour force changes since 1971, but it is clear from the analysis above that the increase in the number of economically active women, while more than compensating for the decline in the supply of men at the national scale, has not prevented many places from experiencing substantial overall contractions in labour supply. Table 4.3 reveals that, to a large extent, the changes in the female labour force have tended to reinforce the patterns experienced by the male section. This is particularly the case in the South where the very high rates of growth in female labour supply in Cities, Towns

Table 4.3   Change in male and female labour force, 1971–81, by LLMA size and regional location (%)

Size Group	Males South	North	Females South	North	Married women South	North
Large Dominants	−11.8	−8.8	−6.1	+0.7	−10.4	+1.3
Cities	+3.5	−3.2	+15.6	+8.6	+16.3	+9.6
Towns	+7.0	−0.0	+19.4	+12.9	+20.7	+16.0
Rural	+6.2	+3.1	+21.6	+17.7	+25.9	+28.5
Total	−1.5	−3.6	+7.4	+7.7	+6.8	+9.6

Source: Population Census Small Area Statistics

and Rural Areas parallel the significant levels of male labour force growth. Moreover, here the Large Dominants of London and Bristol combined have seen no assistance from women in compensating for their loss of economically active males, with the number of married women in their labour force dropping at almost as fast a rate as for men. The situation is somewhat different in the North, in that for Cities and Towns at least the growth in the number of economically active women has more than offset the decline in male labour supply (cf. Table 4.2), but the large Dominants there saw virtually no increase in female labour supply between 1971 and 1981.

Table 4.3 also shows that, just as for the overall labour force, the three population sub-groups are strongly influenced in their growth rate by LLMA size. It is only the marginally slower growth of economically active males in the Rural LLMAs of the South than in the Towns that disturbs the otherwise pervasive negative relationship between LLMA size and labour force growth rate. On the other hand, the regional dimension is much less clear cut than for the labour force as a whole. Not only does the Large Dominants category in the North consistently out-perform London/Bristol across the three population sub-groups, but for the female labour force this effect spills over into the regional totals, giving the North a faster increase in economically active women than the South. A contributory factor is the more rapid increase in the number of active married women in the North than the South – an impressive feature, even if it is basically a catching-up process for a part of the country where female participation rates have traditionally been well below average.

Changes in labour force participation rates

The changing distribution of the overall labour force between different places in Britain can, to a large extent, be explained directly in terms of the patterns of overall population change and broad trends in age structure. Despite the growing importance of retirement migration, migration between places is still strongly selective in favour of younger working-age people and of the economically active within this group, while places with a younger age structure (usually as a result of previous net migration, though in some cases due to higher fertility) tend to have higher school-leaving rates and lower retirement rates than average. Thus the broad geographical patterns of overall labour force growth shown in Figure 4.1 bear a close resemblance to those of population change seen in Figure 2.1, while the nature and relative importance of the LLMA size and regional dimensions is similar for both population and labour force trends.

On the other hand, the relationship between labour force growth and overall population change is not perfect, as we have seen, for instance, from the significantly poorer performance of London compared to the Conurbation Dominants and from faster growth of the female labour force in the North than the South, particularly of married women in Rural LLMAs. Moreover, we have noted the major contrast in growth rates between the male and female parts of the labour force in their rates of growth at particular types of places. This section therefore focuses on the other part of the explanation for changes in the number of people who are economically active, namely the proportion of the working-age population that offers its services on the labour market; in terms of our data source, being those who admitted to having a job or to being actively in search of a job at the time of the Population Census. We use a crude measure of labour force participation which relates the number of economically active people of at least minimum school-leaving age (15 in 1971, 16 in 1981) and below official pensionable age (65 for men, 60 for women) to the total population within those same age bands. Here we do not have the time to go into the details of age-specific economic activity rates, so trends in our overall participation rates can be affected by changes in the distribution of the working-age population between age groups as well as by changes in the proportion of each age group considering themselves as part of the labour force. Owing to their importance nationally, attention is concentrated on married women, though we take a shorter look at trends in male participation rates towards the end of this section.

Married women in the labour force

Between 1971 and 1981 a major increase took place in the proportion of married women of working age who considered themselves as part of the labour force; up from 48.8 to 56.9 per cent, a rise of 8.1 percentage points and a relative increase of one-sixth over the 1971 proportion. This surge was a nationwide phenomenon in that no LLMA experienced a declining activity rate for married women and in that 3 in 5 of all LLMAs recorded an increase of between 7.0 and 10.8 percentage points. On the other hand, LLMAs with a more extreme experience than this fall into clear-cut categories and the 1971–81 changes were superimposed on a pattern of very wide differentials across the country, with the overall effect of the changes being to close the gap between the extremes.

The LLMAs with the most extreme shifts can be identified in Figure 4.2B and Table 4.4. There is a very clear peripheral bias to the types of places which saw the strongest surge in the involvement of married women in the labour force, particularly in more rural areas like Lincolnshire, western Wales, the Borders and northern Scotland, but also in some heavily urbanized areas including South Wales and Clydeside. The 'top ten' are in fact a varied bunch, ranging from remote rural areas (Stornoway and Elgin) to established service centres (Edinburgh and Chester) and traditionally male-dominated heavy industrial towns undergoing transformation (Bridgend, Swansea, Shotton and Greenock), but virtually all these have in common the fact that they started out with below-average, and in many cases well below average, activity rates for married women. Stornoway is a particu-

Table 4.4 Change in economic activity rates for married women of working age, 1971–81, extreme LLMAs

Highest LLMA	% point change 1971–81	(EAR 1971)	Lowest LLMA	% point change 1971–81	(EAR 1971)
Bridgend	+17.2	(38.0)	West Bromwich	+1.6	(55.4)
Stornoway	+15.5	(27.6)	Nelson & Colne	+1.6	(62.9)
Stirling	+13.6	(45.0)	Bradford	+2.6	(57.1)
Didcot	+13.6	(44.9)	Rossendale	+2.7	(64.3)
Edinburgh	+13.3	(49.7)	Burnley	+2.9	(64.8)
Swansea	+13.3	(42.0)	Rochdale	+3.1	(61.1)
Shotton	+13.1	(36.7)	Crawley	+3.3	(59.6)
Elgin	+13.1	(34.8)	Accrington	+3.3	(63.6)
Chester	+13.0	(43.7)	Lowestoft	+3.3	(46.7)
Greenock	+12.7	(41.6)	Yarmouth	+3.5	(45.8)

Source: Population Census Small Area Statistics

Figure 4.2   Economic activity rates for married women of working age, by LLMA –
A: 1971; B: 1971–81 percentage point change
Source: Population Census

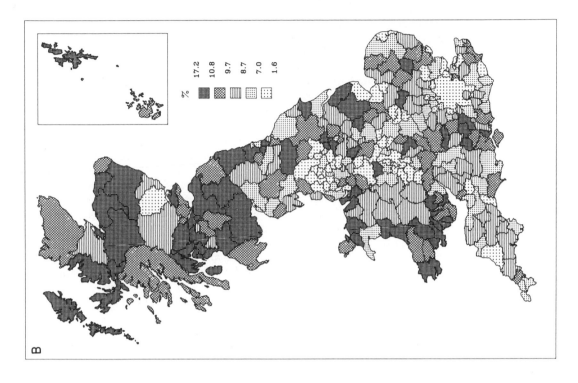

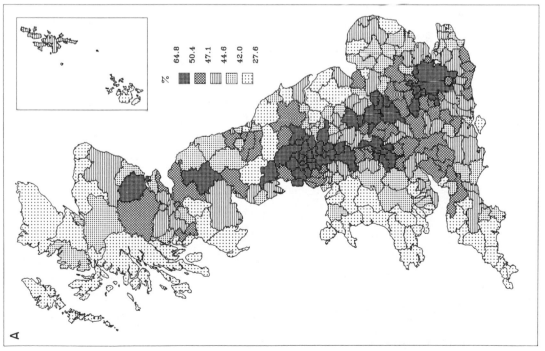

larly extreme example, since the rate in 1971 was only 27.6 per cent and grew to over half as much again by 1981, but all these places have seen their rates increase by over a quarter and several by more than a third (Table 4.4).

The LLMAs experiencing the smallest percentage point rises are even more closely clustered, focusing on London, some more urbanized parts of the Midlands and northern England and a number of seaside resorts and spa towns (Figure 4.2B). The most common denominator of the 'bottom ten' towns in Table 4.4 is that of textile towns with a long tradition of high female labour force participation, with rates in 1971 well over the national figure of 48.8 per cent and in several cases over 60 per cent. Lowestoft and Yarmouth, however, started out with below average rates, so their subsequently pooi showing must be related more to the absence of job opportunities for married women or perhaps to the fact that a greater proportion of their women are in the older working-age groups and not so interested in having jobs.

It seems therefore that, while there has been a general upward shift in labour force participation by married women, the major outcome of recent trends is the narrowing of the gap between the extremes. Indeed between 1971 and 1981 the lowest rate advanced from 27.6 to 40.1 per cent, while the highest rate moved up by less than three percentage points from 64.8 to 67.7 per cent. Moreover, the geographical patterns shown in Figure 4.2 (A and B) are very striking, with most of the textile and other light industrial areas with the highest rates in 1971 having the least increase subsequently (including Dundee but not Hawick & Galashiels) and with many remoter rural areas starting with amongst the lowest rates and seeing the largest increases over the next 10 years.

In terms of the broad frameworks used in our previous analyses, the performances of the Periphery and of Northern Rural Areas are outstanding, with percentage point increases of 10.7 and 10.3 respectively (Table 4.5). At the other extreme, of all the 19 LLMA classes, London had by far the highest participation rate in 1971, but saw by far the smallest increase subsequently. Except at these extremes, however, there is no general progression either across the country or down through the settlement hierarchy, with most groups having followed the national trend quite closely.

Table 4.5 Economic activity rates for married women of working age, 1971–81, by regional division and selected LLMA classes

LLMA Group	1971	1981	1971–81 change	
			% point	%
A Regional division				
London Region	52.0	58.0	+6.0	+11.5
Rest of the South	46.4	55.3	+8.9	+19.2
Heartland	50.6	58.3	+7.7	+15.3
Periphery	44.6	55.3	+10.7	+23.9
B Selected LLMA classes				
London	54.0	59.0	+5.0	+9.3
Conurbation Dominants	50.1	58.8	+8.7	+17.4
Southern Rural	41.7	50.5	+8.8	+21.1
Northern Rural	39.6	49.9	+10.3	+26.1
Great Britain	48.8	56.9	+8.1	+16.6

Source: Population Census Small Area Statistics

Economic activity rates for males

Within the normal working age span up to 65 years old and allowing for the raising of the minimum school leaving age, the overall labour force participation rate for men fell from 91.5 to 90.4 per cent between 1971 and 1981, as the reductions in rates for older working-age groups more than offset the effects of the redistribution of population in favour of the younger age groups. As regards variations between places, there was in 1971 a considerably narrower, but still substantial, range across Britain compared with married women and the effect of the changes over the next 10 years was generally to reduce these differentials. The geographical patterns for both, however, were somewhat different from those for married females, but they indicate some regular factors at work.

Between 1971 and 1981 only 47 LLMAs experienced an increase in economic activity rate for males. Northern Scotland was the most important single area for increasing rates, with Aberdeen and Peterhead most strongly affected in that region. Other notable concentrations of rising male activity rates were parts of the Outer Metropolitan Area round London (particularly on the northern side) and a broad swathe of LLMAs stretching from Avon through Somerset to mid-Devon in the South West. Many of the most rapid increases, however, were recorded by towns with a university, including Cambridge, St Andrews, Aberystwyth, Loughborough, Oxford, Bangor, Lancaster, Exeter, Canterbury and Durham, though this is likely to be a statistical artefact resulting from differences in the timing of the 1971 and 1981 Censuses in relation to the university term rather than to reflect a real factor at work.

The largest concentrations of declining activity rates for working-age males were in south Wales, west Cornwall, south Humberside, Teesside and west central Scotland, but above-average decreases were also widespread in the broad central triangle enclosed by the Mersey and Humber estuaries and the West Midlands conurbation. The most severely affected places are Port Talbot, Ebbw Vale, Consett, Gelligaer, Merthyr Tydfil, Neath, Peterlee, Newport, Llanelli and Scunthorpe – all traditional coal-mining or steel towns where closures and redundancies have forced them into early retirement.

Dependency on the economically active

These changes in economic activity rates, when taken together with the patterns of labour force change described earlier in this chapter and with the trends in population distribution and age structure outlined in Chapters 2 and 3, have produced a very distinctive geography of changing dependency rates. For Britain as a whole, in 1971 there were 113.6 people classed as economically inactive (including children and the elderly) for every 100 persons in the labour force, and over the next 10 years this dependency rate fell to 110.3 people per 100 economically active. This improvement of 3.3 persons took place because the negative effects of the raising of the school-leaving age, the increasing proportion of elderly people and the lower participation rates of older males were more than offset by the major fall in the number of children resulting from the post-1964 decline in fertility and by the shift in the balance of the working-age population towards the younger more active groups.

As can be seen from Figure 4.3A, the biggest improvements in dependency rates were concentrated in two main areas of northern Scotland and central

Figure 4.3   Dependents per 100 economically active persons, by LLMA – A: 1971–81
change; B: 1981
Source: Population Census

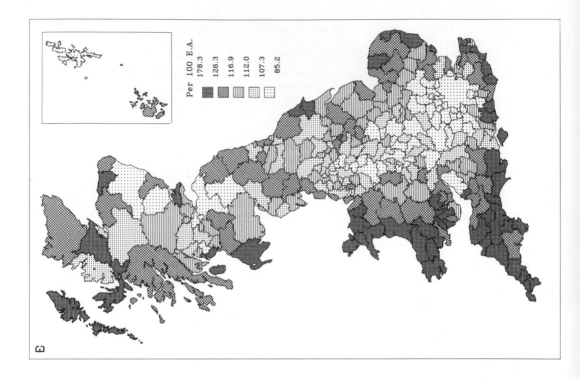

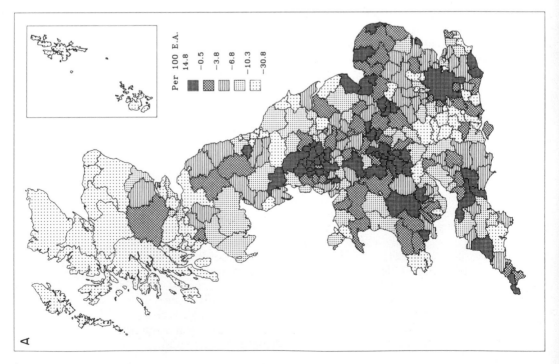

southern England. The former had been characterized by very high dependency rates in 1971 and the improvements over the subsequent 10 years were led by Stornoway (with its dependency rate falling by 30.8 persons per 100 economically active from its very high 1971 level of 179.3), Aberdeen (down by 22.8 from 124.7), Banff & Buckie (down by 19.3 from 154.4), Elgin (down by 19.1 from 141.1) and Inverness (down by 17.6 from 126.5). In the Hampshire–Berkshire–Oxfordshire area, by contrast, dependency rates were already quite low in 1971 and subsequent trends have helped this part of the country to become one of the most favoured in terms of the number of people supported by each member of the labour force. At the other extreme, places which saw an increase in dependency on the economically active between 1971 and 1981 are largely accounted for by three major concentrations – London, the West Midlands and the textiles zones of the North West and West Yorkshire (Figure 4.3A).

In general, however, the 1971–81 changes shown in Figure 4.3A have done little to change the broad geographical pattern of dependency differences across Britain inherited from before 1971. With the exception of the major improvement in dependency rates in north-east Scotland, the overwhelming impression given by the 1981 rates in Figure 4.3B is of a dynamic economic core surrounded by a peripheral rim of more heavily dependent areas. London, the northern and western parts of the rest of the South East and the more urbanized parts of the Midlands constitute the heart of Britain in terms of the high proportion of their total population that is economically active. This favourable situation results from some combination of one or more of the following – fewer than average children, fewer elderly, more of their working-age population in the younger age groups, and higher age-specific activity rates. Very clearly at the other extreme, because of a combination of the opposite factors, lie outer East Anglia, the South Coast towns, the South West peninsula, most of Wales and western parts of Scotland.

The changing patterns are summarized in Table 4.6 on the basis of the three

Table 4.6 Dependents per 100 economically active persons, 1971–81 for alternative aggregations of areas

Area aggregations	Per 100 Economically Active (EA)		
	1971	1981	1971–81
A Regional division			
London Region	100.3	99.9	−0.4
Rest of the South	123.2	117.3	−5.9
Northern Heartland	112.0	110.6	−1.4
Northern Periphery	124.0	115.0	−9.0
B Urban status			
Metropolitan Dominant	105.7	104.2	−1.5
Metropolitan Subdominant	115.5	110.5	−5.1
Freestanding Urban	120.3	115.5	−4.9
Freestanding Rural	133.2	126.1	−7.1
C Zone			
Core	108.8	107.1	−1.7
Ring	120.5	112.5	−8.0
Outer Area	127.9	123.5	−4.4
Rural Area	131.3	124.8	−6.5
Great Britain	113.6	110.3	−3.3

Source: Population Census Small Area Statistics

Functional Regions dimensions that test for core–periphery tendencies at three different scales. At the level of the four broad regional divisions, the principal change is the fall in dependency rate from an originally very high level in the Periphery, contrasting with the very much smaller fall recorded by the Heartland. The reduction is least for the London Region, but the latter retains by far the highest ratio of labour force to dependents. On the metropolitan dimension a similar contrast is evident between the Dominants, which started the 1970s with the lowest dependency rate and subsequently saw the least further improvement, and the Freestanding Rural LLMAs where dependency rates were originally very high and have improved by the largest margin. The pattern at the zone level is, however, rather different in that, while in 1971 the dependency rate rose with distances from the Core, it is the Ring which saw the greatest improvement up to 1981, by which time a distinction appears to have developed between Core and Ring on the one hand and Outer and Rural Areas on the other.

Summary

Trends in the size of the labour force in Britain since 1971 have been affected by a wide range of direct and indirect factors, including international migration, annual variations in the numbers reaching school-leaving and pensionable ages, the raising of school-leaving age, the declining proportion of pensionable-age persons remaining economically active, changes in age- and sex-specific labour force participation rates within working age, and shifts of population between working-age groups. In this complicated context, it is impressive that so many regularities are evident from the study of the experience of individual places with respect to labour force growth, changing activity rates and trends in level of dependency on the labour force. Yet the analysis has revealed the importance of the urban–rural and North–South dimensions in understanding changes between 1971 and 1981 in the distribution of labour supply and has shown that, while labour force trends have broadly paralleled changes in the distribution of total population, some very striking developments have occurred in place-to-place variations in the degree to which working-age people are involved in the labour market. Since 1971, for instance, an increase has occured in labour force participation by married women across the whole country, but it has been particularly dramatic in the peripheral regions and more rural areas; while male economic activity rates have fallen most conspicuously in coal-mining and steel communities where labour shedding has resulted in the premature retirement of older workers and the out-migration of younger ones.

In general, these processes have been leading to the reduction of differences between places. With the massive cutbacks in the labour supply available in the largest cities, Britain's workforce has been becoming more evenly distributed across the national territory. With the labour force participation of married women growing most rapidly in places where it was previously least and vice versa, there has been a marked closing of the gap between the extremes. Moreover, some of the areas which saw the largest increases in dependency rates had started the decade with the fewest dependents per 100 economically active. On the other hand, 10 years of change have not been sufficient to alter significantly the overall picture of a comparatively young, highly active and dynamic population in the heart of England and a much more heavily dependent rim of remoter and more rural areas. In particular, in relation to national balance there must be cause for concern over the substantial falls in dependency rates occurring in central southern England and some other parts of the outer South East, which were already supporting fewer than average proportions of dependents in 1971. This source of imbalance, however, is highlighted much more closely in relation to employment and unemployment trends in the next two chapters.

Further reading

A thorough introduction to labour supply trends is provided by Metcalf, D. and Richardson, R. 1984: Labour, in Prest, A.R. and Coppock, D.J. (eds.) *The UK economy: A manual of applied economics* (London: Weidenfeld & Nicolson, 10th ed). Changes in Britain's labour force between the 1971 and 1981 Censuses are outlined by Beacham, R. 1984: Economic activity: Britain's workforce 1971–81, *Population Trends* 37, 6–14, and future trends are estimated in the Department of Employment 1984: Regional labour force outlook for Great Britain, *Employment Gazette* 92, 56–64.

The demographic background to recent national trends and future expectations is given by Ermisch, J. 1983: *The political economy of demographic change* (London: Heinemann), especially chapter 4, while geographical aspects are dealt with by Lawton, R. 1982: People and work, in House, J.W. (ed.) *The UK space: resources, environment and the future* (London: Weidenfeld & Nicolson, 3rd ed).

The three separate components of changing labour supply – natural change, migration and trends in labour force participation rates – are examined at national and regional level for Britain by the Cambridge Economic Policy Group 1980: Urban and regional policy with provisional regional accounts 1966–78, *Cambridge Economic Policy Review* 6. A similar methodology was applied to Britain's 280 Local Labour Market Areas by Owen, D.W., Gillespie, A.E. and Coombes, M.G. 1984: 'Job Shortfalls' in British Local Labour Market Areas: a classification of labour supply and demand trends 1971–81, *Regional Studies* 18, 469–88.

The role of women in the labour force is examined by Ermisch, J. 1980: Women's economic position and demographic changes, *Occasional Paper* 19/1, (London: Office of Population Censuses and Surveys) 36–63, and by Joshi, H., Layard, R. and Owen, S.J. 1985: Why are more women working in Britain? *Journal of Labour Economics* 3, 147–77. The increase in economic activity rates for married women and its relationship to the growth of jobs in rural and peripheral areas is examined by Massey, D. 1983: Industrial restructuring and class restructuring: production decentralisation and local uniqueness, *Regional Studies* 17, 73–90. Trends in male activity rates are described by Greenhalgh, C. 1979: Male labour force participation in Great Britain, *Scottish Journal of Political Economy* 26, 275–86.

5
Employment change

The challenge of ensuring sufficient jobs for Britain's growing labour force has provided successive governments with their most consistently important policy issue since the end of the Second World War, though the means selected for tackling it have varied considerably. Likewise, trends in the nature and distribution of jobs constitute a fundamental key to understanding the way in which places in Britain have been changing in recent years. The decade 1971–81 constituted a watershed for Britain in employment terms. From the end of the Second World War to the mid-1970s, employment grew overall (with cyclical fluctuations), broadly keeping pace with the growth of population. After 1966, employment in manufacturing industry began to decline, and during the 1970s, as economic crises became more severe, employment growth came to a halt. Employment peaked in 1979 and then went into a rapid decline, with more than two million jobs being lost by June 1983. Since then, there has been some recovery of employment, but this in no way matches the scale of previous job losses (Figure 5.1).

This chapter concentrates on the nature and scale of the employment changes which took place during the critical years between 1971 and 1981 when national employment growth came to a halt. It begins by outlining the national pattern of employment change by sector and industry, showing not only the main areas of job loss, but also pointing to the areas of growth during this decade, particularly in the service sector, in part-time jobs for women and in self-employment. The geography of employment change is then considered at the level of the Local Labour Market Area (LLMA) in order to see how these national trends have impacted on individual places and to identify the principal dimensions which appear to have influenced the fortunes of these places in terms of job availability. This analysis is based on the results of the Censuses of Employment, and a distinction is made between the trends associated with the main period of job growth up to 1978 and the more recent period of massive overall employment decline (1978–81).

The national context

The pattern of industrial employment change

Employment changes for the 27 'Orders' of the 1968 Standard Industrial Classification are presented for the period 1971–81, with the periods before and after 1978 contrasted, in Table 5.1. Clearly, the broad trends were fairly constant over the decade. Employment decline was almost universal in the Primary, Manufacturing and Construction sectors, but strong employment growth was displayed by many industries in the Service sector. Within the manufacturing sector, the older industries such as Textiles, Clothing and Footwear, Metal Manufacture and Shipbuilding continued their long-term employment decline in the period 1971–78. Under the combined pressure of

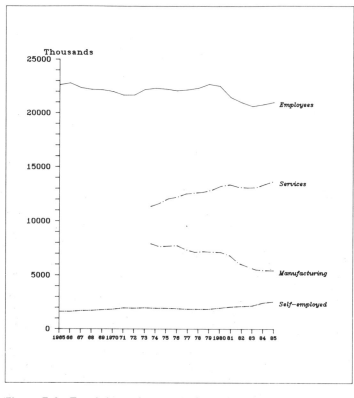

Figure 5.1 Trends in employment in Great Britain, 1965–85
Source: Employment Gazette April 1985 and June 1986

high exchange rates, high interest rates and high energy costs, employment in the older industries fell dramatically in the years 1978–81. These pressures also led to high rates of job loss in previously successful industries; Chemicals, Engineering and Motor Vehicle and Car Component Manufacture all lost more than 10 per cent of their 1978 employment by 1981, amounting to some 194,000 jobs.

The Service sector was the main source of new jobs during the 1970s, but it too was severely affected by recession conditions from mid-1979 onwards. Within this sector, employment in the public utilities and the 'Transport and Communications' Order declined both before and after 1978, but all other Orders increased in employment between 1971 and 1978. The greatest increases in employment occurred in public sector services; in national and local government and particularly in the 'Professional and Scientific Services', the latter resulting from rapidly increasing employment in education and health services. Recession conditions and monetarist economic policies led to reduced public spending and hence job losses in public administration and a slower rate of growth in education and health service employment after 1978.

The private sector created jobs at a slower rate than the public sector services during the years 1971–78, with extra jobs concentrated in retailing and wholesaling, financial services and the Miscellaneous (increasingly leisure-related) Services Order. In contrast to the public sector, employment in these industries increased at a similar rate after 1978, with the exception of

Table 5.1   Employment change by industry, 1971–81

Sector and SIC (1968) Order	Employed 1971 (000s)	Percentage change 1971–78	1978–81	1971–81
Primary production	812	−11.1	−6.2	−16.6
I Agriculture, forestry and fishing	419	−11.1	−8.3	−18.4
II Mining and quarrying	393	−11.2	−4.0	−14.7
Manufacturing industry	7,886	−9.7	−16.2	−14.7
III Food, drink and tobacco	744	−8.1	−7.6	−15.0
IV Coal and petroleum products	44	−13.9	−4.3	−17.6
V Chemicals and allied industries	435	0.7	−11.1	−10.5
VI Metal manufacture	556	−16.4	−31.7	−42.9
VII Mechanical engineering	1,038	−11.5	−11.5	−21.7
VIII Instrument engineering	164	−9.6	−9.0	−17.8
IX Electrical engineering	799	−6.0	−10.0	−15.4
X Shipbuilding and marine engineering	183	−6.0	−18.6	−23.5
XI Vehicles	807	−7.4	−18.9	−24.9
XII Other metal goods NES	572	−6.2	−21.6	−26.4
XIII Textiles	581	−21.3	−29.7	−44.7
XIV Leather, leather goods and fur	46	−18.9	−16.0	−31.9
XV Clothing and footwear	429	−16.3	−24.8	−37.0
XVI Bricks, pottery, glass and cement	301	−14.1	−17.9	−29.5
XVII Timber, furniture, etc.	264	−4.8	−15.1	−19.2
XVIII Paper, printing and publishing	589	−8.6	−7.4	−15.3
XIX Other manufacturing	331	−3.2	−21.2	−23.7
Construction (Order XX)	1,222	−0.1	−8.0	−8.1
Service Industries	11,718	12.3	1.0	13.4
XXI Gas, electricity and water	369	−10.5	2.4	−8.3
XXII Transport and communication	1,545	−5.7	−3.0	−8.6
XXIII Distributive trades	2,555	6.3	−1.2	5.1
XXIV Insurance, banking, etc.	963	23.0	9.6	34.9
XXV Professional and scientific services	2,916	22.8	2.6	26.0
XXVI Miscellaneous services	1,906	23.2	6.3	31.0
XXVII Public administration and defence	1,465	5.4	−9.9	−5.0
Great Britain	21,638	2.7	−5.1	−2.5

Source: Census of Employment

retailing and wholesaling, in which employment declined. It is these private 'producer' and 'consumer' services which have continued to provide the main source of employment growth since 1981, though they compensate for only a small part of the employment shed by the manufacturing sector since 1978 – and indeed, even in the mid 1980s, manufacturing was still losing jobs faster than it was creating new ones.

The growth of new forms of employment

Just as the low overall rate of population growth has not prevented marked changes in the structure and composition of the population from taking place (see Chapters 2–4), so have major changes in the structure of employment been occurring, even during the period of slow employment growth up to 1978, and particularly during the subsequent years of restructuring. It has been notable that whilst job losses have affected full-time male workers disproportionately, the majority of the new jobs have been part-time and for women. As suggested by the trends in labour force participation rates shown in the previous chapter, many of these new jobs have been filled by married women who were previously economically inactive. Over the decade, the number of part-time female jobs increased by nearly a million, and the proportion of all employment represented by such jobs grew from 12.7 per cent in 1971 to 17.7 per cent in 1981.

Another significant feature of employment change has been the growing importance of self-employment. In June 1971, 1.95 million persons were estimated to be self-employed; a number which remained fairly stable until 1976, declined slightly in the next three years and then increased rapidly after 1979. According to the Department of Employment self-employment increased by 457,000 between March 1983 and December 1985; 301,000 of this increase was accounted for by males – in contrast to the number of male employees which declined by 21,000 over the same period.

Self-employment is largely concentrated in agriculture, construction, retailing, hotels, catering, leisure services and business services, most of the self-employed being managers or skilled manual workers and predominantly aged over 30. The highest rates of self-employment are found in the South East (which had 35.4 per cent of all the self-employed in 1984) and the rural regions. This form of employment is thus largely found in those parts of the country and in those industries which have seen the greatest economic recovery since 1982.

Spatial patterns of employment change

Clearly, changes in the level and nature of employment in Britain have been profound and complex. At the same time, there have been substantial changes in the location of employment. The remainder of this chapter is concerned with tracing the spatial expression of the trends in employment discussed so far during the period 1971 to 1981, using the 280 LLMAs and aggregations thereof, and drawing comparisons between the trends before and after 1978.

Figure 5.2 depicts the spatial pattern of employment change over the decade. The most striking feature is the stark division of the nation into areas of severe employment decline and rapid employment growth. The former occur predominantly in the areas of greatest population concentration, notably London, the North West, West and South Yorkshire, central Scotland, north-east England and the South Wales valleys. These areas all lost at least 8.4 per cent of their 1971 employment in the ensuing 10 years. In contrast, large parts of the south-eastern corner of England, together with parts of the rural South West, west Wales and northern Scotland increased their 1971 employment levels by more than 13.4 per cent over the decade, strongly contrasting with the national employment loss of 2.5 per cent.

Table 5.2 presents results for the LLMAs which experienced the 'best' and 'worst' employment trends during the period 1971–81. The most successful places were located in two areas. Particularly impressive is the 'doughnut' of employment growth located at a radius of 50–140km from central London, which includes successful New and Expanded Towns such as Milton Keynes and Basingstoke, and Winchester, a county town which has gained from the growth of public services and from being at the centre of a region of rapid economic growth. The other is northern Scotland where oil-related development has created large numbers of new jobs, notably in the 'boom town' of Aberdeen. Decline was a feature of the regions with heavy industry and large

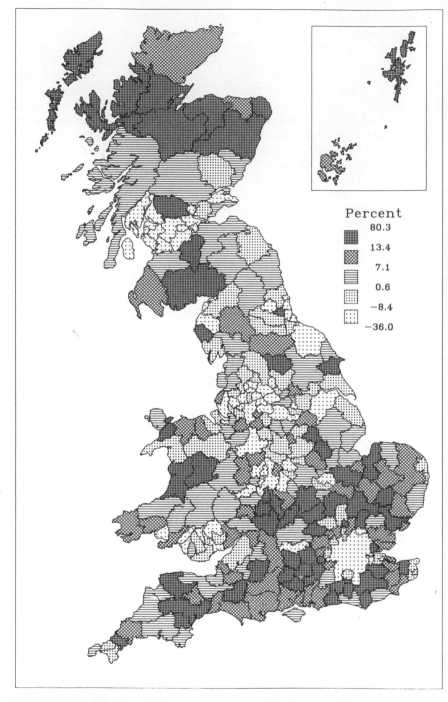

Figure 5.2   Employment change 1971–81, by LLMA
Source: Census of Employment

Table 5.2 LLMAs growing and declining fastest in employment, 1971–81

A) The 10 'best' and 'worst' LLMAs in terms of absolute change

Growing LLMAs			Declining LLMAS		
	New jobs (000s)	Rate of growth (%)		Jobs lost (000s)	Rate of decline (%)
1 Aberdeen	45.2	39.9	London	−378.8	−8.9
2 Milton Keynes	27.5	80.2	Liverpool	−99.7	−20.7
3 Reading	26.0	23.5	Birmingham	−81.4	−11.7
4 Southampton	20.0	11.7	Glasgow	−74.9	−13.2
5 Northampton	19.1	22.1	Manchester	−64.5	−10.8
6 Cheltenham	18.5	33.1	Coventry	−40.1	−17.3
7 Aldershot	17.7	23.5	Newcastle upon Tyne	−31.4	−8.3
8 Bournemouth	17.1	12.6	Sheffield	−30.6	−10.6
9 Cambridge	16.3	18.4	Wolverhampton	−29.0	−17.6
10 Winchester	15.5	59.6	Smethwick	−27.0	−25.9

B) The 10 'best' and 'worst' LLMAs in terms of rates of change

Growing LLMAs			Declining LLMAs		
	Rate of growth (%)	New jobs (000s)		Rate of decline (%)	Jobs lost (000s)
1 Milton Keynes	80.2	27.5	Harlow	−35.9	−15.6
2 Winchester	59.6	15.5	Corby	−33.1	−9.6
3 Dingwall	58.2	4.9	Consett	−29.5	−7.9
4 Stornoway	53.0	3.7	Port Talbot	−27.2	−13.1
5 Stirling	41.4	10.8	Smethwick	−25.9	−27.0
6 Aberdeen	39.9	45.2	Mexborough	−22.8	−6.7
7 Basingstoke	36.7	13.2	Rossendale	−21.4	−4.4
8 Horsham	35.7	6.2	Kilmarnock	−20.8	−7.1
9 Inverness	35.3	9.2	Liverpool	−20.7	−99.7
10 Truro	33.6	4.5	Coatbridge & Airdrie	−20.6	−8.3

Source: Census of Employment

populations. The highest rates of job loss were recorded by towns specializing in one particular industry – the most famous being the 'steel closure' towns of Consett and Corby (though it should be noted that the Census of Employment found the single highest rate of job loss to be at Harlow). However, the bulk of job loss was accounted for by the decline of London and the major cities, the worst affected being Liverpool, which lost nearly a fifth of its employment over the decade; it is salutory to note that the number of jobs lost in this city alone exceeds the total of new jobs created in Aberdeen, Milton Keynes and Reading.

1971–78 was a period of slow and erratic employment growth nationally, while 1978–81 saw a rapid contraction of employment. In some places the rate of job loss was near catastrophic. It is important to note that employment decline 1971–81 was dominated by the events of the latter period.

Local employment change, 1971–78

Figure 5.3A presents the spatial pattern of variation in rates of employment change within Britain during the first seven years of the decade. Clearly, substantial variations existed between places in which rapid growth of employment occurred, such as Winchester and Milton Keynes, which increased employment by 49.2 per cent and 47.3 per cent respectively, and at the other

Figure 5.3 Employment change by LLMA – A: 1971–78; B: 1978–81
Source: Census of Employment

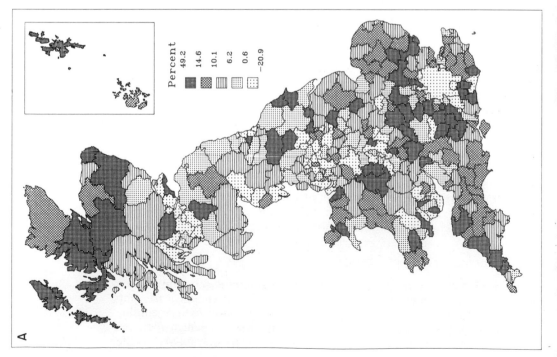

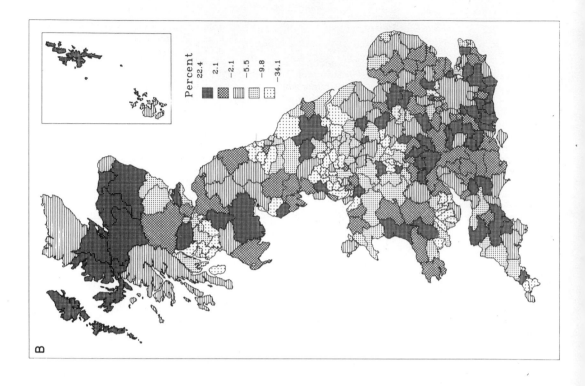

extreme, Port Talbot and St Andrews which lost 20.9 per cent and 18.0 per cent respectively of their 1971 employment by 1978. Whilst these are extreme rates of change, they all relate to medium-sized or small places, and the absolute number of jobs involved is not great (only 16,204 in the case of Milton Keynes). The greatest numbers of jobs were created in some larger cities such as Aberdeen (28,842 or 25.5 per cent), Reading (22,412 or 20.3 per cent) and Northampton (21,603 or 25.0 per cent). At the other extreme, job losses took place in London and the centres of the major conurbations; London lost 253,052 jobs (5.9 per cent of its 1971 employment), Liverpool lost 44,217 jobs (a rate of decline of 9.2 per cent), Glasgow lost 26,717 jobs (4.7 per cent) and Birmingham and Manchester lost 21,165 and 17,626 jobs respectively (corresponding to rates of decline of 4.7 per cent and 3.0 per cent). On the other hand, some major cities such as Newcastle and Edinburgh gained significant numbers of new jobs, despite their location within regions of long-term employment decline, and with 203 out of 280 LLMAs gaining more than 1,000 jobs during this period, national employment grew by 588,460 or 2.7 per cent.

The overall impression given by Figure 5.3A is that employment decline and slow growth is largely a feature of the more urbanized parts of the country, following the 'coffin'-shaped belt of urban development stretching from London to Manchester, together with the areas of nineteenth-century industrialization in north-east England, west Cumbria, south Wales and central Scotland. In contrast, employment growth was characteristic of the outer South East, the South West, eastern England, and in dramatic contrast to the period up to 1971, northern Scotland, particularly the Grampian region, where most of the jobs created by North Sea Oil development were concentrated. However, the picture is more complex than this summary implies. Not all LLMAs in the South East were successful; there was only sluggish employment growth in the larger London Subdominant Cities, such as Watford and Slough, and job losses were recorded in places like Welwyn (– 2,301 or – 4.7 per cent) and Harlow (– 1,193 or – 2.8 per cent). Conversely, there were some pockets of employment growth in the declining regions of peripheral Britain, notably Stirling (where employment grew by 8,988 or 34.6 per cent) and Durham (a growth of 8,119 jobs, or 26.4 per cent). As in the growing regions of the South West and East Anglia, relatively rapid employment growth occurred in some of the more rural areas, notably rural west Wales, south-west Scotland and especially North Yorkshire where employment in Northallerton & Richmond grew by 4,005 (20.1 per cent) and that in Harrogate by 5,309 (14.6 per cent).

This tendency for smaller and more rural areas to have more favourable employment trends than larger urban areas has already been indentified for the 1960s and early 1970s by Fothergill and Gudgin (1982) and Keeble (1980). As noted in Chapter 1, this phenomenon has been dubbed the 'urban–rural' shift of employment, but this term is something of a misnomer because it simply refers to broad differences in average rates of employment change for different size categories of towns and carries no special significance in relation to the underlying processes. Indeed, Fothergill, Kitson and Monk (1985) argue that the 'shift' does not result from a physical transfer of employment from the larger cities to the rural areas, but instead reflects the better employment performance of firms located in the smaller towns and rural areas and the location of declining industries in the inner cities, along with the ability of land-intensive activities to expand in the less urbanized areas. Whatever the mechanism responsible for this empirical regularity,

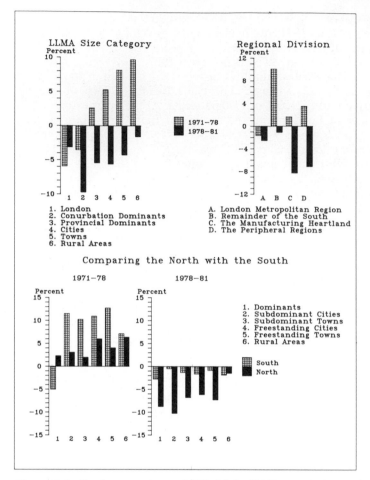

Figure 5.4 Employment change 1971–81, by LLMA aggregations – A: Size of LLMA;
B: Regional location; C: Type of LLMA in North and South
Source: Census of Employment

Figure 5.4A clearly demonstrates its existence in the period 1971–78, with a
clear gradation in rates of employment change related to urban size, from the
employment decline of London and the Conurbation Dominants to vigorous
employment growth in the Towns and Rural Areas.

On the other hand, the effect of LLMA size on 1971–78 employment
changes is tempered by a second dimension, as the more detailed breakdown
in Figure 5.4C shows. LLMAs in both the Metropolitan and Freestanding
areas of the South grew in employment much faster than the corresponding
areas of the North. Thus, the apparent urban–rural shift in employment at
the national scale obscures the rapid growth of employment in the Cities and
Towns of the South (particularly in the Freestanding areas, where the bulk of
new employment – 379,178 jobs – was created) and the comparatively poor
performance of LLMAs in these size categories in the North, particularly in
the Northern Metropolitan Regions. It is notable, however, that rural areas
grew in employment at a similar rate in both the North and the South.

Spatial patterns of employment change, 1978–81

Though this second period was one of severe employment decline nationally, we have already shown that it was by no means one of universal employment loss across all industrial sectors. As a result there were substantial geographical variations in rates of employment change (Figure 5.3B). These range from increases of 11,277 jobs (up by 22.3 per cent in the three years) in Milton Keynes and 3,964 new jobs in Newark (up by 18.8 per cent) to the declines of 33.6 per cent (9,542 jobs) in Consett and 34.1 per cent in Harlow (14,403 jobs) (Table 5.2). In all, 43 of the 280 LLMAs enjoyed increases of employment greater than 1,000; but in contrast to the earlier period, 150 LLMAs lost more than 1,000 jobs. Though the period covered is half the length of the earlier period, the scale of job losses in the larger cities was much greater than in 1971–78; each of the Conurbation Dominants lost more than 44,000 jobs, and Sheffield, Leeds and Coventry all lost more than 20,000 jobs. Whilst the recession was felt by all parts of manufacturing industry, the steel, vehicle manufacturing and textiles industries saw their employment cut more sharply than the others, often as a result of the closure of major plants, which had particularly severe effects on 'company towns' such as Consett and Corby.

The impact of employment loss was generally most marked in the regions which had suffered the worst employment performances in the earlier part of the decade. The principal exception was the formerly prosperous West Midlands, in which the loss of employment in the vehicle, car components, metal and mechanical engineering industries was so severe that it 'raised' the West Midlands Conurbation to the status of an Assisted Area in 1984. In addition, the relatively rapid growth of parts of the South West Peninsula in 1971–78 was replaced by substantial employment loss in the next three years; for example, Plymouth gained 10,149 jobs (9.2 per cent) in the former period, but lost 5,804 (4.82 per cent) in the latter and Launceston, Falmouth, Redruth and Penzance all lost more than 5 per cent of their 1978 employment, following earlier employment growth (Figure 5.3A and 5.3B)

Employment growth was again largely concentrated in the south and east of England, with the most successful areas being located to the south and west of London (notably Brighton and Portsmouth), in the Cotswolds, and again in the Milton Keynes–Peterborough area (Figure 5.3B). Employment declined at a rate of 2.5 per cent in the London Metropolitan Region in these three years (largely due to decline in London itself, but some of its northern and eastern Subdominants also lost employment at a relatively rapid rate), but at only 1.1 per cent in the remainder of the South (Figure 5.4B). Elsewhere, notable employment growth occurred in west Wales, south west Scotland, and North Yorkshire. Townsend (1986) also notes the employment growth of service centres in the North such as Chester, York and Preston, which he ascribes to the growth of retailing and of the leisure and producer services.

It has been suggested by Townsend (1983) and the Regional Studies Association (1983) that the dramatic overall loss of employment in the years 1978–81 resulted in the stagnation or indeed reversal of the urban–rural shift of employment. Figure 5.4A relates employment change rates to urban size, and seems to confirm that the previously close inverse relationship between urban size and employment change had broken down. As noted by Fothergill, Kitson and Monk (1985) this is essentially caused by the remarkable turnaround in the relative performance of London, because at lower levels in the urban hierarchy, the inverse relationship appears to be maintained, with the Conurbation Dominants losing the largest proportion of jobs between 1978 and 1981 and Rural Areas the least.

It is again instructive, however, to examine the pattern of employment change in greater detail, using Figure 5.4C. The major dimension of employment change is the great contrast in rates of employment decline between the South (– 1.9 per cent) and the North (– 7.8 per cent). Within the South, there was relatively little variation in rates of employment loss between Metropolitan and Freestanding areas, but London itself continued to exhibit a poorer employment performance than the rest of the South, though losing jobs at a much slower rate than the major cities of the North. The association between urban size and employment change was quite weak in the smaller southern LLMAs, with the Cities losing employment more slowly than Towns in the Metropolitan Regions while the Towns had the more favourable employment performances in Freestanding areas, and Rural Areas displayed relatively high rates of employment loss. In the North, variations in rates of employment loss between types of LLMA were much greater, and there was stronger evidence for an 'urban–rural shift'. The bulk of job loss was concentrated in the Metropolitan Regions, in which the Subdominant Cities lost employment at an even faster rate than the Dominants. Freestanding areas maintained their employment rather better, but some of the largest factory closures occured in Northern Freestanding Towns, which thus lost employment faster than the Cities in Freestanding areas. The Northern Rural Areas again displayed a similar employment performance to those in the South.

Summary

The cumulative impact of employment change over the decade as a whole has been a relative North–South shift of employment, and within this, employment in the provincial conurbations has contracted dramatically, while the decline of London has slowed down. Across the whole of Britain, the most vigorous LLMAs in employment terms have been located in the Freestanding parts of the country, with the highest rates of growth occurring in the service centres, mostly in smaller cities and towns, and some Rural Areas. However, the bulk of new jobs have been created in the growing Peterborough–Milton Keynes axis, and in the Southampton–Portsmouth–Reading triangle, a focus of much new 'high-tech' employment. Employment decline is clearly associated with specialization in the older manufacturing industries which suffered so greatly from recession and rationalization pressures in the 1970s and 1980s, and it is these areas that continue to suffer manufacturing redundancies and fail to attract the newer industries.

The geography of employment growth: two case studies

Increasingly the service sector has come to replace manufacturing as the main source of employment, and this trend accelerated during the decade 1971–81, with overall employment decline taking place only because manufacturing job loss was greater than service employment gains. Within the service sector the most dynamic industries of the past few years have been those classed as 'producer services', while associated with the general increase in service employment has been a massive rise in the number of part-time jobs. This section outlines the background to these two 'growth sectors' in the otherwise generally dismal national employment record of this period and traces the way in which different parts of the country have contributed to them and been affected by them.

Producer services

This term covers a group of activities which are considered essentially 'basic' to the economy of a place in the sense that, like most manufacturing industry, their work is geared to national and international markets rather than simply depending on local demand. These activities include insurance, banking, accountancy, advertising, market research and other 'professional' services needed by the other sections of the economy. Employment in Britain's producer service industries grew by 33 per cent over the period 1971–81, creating some 484,000 new jobs; and increases occurred very widely across the country, with only 9 LLMAs having fewer jobs in this sector in 1981 than 1971 (Figure 5.5A).

Employment in producer services was highly concentrated in London, the South East and the major provincial cities in 1971, and these areas also gained substantial numbers of these new jobs by 1981. One-sixth of the increase, 79,800 jobs, was accounted for by London itself, representing a rate of growth of 14.7 per cent for this sector, starkly contrasting with the overall decline of employment in the capital of 8.9 per cent. However, there was also significant decentralization of employment in producer services, notable gains being made by the Subdominant Cities such as Reading (which gained 9,699 jobs, a rate of increase of 98 per cent), Freestanding Cities such as Leicester (an increase of 6,458 or 76 per cent) and Swindon (which grew by 6,249 jobs, or 29.1 per cent), New Towns such as Milton Keynes and Redditch (up by 29.5 per cent and 23.6 per cent respectively) and Freestanding Towns such as Winchester, which gained 3,844 of these jobs (a rate of increase of 34.0 per cent).

From Table 5.3 it can be seen that there is some evidence for an 'urban–rural shift' in producer service jobs during the decade, but this is largely a result of the very small number of these jobs in the smaller LLMAs at the start of the period; the bulk of the jobs then were located in London and the larger Cities. Table 5.4 suggests that there was also some regional decentralization, with the North increasing employment by 39.8 per cent, compared with 33.2 per cent in the South. The Northern Dominants, with fewer jobs in 1971, grew more rapidly over the period than those in the South, but the main contrast lay in the much faster rate of employment growth in

Table 5.3 Change in producer services, part-time and all employment 1971–81, by LLMA size (%)

Size category	Producer services	Part-time employment	All employment
London	14.7	13.2	−5.9
Conurbation Dominants	24.2	17.4	−3.6
Provincial Dominants	46.0	25.6	2.6
Cities	60.2	37.0	5.3
Towns	57.9	47.0	8.2
Rural Areas	52.0	51.9	9.7
Great Britain	35.6	32.6	2.7

Source: Census of Employment

Figure 5.5 1971–81 change in employment sub-groups, by LLMA – A: Producer services; B: Part-time employment
Source: Census of Employment

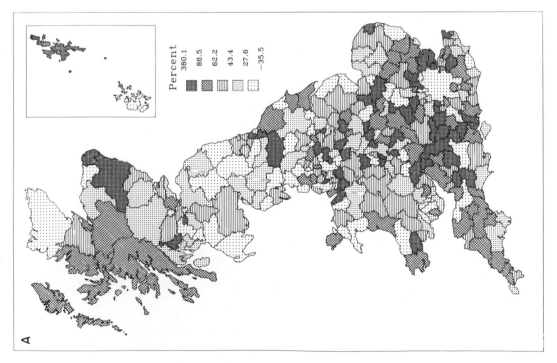

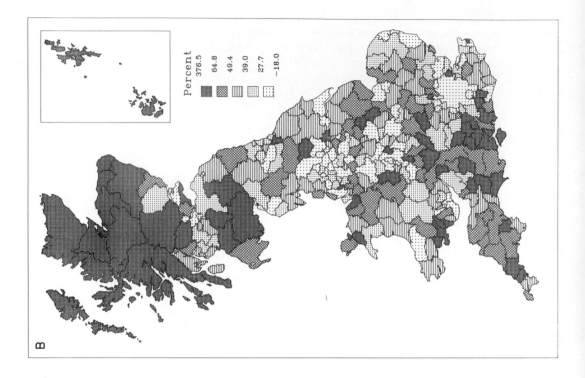

Table 5.4 The North–South contrast in employment change 1971–81: producer services and part-time employment (%)

LLMA groups	% change in producer services employment		% change in part-time employment	
	South	North	South	North
Dominants	18.2	31.6	16.1	21.9
Subdominants	61.3	61.6	41.7	37.2
Cities	*59.5*	*61.9*	*42.9*	*30.7*
Towns	*62.4*	*64.4*	*40.7*	*44.0*
Freestanding	68.0	41.7	52.1	39.6
Cities	*69.9*	*44.8*	*46.3*	*33.4*
Towns	*63.8*	*40.5*	*58.7*	*41.5*
Rural Areas	80.1	34.0	45.4	56.2
All LLMAs	33.2	39.8	33.7	31.6

Source: Census of Employment

Freestanding areas in the South than in the North – more than twice as many jobs were created in the former areas than in the latter. Clearly then, the decade 1971–81 was one in which the distribution of employment in producer services became much more spatially even compared with the relatively concentrated pattern in 1971, as a result of decentralization of office activities by major financial organizations and of the growth of high street services throughout Britain. However, London remained predominant in 1981, having 34 per cent of all employment in producer services.

Part-time employment

The number of part-time jobs increased by 1.09 million or 32.6 per cent between 1971 and 1981. It was associated with a shift away from the employment of full-time, mainly male, workers over the decade and with the substantial growth of female labour force participation seen in Chapter 4. The growth in numbers of part-time workers is largely due to their low wages, lack of employment protection and low level of unionization. The switch from full-time to part-time employees is partly a result of the rapid growth of the service sector, in which part-time workers are particularly significant, but is also due to a real substitution between the two types of worker, particularly in manufacturing where it permits firms more easily to adjust their workforces to changing levels of demand.

Figure 5.5B shows that almost everywhere contributed to the growth of part-time working between 1971 and 1981. Only five LLMAs experiencing a decline, the most extreme case being Smethwick with a loss of 2,784 or 17.9 per cent. The fastest rates of growth occurred in Scotland outside the main centres of population, central southern England, a zone stretching from London along the south coast to the tip of the South West Peninsula, and in the rural areas fringing the main belt of population in England. Lower rates of growth occurred in the Metropolitan Regions, in which female employment was relatively important in 1971, in East Anglia, Kent, west Cumbria and parts of Wales. The highest rate of growth was experienced in Winchester (37.7 per cent, representing 14,160 new jobs), and in the surrounding area part-time employment grew by some 15 per cent in Basingstoke, 12 per cent in Andover, 11 per cent in Gosport and Fareham, 85 per cent in Aldershot, 68 per cent in Southampton and 53 per cent in Portsmouth.

Table 5.3 demonstrates that there were much higher rates of part-time employment growth at the lower end of the urban hierarchy than at the top, with the bulk of new jobs being created in the smaller Cities and Towns. Table 5.4 shows that the overall rate of growth was similar in both the South and the North. The main regional dimension is the faster growth of part-time employment in Freestanding areas in the South than in the North; but part-time employment also grew faster in the southern Subdominants than in those in the North.

Conclusion

Clearly, patterns of employment change in Britain over the period 1971–81 were extremely complex. It is easy to regard it as a period of unmitigated decline, because of the severity of the post-1978 recession, and indeed, for many areas, the scale of job loss during these years was sufficient to eclipse whatever growth had occurred in earlier years. However, this chapter has demonstrated that substantial amounts of new employment were created in the producer service industries and in part-time jobs, and that this type of employment growth was felt throughout the country. Nevertheless, the decline of manufacturing employment in the North occurred on such a scale that a marked North–South divide in employment change grew up over the decade.

This had the effect of overshadowing the influence of urban size on employment change which had been more clearly marked in the earlier part of the decade. It also helped to reverse the trend towards regional convergence in employment opportunities which had been evident in the 1960s and early 1970s. By the end of the decade, the economies of Northern LLMAs, and in particular the major cities, had been severely damaged, and the scale of job loss was too great for the growing service sector to offset fully. Since the growth of the service sector has been weakest in these cities, it is likely that the 'North–South divide' in employment opportunities will persist throughout the 1980s.

Further reading

For a detailed discussion of the factors underlying the long-term decline in British manufacturing employment see Blackaby, F. (ed.) 1979: *De-industrialisation*, NIESR Policy Papers 2 (London: Heinemann), and for the characteristics of the recession of 1979–83 see Worswick, G.D.N. 1984: Two Great Recessions: the 1980s and the 1930s in Britain, *Scottish Journal of Political Economy* 31, 209–28.

Spatial transformations in the nature of employment in Britain are investigated by Keeble, D. 1976: *Industrial location and planning in the United Kingdom* (London: Methuen); Massey, D. 1984: *Spatial divisions of labour: social structures and the geography of production* (London: Methuen) and Fothergill, S. and Gudgin, G. 1982: *Unequal growth: urban and regional change in the UK* (London: Heinemann).

For the growth of service sector employment see Robertson, J.A.S., Briggs, J.M. and Goodchild, A. 1982: Structure and employment prospects of the service industries, *Department of Employment Research Paper 30*, and Damesick, P. 1986: Service industries, employment and regional development in Britain: a review of recent trends and issues, *Transactions of the Institute of British Geographers, New Series*, 11, 212–26.

For the growth of part-time employment see Robinson, O. and Wallace, J. 1984: Growth and utilisation of part-time labour in Britain, *Employment Gazette*, September 1984, 391–7.

6
The rise in unemployment

The increase in unemployment is one of the main socio-economic changes that has occurred in Britain since 1971. This rise in unemployment is essentially a nationwide phenomenon – affecting virtually all places and all population sub-groups – although some have suffered more than others. In this chapter, the emphasis is on identifying the 'winners' and 'losers' in the face of unemployment increase, on investigating whether spatial divisions have remained the same or whether new cleavages have emerged, and assessing whether urban and regional differentials in the incidence of unemployment have grown wider as unemployment has increased.

In the first section, the national context is described and the rise in unemployment from the early 1970s to the mid 1980s is outlined. Concepts of relative (percentage) and absolute (percentage point) changes in the unemployment rate over time are discussed. This section also includes a note on the data sources. In the second section the focus of attention shifts to spatial variations in unemployment experience. The geographical pattern of unemployment rates in 1971 and 1981 is investigated using data from the Census of Population, and key urban and regional dimensions of change over the decade are analysed. The majority of this analysis is conducted at the LLMA scale, but reference is also made to the existence of unemployment blackspots within LLMAs. In the third and fourth sections attention is focused on two sub-groups for whom the effects of the rise in unemployment have been particularly severe: young people and the long-term unemployed (defined as those unemployed for at least one year). The final section summarizes the key urban and regional dimensions of unemployment change.

The national context

The rise in the number of unemployed and the national unemployment rate

Between June 1972 and June 1985 the number of unemployed increased by 2.29 million, from 0.77 million in June 1972 to 3.06 million in June 1985 (see Figure 6.1). This increase is massive in absolute terms but to give a clearer assessment of its significance, it is necessary to place it in the perspective of the size of the economically active population (i.e. those in work or seeking employment) by calculating an unemployment rate. Thus the unemployment rate was 3.4 per cent in June 1972 but 12.9 per cent by June 1985 (see Figure 6.1); representing an absolute increase of 9.5 percentage points and a relative increase of 279 per cent. These two change measures together provide a full perspective of the extent of the impact of growth in unemployment over the decade. This increase was due to the combination of two factors, with the rise in the economically active population outlined in Chapter 4 coinciding with a dramatic decrease in employment opportunities described in Chapter 5.

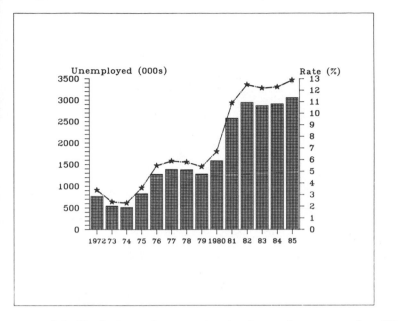

Figure 6.1   Rise in the number unemployed and unemployment rate, June 1972 –
June 1985, Great Britain
Source: Department of Employment

A note on data sources

Comprehensive spatially disaggregated unemployment data can be derived
from two sources – the Census of Population and Department of Employment Statistics – both of which are drawn on in this chapter. Data from these
two sources are not strictly comparable. The unemployment data from the
Census of Population (used here to describe urban and regional dimensions
of unemployment change, 1971–81) is a count of those declaring themselves
to be unemployed. The Department of Employment count has been the
subject of changes in calculation methods over time: before October 1982
representing a count of those registered as unemployed and from October
1982 onwards representing a count of those claiming unemployment benefit.
Furthermore, institutional factors, such as the introduction of special
employment schemes for certain sub-groups of the unemployed, affect the
unemployment count and hinder direct comparison of change over time.

Spatial variations in unemployment rates

Unemployment rates in 1971 and 1981

The pattern of unemployment rates at the LLMA scale, as measured by data
from 1971 and 1981 Censuses of Population, is shown in Figures 6.2A and
6.2B respectively. The most clear-cut feature of this pattern is the concentration of LLMAs with highest unemployment rates in Northern Britain. This is
particularly apparent in 1981, suggesting an increase in the significance of the
regional dimension in the spatial pattern of unemployment rates with the
growth of unemployment.

  The strength of North–South contrasts is also indicated by the location of

Figure 6.2   Unemployment rate by LLMA – A: 1971; B: 1981
Source: Population Census

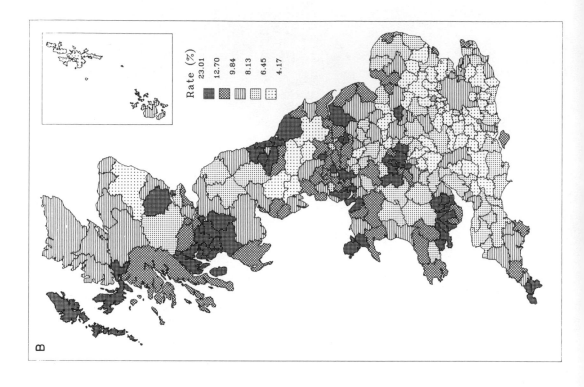

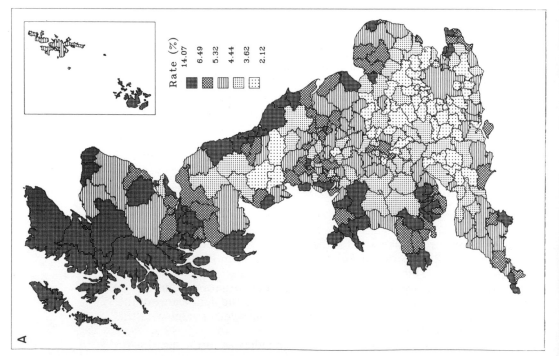

Table 6.1   Unemployment rates 1971, extreme LLMAs

Highest LLMAs	%	Lowest LLMAs	%
Stornoway	14.06	Hertford & Ware	2.13
Bangor	11.33	Chippenham	2.39
Gelligaer	10.72	Horsham	2.48
Merthyr Tydfil	10.09	Bishops Stortford	2.50
South Shields	9.72	Aylesbury	2.57
Hartlepool	9.59	Crawley	2.57
Coatbridge & Airdrie	9.55	Letchworth	2.59
Glasgow	9.43	Milton Keynes	2.60
Liverpool	9.39	Haywards Heath	2.62
Yarmouth	8.84	Reigate & Redhill	2.66

Source: Population Census Small Area Statistics

Table 6.2   Unemployment rates 1981, extreme LLMAs

Highest LLMAs	%	Lowest LLMAs	%
Consett	23.00	Winchester	4.18
Corby	21.33	Horsham	4.24
Coatbridge & Airdrie	19.24	Haywards Heath	4.27
Liverpool	18.17	Guildford	4.28
Hartlepool	17.91	Bishops Stortford	4.34
Port Talbot	17.50	Hertford & Ware	4.36
West Bromwich	17.31	Woking & Weybridge	4.36
Merthyr Tydfil	17.03	Reigate & Redhill	4.51
Irvine	17.00	St Albans	4.55
Motherwell	16.92	Aldershot & Farnborough	4.56

Source: Population Census Small Area Statistics

LLMAs with the most extreme unemployment rates (Tables 6.1 and 6.2). In 1971 (Table 6.1) there was one LLMA from the South – Yarmouth – amongst those with the highest unemployment rates; a fact indicative of higher than average unemployment rates in many seaside resorts outside the peak holiday season. Also among the LLMAs with the highest unemployment rates in 1971 are two LLMAs classified as Rural Areas – Stornoway and Bangor, reflecting the unemployment problems facing many peripheral areas at that time. By contrast, in 1981 (Table 6.2) the highest unemployment rates are recorded by two steel closure areas – Consett and Corby – and there are no Rural Areas amongst the worst affected LLMAs. On this basis it would appear that in relative terms, unemployment was less of a problem of the rural periphery in 1981 than in 1971. At the other extreme, LLMAs with the lowest unemployment rates in 1971 and 1981 are located exclusively in the South. Over the decade 1971–81, however, there is evidence for an increasing representation of London Subdominant LLMAs amongst the LLMAs least affected by unemployment, squeezing out representatives of the Southern Freestanding Towns located at somewhat greater distances from London, such as Aylesbury, Chippenham, Letchworth and Milton Keynes.

The importance of urban size and regional location dimensions in the pattern of unemployment rates is summarized in Figure 6.3, which shows that in both 1971 and 1981 LLMAs in the South recorded lower unemployment rates than LLMAs from comparable size categories in the North. Urban size differentials in the patterning of unemployment rates, however, are more

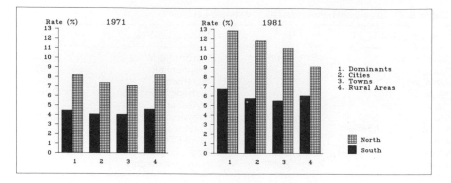

Figure 6.3   Unemployment rates by LLMA size and regional location, 1971 and 1981
Source: Population Census

apparent in the North than in the South. In 1981, for instance, there was a
clear positive relationship between increasing urban size and unemployment
rates in the North, with the Rural Areas having improved their relative
position dramatically over the decade after recording higher unemployment
rates than Cities and Towns in 1971. In the South, however, the highest
unemployment rates in both 1971 and 1981 were recorded in the Rural Areas
and the Dominants.

Change in unemployment rates

The pervasiveness of the increase in unemployment between 1971 and 1981 is
illustrated by the fact that in only one LLMA – Winchester – did the unemployment rate decline. On the other hand, the incidence of the rise in unemployment varied considerably from place to place, for at the other extreme
the steel closure areas of Consett and Corby experienced an absolute increase
in their unemployment rates of over 16 percentage points, corresponding to a
quadrupling of their 1971 levels. The pattern of absolute change in unemployment rates 1971–81 by LLMA is shown in Figure 6.4A, and the LLMAs
experiencing the most extreme changes are listed in Table 6.3. It is clear that
the traditional problem regions of Northern Britain, such as North East
England, the North West, West Central Scotland and South Wales, displayed
amongst the highest percentage point increases in unemployment rates. In

Table 6.3   Absolute (percentage point) change in unemployment rates, 1971–81,
extreme LLMAs

Highest LLMAs	%	Lowest LLMAs	%
Consett	17.21	Winchester	−0.26
Corby	16.10	Aberdeen	0.39
West Bromwich	12.84	Stornoway	0.45
Port Talbot	10.54	Dingwall	0.76
Shotton	10.42	Banff & Buckie	0.94
Coatbridge & Airdrie	9.69	Peterhead	1.21
Llanelli	9.46	Dover	1.33
Smethwick	9.33	Bury St Edmunds	1.46
Middlesbrough	9.23	Aldershot & Farnborough	1.52
Walsall	9.20	Woking & Weybridge	1.52

Source: Population Census Small Area Statistics

Figure 6.4 1971–81 change in unemployment rate by LLMA – A: Percentage point change; B: Percent change
Source: Population Census

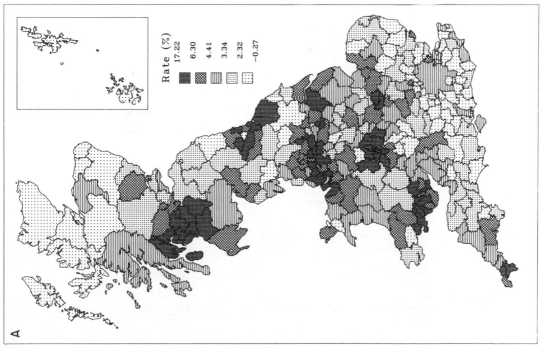
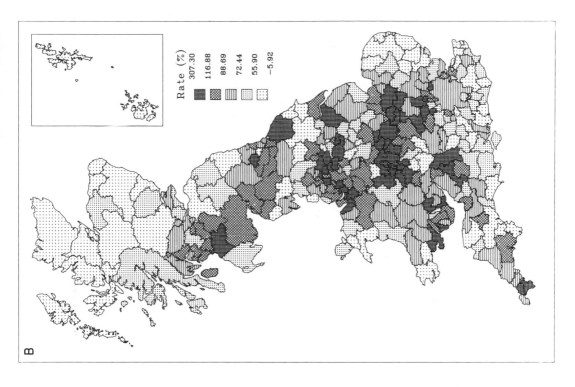

addition, massive increases in unemployment rates were recorded in many West Midlands LLMAs: with West Bromwich, Smethwick and Walsall all appearing in the list of extreme LLMAs in Table 6.3. The list of LLMAs with lowest absolute increases in unemployment rates 1971–81 is dominated by LLMAs from northern Scotland: a region of relative buoyancy during the 1970s and early 1980s, benefiting from North Sea oil associated developments. Many of these Northern Rural Areas initially had very high unemployment rates.

These same LLMAs in northern Scotland also dominate the list of LLMAs with lowest relative increases in unemployment rate over the decade (Table 6.4). The London Subdominant LLMAs are not represented in this bottom 'ten': indeed many of these most prosperous LLMAs suffered greater than average relative increases in the unemployment rate (Figure 6.4B); indicating the impact of recession on areas where unemployment problems were formerly absent. At the other extreme, the single largest regional grouping of LLMAs with highest relative increases in the unemployment rate is the West Midlands, the former manufacturing powerhouse of Britain, and includes West Bromwich, Smethwick, Dudley, Walsall and Telford. The presence of New and Expanded Towns such as Telford and Milton Keynes within this list illustrates that massive increases in unemployment were a feature of areas of employment growth as well as areas of large industrial closures.

The differential impact of increase in unemployment rates was such, however, as to shift the position of the line demarcating the division between North and South. Figure 6.5 shows that in 1971 the level of unemployment rates in the Heartland was more akin to those of the London Metropolitan Region and the Rest of the South than to the Periphery. In the period 1971–81, the Heartland experienced the greatest increases in unemployment rates in both absolute (see Figure 6.5) and relative terms: the 109 per cent increase in the unemployment rate in the Heartland contrasted with relative increases of 77–79 per cent in the London Metropolitan Region, the Rest of the South and the Periphery. Thus, by the end of the decade unemployment rates in the Heartland were more similar to those in the Periphery than those of Southern Britain.

Unemployment blackspots

As well as spatial differentials at this broad regional scale, there are often

Table 6.4   Relative (%) change in employment rates, 1971–81, extreme LLMAs

Highest LLMAs	%	Lowest LLMAs	%
Corby	307.3	Winchester	− 5.9
Consett	297.4	Stornoway	3.2
West Bromwich	287.0	Aberdeen	7.3
Smethwick	255.7	Dingwall	10.2
Kettering	237.3	Banff & Buckie	12.8
Dudley	233.1	Peterhead	17.2
Milton Keynes	227.2	Bangor	20.2
Shotton	224.0	Durham	21.8
Walsall	208.9	Inverness	24.0
Telford	195.5	Thurso	24.6

Source: Population Census Small Area Statistics

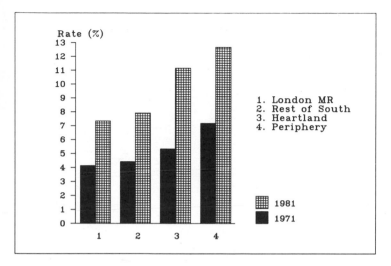

Figure 6.5   Unemployment rate by broad regional division, 1971 and 1981
Source: Population Census

relatively large disparities in residential unemployment rates within LLMAs; thus creating localized 'blackspots' in more prosperous LLMAs, as well as 'whitespots' in LLMAs with relatively high unemployment rates overall. At the micro scale, represented by the Census ward, the existence of unemployment blackspots outside traditional problem regions and even in prosperous LLMAs is clear. Figure 6.6 shows the distribution of wards where unemployment rates are amongst the worst 10 per cent in Britain. Problem regions of Merseyside, Clydeside, South Wales and North East England stand out, having large numbers of wards with high unemployment rates. Elsewhere, high unemployment rate wards tend to be concentrated in inner city areas, a pattern that is particularly apparent in the case of London (see Figure 6.6).

The unemployment dimension of the inner city problem is reflected at the zone level of the Functional Region framework. Using the zonal disaggregation, it is clear that those living in the Cores are most disadvantaged; moreover, this disadvantage extends beyond the Cores of the Dominant Cities across the urban system to those of Subdominant and Freestanding Functional Regions (Table 6.5). Outside the Cores, there is no clear relationship between degree of population concentration and unemployment rates, although the relatively high unemployment rates in the Rural Areas of Freestanding Functional Regions is possibly indicative of accessibility problems in remote areas. Furthermore, the change statistics in Table 6.5 show that the disparity in unemployment rates between Cores and other zones increased over the decade, with the Cores displaying the greatest increase in unemployment rates 1971–81, in both absolute and relative terms, from the highest initial base.

Youth unemployment

While in spatial terms inequalities in access to employment fall particularly heavily on those resident in Cores, in non-spatial terms young people are one of the sub-groups within the population who have suffered most of all in the face of the rapid growth in unemployment in the late 1970s through to the

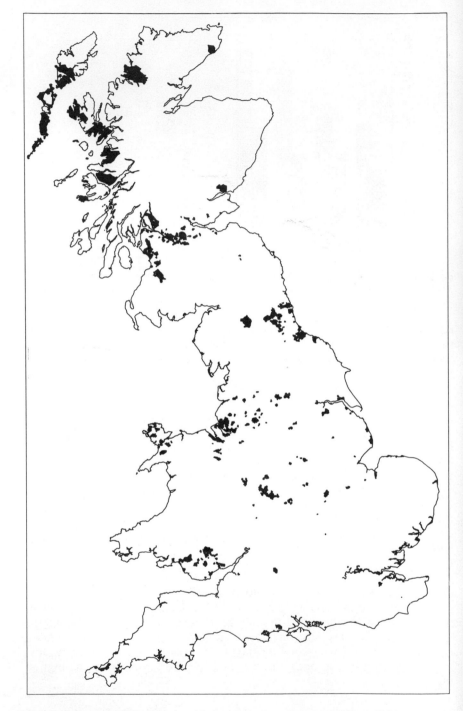

Figure 6.6   The 10% of wards with the highest unemployment rates, 1981
Source: Population Census

Use

Table 6.5 Unemployment rates by zone and Functional Region type, 1971 and 1981 (%)

Type of FR	Cores	Rings	Outer Areas	Rural Areas
Dominant				
1971	5.7	4.6	4.2	4.3
1981	11.2	8.5	6.9	7.4
1971–81*	5.5	3.9	2.7	3.1
1971–81†	96.5	84.8	64.3	72.1
Subdominant				
1971	5.0	4.5	4.4	4.4
1981	10.7	8.1	8.3	7.5
1971–81*	5.7	3.6	3.9	3.1
1971–81†	114.0	80.0	88.6	70.5
Freestanding				
1971	5.5	4.3	4.6	5.7
1981	10.8	7.3	7.8	8.9
1971–81*	5.3	3.0	3.2	3.2
1971–81†	96.4	69.8	69.6	56.1
All FRs				
1971	5.5	4.4	4.5	5.5
1981	11.0	7.9	7.8	8.7
1971–81*	5.5	3.5	3.3	3.3
1971–81†	100.0	79.5	73.3	60.0

Note: * percentage point change in rate
  † percentage change in rate
Source: Population Census Small Area Statistics

mid 1980s. What has exacerbated the problem is that the severe downturn in the economy has coincided with the entry of large numbers of young people into the economically active age groups.

It is possible to estimate youth unemployment rates for LLMAs by combining Census of Population data on the numbers economically active by age group and Department of Employment unemployment data disaggregated by age and sex. Table 6.6 shows unemployment rates for both 18 year olds and 20–24 year olds by gender in selected LLMA classes in April 1982. The highest unemployment rates for both sexes and both age groups were recorded in the Conurbation Dominants, while the lowest rates were to be found in the London Subdominant Towns. This reflects the fact that a vulnerable sub-group – such as young people – suffer and benefit disproportionately from location in an area of high and low unemployment, respectively. The youth unemployment rate estimates for April 1982 (towards the end of the period of most rapid increase in unemployment) indicate that the problem of youth unemployment is particularly severe in the traditional problem areas and that the North–South differential is particularly significant in understanding the geography of youth unemployment. Table 6.6 reveals that there are also quite marked differentials in unemployment experience by gender, with female unemployment being more pronounced than male unemployment in rural areas and relatively less severe in the larger metropolitan areas. The high levels of youth unemployment indicate the nationwide nature of the problem of youth unemployment.

Table 6.6   Youth unemployment rates in selected LLMA classes, April 1982 (%)

	18 year olds		20–24 year olds	
LLMA class	Males	Females	Males	Females
Dominant				
London	21.0	16.2	21.6	26.3
Conurbation Dominants	35.2	27.7	36.8	45.7
Subdominants				
London Subdominant Towns	15.8	11.6	13.7	18.3
Conurbation Subdominant Towns	28.9	25.7	27.8	41.5
Freestanding				
Southern Commercial Towns	19.3	15.6	18.7	27.2
Northern Commercial Towns	22.1	20.7	23.5	38.1
Rural				
Southern Rural Areas	20.4	17.0	18.0	31.2
Northern Rural Areas	19.8	20.1	21.5	41.6

Source: calculated from data from Department of Employment and Census of Population

Long-term unemployment

The increase in unemployment rates is not the only significant measure of the growth in unemployment during the recession; not only has the incidence of unemployment increased but so too has the duration of unemployment spells. In recent years just as youth unemployment has assumed a higher profile in policy initiatives, so too increasing attention and resources have been focused on the long-term unemployed, those unemployed for one year or more.

Measures of unemployment duration and the number of long-term unemployed can be calculated from Department of Employment statistics. The rise in long-term unemployment during recession has been more specta-cular, in relative terms, than the rise in unemployment. At the national scale the number of long-term unemployed increased from 0.3 million in April 1979 to 1.3 million in January 1986 (although it should be noted that the way of counting the unemployed and exactly which sub-groups are included in a count of the long-term unemployed has changed somewhat during this period). This rise in the numbers of long-term unemployed has economic, social and individual costs.

As with unemployment rates, although the increase in unemployment duration and long-term unemployment has been nationwide, acute problems of long-term unemployment are localized in some LLMAs. Table 6.7 lists those LLMAs with the highest and lowest proportions of long-term unemployed amongst the unemployed in April 1985. In those regions suffering most acute job losses in recession – notably the West Midlands, Merseyside and Teesside – up to half of the unemployed are long-term unemployed, and often one-third of the total have been out of work for at least two years. At the opposite extreme, even in the LLMAs with the lowest proportions of long-term unemployed amongst the unemployed, approx-imately one-quarter of the total unemployed have been unemployed for more than one year.

The significance of urban size and regional dimensions in the spatial distri-bution of long-term unemployment is indicated in Figure 6.7. With the excep-

Table 6.7 Proportion of long-term unemployed amongst total unemployed, April 1985, extreme LLMAs (%)

Highest LLMAs	Over 1 yr	Over 2 yrs	Lowest LLMAs	Over 1 yr	Over 2 yrs
West Bromwich	55.0	37.4	Dingwall	21.3	10.3
Liverpool	53.4	36.3	Crawley	23.2	11.4
Sunderland	52.7	33.3	Aberdeen	23.4	11.8
St Helens	52.1	34.2	Andover	24.6	11.8
Wolverhampton	51.2	33.4	Bishops Stortford	24.6	11.0
Smethwick	50.3	31.8	Winchester	25.3	12.6
Birmingham	50.3	32.8	Woking & Weybridge	25.3	11.9
Middlesbrough	49.9	31.2	Huntingdon	25.5	13.3
Walsall	48.9	32.7	Aldershot & Farnborough	25.5	12.5
Stockton-on-Tees	48.5	29.6	Bury St Edmunds	25.6	13.4

Source: calculated from Department of Employment data

tion of the Rural Areas, long-term unemployment is obviously a greater problem in the North than in the South since comparable LLMA categories exhibit higher proportions of long-term unemployed amongst the unemployed in the North than their counterparts in the South. As well as this regional dimension, however, there is an important urban size dimension, with the highest proportions of long-term unemployed being found in the largest Dominants and the Cities. In the North, the smallest proportions of long-term unemployed are found in the Rural Areas – indeed only the Southern Towns exhibited a smaller proportion than the Northern Rural Areas – whereas in the South the Towns and Rural Areas display similar proportions.

Conclusion

The foregoing analyses indicate that the rise in unemployment has had a nationwide impact, with very few localities emerging from recession

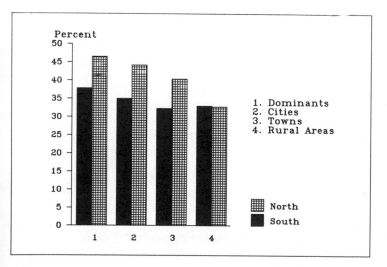

Figure 6.7 Proportion of long-term unemployed among total unemployed, by LLMA size and regional location
Source: Department of Employment data

unscathed. However, some places emerge more scarred than others. The foremost spatial distinction is the regional differentiation between Northern and Southern Britain with the former faring consistently worse than the latter. Indeed, in absolute terms – as measured by percentage point change in unemployment rates – the gap between North and South widened, although in relative terms – as measured by the local : national ratio in unemployment rates – there was overall convergence in unemployment rates as the numbers unemployed increased.

In terms of new spatial divisions emerging as a result of the growth in unemployment, particular attention is drawn to three salient changes. First, considering the regional dimension, the Heartland of Britain, having had an unemployment experience similar to that of Southern Britain in the pre-recession era, became more akin to the Peripheral regions of the North, Wales and Scotland, characterized by problems of high unemployment. Secondly, turning to the hierarchical dimension, the large urban areas (particularly the large urban areas of Northern Britain) suffered disproportionately from the increase in unemployment, and more notably long-term unemployment; while the Rural Areas (again, particularly those of Northern Britain) emerged least scathed from the recession. Finally, at the intra-LLMA scale, unemployment problems became more pronounced in the urban cores which had previously suffered most acutely from long-standing unemployment problems.

Further reading

For a general text on Unemployment, see Hawkins, K. 1984: *Unemployment* Harmondsworth: (Penguin), 2nd ed.

Spatial disparities in unemployment are comprehensively dealt with in Chapter 8: Regional Unemployment Disparities pp. 141–68 in Armstrong, H. and Taylor, J. 1985: *Regional economics and policy* (Oxford: Philip Allan).

For an introduction to spatially disaggregated unemployment data, see Goddard, J.B. and Coombes, M.G. (1983): Local employment and unemployment data, in Healey, M. (ed.) *Urban and regional industrial research; the changing UK data base*, Norwich: Geobooks.

A summary of a survey into long-term unemployment may be found in White, M. 1983: Long-term unemployment – labour market aspects, *Employment Gazette*, 91, 437–43.

For an examination of variations in unemployment duration during the recession, using the Functional Region framework, see Green, A.E. 1985: Unemployment duration in the recession: the Local Labour Market Area scale, *Regional Studies* 19, 111–29. For a more detailed analysis of this topic see Green, A.E. 1986: The likelihood of becoming and remaining unemployed in Great Britain, 1984, *Transactions, Institute of British Geographers New Series* 11, 37–56.

A useful account of the nature and patterns of unemployment rate changes in Britain between 1963 and 1982 is provided by Frost, M.E. and Spence, N.A. 1983: Unemployment change, in Goddard, J.B. and Champion, A.G. (eds.) *The urban and regional transformation of Britain*, (London: Methuen), 239–59.

7
Socio-economic characteristics

Levels of unemployment and the structure of employment have a powerful influence on the prosperity and spending power of people living in a place. Hammond (1968) and Coates and Rawstron (1971) have shown how much living standards varied across the country in the 1960s with some places having considerably higher incomes (particularly from investment), longer life expectancy and better access to transport, medical and other facilities than others. By and large, it would seem from the previous two chapters that the events of the last 15 years have tended to exacerbate regional and local differentials in access to higher-paid jobs, with the strong growth of high-level service jobs in London and the South East, the massive cutback in full-time jobs for men in the older industrial regions and the surge in low-paid part-time jobs for women in more rural and peripheral parts of Britain.

This chapter examines the evidence to assess whether the socio-economic differences between Britain's 'Two Nations', insofar as they can be expressed in spatial terms, have been widening since the early 1970s. Because of the difficulty of obtaining access to local information on incomes, this chapter concentrates on three commonly used alternative measures of social well-being; the importance of higher-status Socio-Economic Groups (SEGs), the availability of cars to households, and the proportion of households living in owner-occupied accommodation. Though all such indicators pose problems of measurement and interpretation at the level of the individual person or household, they provide some clear-cut patterns when used as a proxy for the average standards of living faced by a whole community. As in previous chapters, the Functional Regions framework allows some insights into the relative importance of North–South, urban–rural and other dimensions of variability, as well as providing a set of consistently defined 'places' which can be compared with each other on a common basis. We begin, however, with a look at the national picture and an examination of variations in socio-economic characteristics at the zone level within Functional Regions.

National context

In spite of the increasing problems over employment decline and unemployment, the period since 1971 has seen some remarkable improvements in the average living conditions of the British population. This is particularly noticeable in the realm of the traditional indicators of housing amenities and overcrowding. The proportion of households with exclusive use of the three basic amenities of hot and cold water supply, fixed bath and inside WC rose from 82.7 to 95.6 per cent between the 1971 and 1981 Censuses, leaving only 1.8 per cent of households without a fixed bath in 1981 and 3.7 per cent without unshared use of an inside WC. Similarly, with overcrowding, the proportion of households living at a density of 1.5 or more persons per room, fell from 1.9 to 0.8 per cent over the decade, while the proportion with 1.0 or more persons per room dropped from 7.2 to 4.3 per cent.

There is more scope for place-to-place variability in the three social indicators selected for this chapter, though each again reflects significant improvements in real incomes and living standards. The proportion of households owning or buying their own homes grew from 48.1 to 55.9 per cent between the two Censuses. Levels of car availability changed dramatically, as the proportion of households with access to two or more cars rose from 8.7 to 15.5 per cent and those with no car at all fell from 49.1 to 39.5 per cent. As regards the proportion of people in the highest social groups, changes in definition between the two Censuses force us to treat employees and professional and managerial workers (SEGs 1–4 and 13) together with the intermediate category of non-manual workers (SEG 5). The share of economically active or retired persons in this broad higher-status grouping increased from 21.7 to 26.5 per cent between 1971 and 1981, reflecting the shift from manual to non-manual occupations partly associated with the decline in manufacturing and the growth of the service sector.

Variations between zones

As noted in Chapter 1, much attention has been given in recent years to the polarization of social groups and living standards between inner and outer parts of cities, as the former have lost more mobile people to the latter and as rising unemployment has been focused disproportionately on the so-called 'inner city areas' which nowadays are defined to include the local authority problem estates built towards the edge of the main built-up areas of the larger cities. The zone level of the Functional Regions framework, which distinguishes the whole built-up area of the central city as the Core from the surrounding commuting Ring and other zones, can be used to examine the extent of polarization and whether it has been increasing over time.

The evidence presented in Table 7.1 shows that, across the nation as a whole, the Cores are the most deprived zone on each of the criteria shown, having the smallest proportions of people in the higher social groups, the smallest proportions of owner-occupying and two-car households and the largest proportions of households with no car at all. Moreover, though the performance of the Cores improved between 1971 and 1981 on all these indicators, the rate of improvement was below the national rate in each case and therefore the gap between the Cores and the national level has widened. The degree of increasing polarization is reinforced by the changes taking place in the Rings and Outer Areas, which present a complete mirror image of the Cores because of their already privileged positions in 1971 and their faster-than-average improvements subsequently, particularly in terms of two-car households (Table 7.1).

Socio-economic composition by Local Labour Market Areas (LLMAs)

The national figures of 21.7 per cent (1971) and 26.5 per cent (1981) for the proportion of economically active or retired persons in the higher socio-economic groups (SEGs 1–5 and 13) represent merely the averaging of a wide range of variability across Britain. In 1971 St Albans, at the upper extreme, registered a level of 36.3 per cent in these groups, over three times the level at the lowest place (West Bromwich, 11.3 per cent). Ten years later, these same

Table 7.1 Socio-economic characteristics, 1971–81, by Functional Region zone

Characteristic	Core	Ring	Outer	Rural	All Zones
% Persons in SEGs 1–5, 13					
1971	20.4	24.0	24.6	23.2	21.7
1981	24.7	29.9	29.4	26.9	26.5
1971–81	+4.2	+5.9	+4.9	+3.7	+4.8
% Households without a car					
1971	54.0	39.6	40.1	39.6	49.1
1981	45.1	29.9	30.4	30.8	39.5
1971–81	−8.9	−9.8	−9.8	−8.9	−9.6
% Households with 2+ cars					
1971	7.0	12.1	12.0	11.3	+8.7
1981	12.3	21.4	20.2	18.5	15.5
1971–81	+5.3	+9.2	+8.2	+7.1	+6.8
% Owner occupiers					
1971	45.7	53.7	52.4	48.5	48.1
1981	52.7	62.4	60.6	56.1	55.9
1971–81	+7.0	+8.7	+8.2	+7.6	+7.8

Source: Population Census Small Area Statistics

two places continued to occupy the extreme positions, but though they had both increased their representation of this group of people, the proportion at West Bromwich had grown only marginally to 12.5 per cent while that for St Albans had leapt ahead to 43.1 per cent. Thus over the decade the range between the two extremes widened from 25 to over 30 percentage points. The identity of the top and bottom 10 LLMAs on this indicator in 1981 is shown in Table 7.2.

In terms of geographical patterns there is in 1981 a clear distinction between the places at the two extremes (Figure 7.1A). Most notable is the ring of most privileged LLMAs around London, extending down to the South Coast and forming a virtually complete arc on the other flanks; the only exception being along both sides of the Thames estuary. There are also significant clusters of better-off LLMAs further westwards along the South Coast and in the southern parts of the West Midlands. The prosperity of the South can be gauged in terms of the fact that south of a line between the Severn Estuary and Lincolnshire there are only three representatives of the lowest

Table 7.2 Proportion of economically active or retired persons in SEGs 1–5 and 13, extreme LLMAs 1981

Highest LLMAs	%	Lowest LLMAs	%
St Albans	43.1	West Bromwich	12.5
Maidenhead	40.2	Peterlee	14.3
Haywards Heath	39.8	Mexborough	14.5
Guildford	39.6	Mansfield	16.7
Woking & Weybridge	39.4	Gelligaer	16.8
High Wycombe	38.6	Corby	16.9
Bishop's Stortford	37.4	Castleford & Pontefract	16.9
Winchester	37.1	Merthyr Tydfil	17.0
Aldershot & Farnborough	37.1	Bathgate	17.3
Horsham	36.1	Smethwick	17.3

Source: Population Census Small Area Statistics

Figure 7.1   Proportion of economically active or retired persons in SEGs 1–5 and 13, by LLMA – A: 1981; B: 1971–81 percentage point change
Source: Population Census

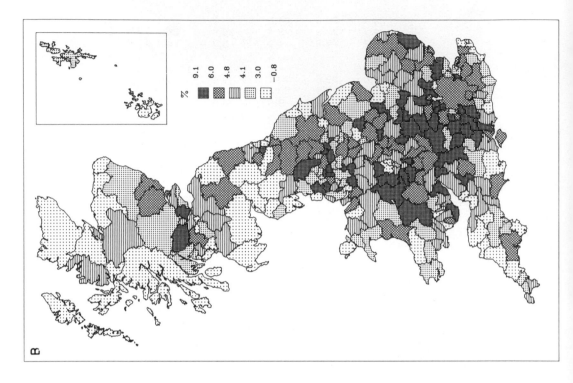

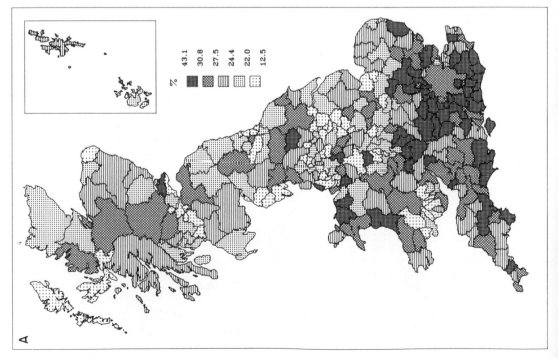

quintile on this indicator, namely Corby, Spalding and Wisbech, and, of Britain's bottom 112 places, the South accounts for only 11, all but one of which are located on the margins of the region in East Anglia and the East Midlands (Figure 7.1A).

North of the Severn–Wash line, the LLMAs which perform most poorly on this indicator present a much more disparate geographical pattern, but relate to a similarly distinctive set of places. These are essentially the older industrial and mining settlements situated on the coalfields of South Wales, South Yorkshire, the East Midlands, Lancashire, West Cumbria, County Durham and Central Scotland, together with the Black Country and Potteries of the West Midlands. In the North the most favoured LLMAs comprise a group of well known high-status residential towns, particularly resort and retirement areas, including Harrogate, Southport, Macclesfield, Malvern, Aberystwyth, St Andrews, Llandudno, Stockport and Chester (Figure 7.1A).

The changes which took place in the preceding 10 years very largely served to reinforce a pattern of regional imbalance which already existed in 1971. It is particularly impressive that so few places in Scotland and the Northern Region of England saw their proportion of these SEGs increase by more than the national amount (Figure 7.1B). Similarly outstanding is the extensive and relatively unbroken block of places in central southern England which increased their proportions by over 6.0 per cent, stretching from Portsmouth to Leicester and from Gloucester to St Albans. Perhaps the most surprising aspects of the 1971–81 changes in the South are the relative lowering of the status of the South Coast towns, albeit from very high levels in 1971 except in Kent, and the above-average performance of London, despite its carrying various negative features like an ageing population, increasing concentrations of immigrants and rising unemployment. Places in the North which improved their proportion of the higher SEGs most markedly are largely grouped around major conurbations, particularly in the West Midlands and the North West, but also include some smaller more independent towns, such as Durham, Newark, Stamford, Loughborough and Stirling (Figure 7.1B).

These patterns reflect some of the principal changes which have taken place in the distribution of population and jobs during the decade (see Chapters 2, 3 and 5). Of particular importance has been the growth of relatively high-level employment in both manufacturing and service sectors in southern England along the M4, M3 and M1 corridors. The strongest performances in the North can mainly be attributed to the surge in residential decentralization which took higher-status people out of the major cities into surrounding towns with a long manufacturing tradition, but some of the more successful freestanding settlements experienced significant growth in their service sectors, partly in connection with the expansion of higher education. The lack of improvement in the more rural and peripheral regions of the North can be associated in part with the swelling of the labour force by low-paid part-time female labour and low-skilled manual jobs for men, while the falling status of the South Coast towns reflects a partial substitution of their traditional high-class retirement role by a wider range of locally based jobs and by long-distance commuters seeking out lower house prices.

In terms of the dimensions of the Functional Regions framework, the size factor seems to play a relatively minor role (Figure 7.2). In both North and South the Rural LLMAs have experienced the smallest increases in their proportions of the higher SEGs, but whereas in the South they constitute the least privileged places, in the North they continue to have the largest proportions of these people. Instead, from this analysis the regional dimension

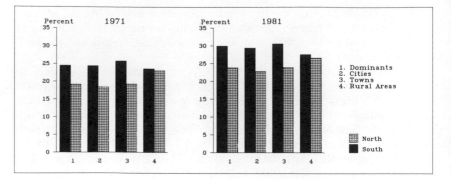

Figure 7.2   Proportion of economically active or retired persons in SEGs 1–5 and 13, by LLMA size and regional location
Source: Population Census

appears paramount, as seen from the rankings of the eight settlement categories. These remained unchanged between 1971 and 1981, beginning with the three more urban representatives of the South, continuing with the two rural groups and finishing up with the three urban categories of the North.

Car availability by LLMAs

On this indicator, too, a wide range separates the most privileged places from the most deprived. The places which were most favourably situated in 1981 are identified in Table 7.3. In High Wycombe and Maidenhead one in three of all households had access to two or more cars and the proportion was over one in four in another 15 LLMAs. Virtually all of these are located in London's Metropolitan Region, including (besides those shown in Table 7.3) Bracknell, Reigate & Redhill, Reading, Slough, Newbury and Hemel Hempstead. The only comparable places lying outside this area are Stratford-on-Avon and Evesham, situated adjacent to each other in the southern part of Birmingham's Metropolitan Region and reinforcing the 'cocktail belt' nature of the most privileged places. Moreover, none of the top 10 places in Table 7.3 had more than a quarter of its households without access to a car.

By contrast, the 10 LLMAs with the lowest proportions of two-car households in 1981 were all located to the north of the Severn–Lincolnshire line and

Table 7.3   Proportion of households with 2 or more cars, 1981, extreme LLMAs

Highest LLMAs	2 + cars %	(No car) %	Lowest LLMAs	2 + Cars %	(No car) %
High Wycombe	34.3	(20.7)	Mexborough	6.8	(54.8)
Maidenhead	33.6	(21.2)	South Shields	6.8	(59.5)
Woking & Weybridge	30.9	(21.5)	Sunderland	7.0	(57.3)
Bishop's Stortford	30.6	(21.4)	Peterlee	7.1	(54.8)
Aldershot	29.4	(21.0)	West Bromwich	7.5	(53.2)
Guildford	29.4	(23.9)	Coatbridge & Airdrie	7.6	(56.0)
St Albans	29.2	(23.6)	Merthyr Tydfil	7.8	(52.0)
Hertford & Ware	29.0	(23.0)	Glasgow	8.3	(59.5)
Stratford-on-Avon	28.2	(24.4)	Newcastle upon Tyne	8.4	(52.8)
Horsham	27.2	(21.9)	Bathgate	8.5	(51.0)

Source: Population Census Small Area Statistics

comprised industrial and mining centres and large cities (Table 7.3). The levels at Mexborough and South Shields were only one-fifth of High Wycombe's figure and none of these bottom 10 LLMAs had more than one in 12 households with two or more cars. Furthermore, in all 10 cases over half the households had no car at all. Other places with more than 50 per cent of households without a car in 1981 were Greenock, Liverpool, Paisley, Hartlepool, Bradford, Dundee, Motherwell and Oldham.

The detailed geographical patterns of places with low car availability in 1981 are shown in Figure 7.3A. Most impressive are the large urban concentrations in central Scotland, north east England, the Pennine industrial towns (basically the M62 corridor) and the South Wales coalfield. The urban factor, associated with higher levels of public transport services and greater difficulties in using and garaging vehicles as well as with consumer spending power, is also evident in London and in the 'motor cities' of the West Midlands conurbation, while the above-average proportions on the South Coast, and parts of the East Coast too, reflect the relatively large numbers of households there which comprise only persons of pensionable age.

The places with the highest levels of car availability are also highly distinctive in their distribution (Figure 7.3A). They occur predominantly to the south of the Severn–Wash line and the best-off places are particularly concentrated in the outer parts of the London Metropolitan Region, following the line of the recently opened M25 motorway and reflecting the distribution of the higher social groups (cf. Figure 7.1A). In the North of Britain the relatively few places with high levels of car availability comprise either wealthy dormitory towns, as in the West Midlands and North West, or more rural LLMAs as in central Wales and the northern Pennines where lower levels of public transport place a premium on the availability of private cars. Even so, it is impressive that in many of the most remote areas in Britain at least one-third of households had no car in 1981 despite a decade of rapid growth in car ownership.

It is, however, the growth in the proportion of households with two or more cars that provides the most marked indication of regional imbalance. As Figure 7.3B shows, well above average increases were grouped together in a block of LLMAs around London and westwards along the M4 corridor across central southern England and into Gloucestershire, signifying the single most important concentration of wealth in Britain. The metropolitan-ring effect is much more weakly developed in the West Midlands and North West. North of the M62 only Aberdeen is outstanding, while only a handful of places like Stirling and Harrogate and some smaller and more rural parts of the northern Pennines recorded increases anywhere near the national figure of 6.8 per cent. Because the absolute increase in proportion of two-car households occurred fastest in those areas which were already the most favoured in 1971, the gap between highest and lowest LLMAs on this criterion widened substantially over the decade from 17.6 to 27.5 percentage points.

In terms of the dimensions of the Functional Regions framework, it is therefore the broad regional division that provides the clearest description of changing patterns of car availability (Figure 7.4). With respect to both households without a car and those with two cars the major divide occurs between North and South. In 1971 over 10 per cent of households in both the London Metropolitan Region and the Rest of the South had two or more cars, three or more percentage points clear of the two Northern regions. The subsequent 10 years opened up this gap still further, with the proportion increasing by 8.2

Figure 7.3   Car availability 1971–81, by LLMA – A: Proportion of households with no car, 1981; B: Percentage point change in proportion of households with two or more cars, 1971–81
Source: Population Census

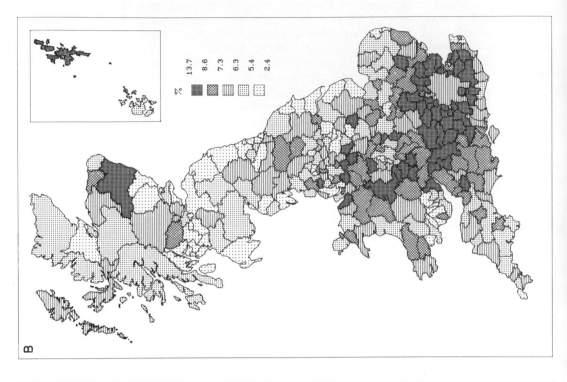

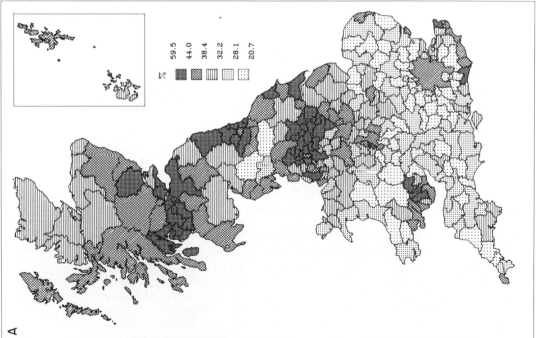

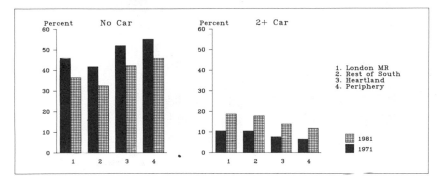

Figure 7.4 Car availability, 1971 and 1981, by broad regional division
Source: Population Census

percentage points in the London Region and being progressively smaller for
the other regions.

Housing tenure by LLMAs

Considerable changes have taken place in housing tenure since the early
1970s. These changes have, however, not followed such consistent lines as for
socio-economic composition and car availability – partly due to the variety
of housing types found in each of the main tenure groups, but also due to
switches in central government policy. The 1974 Housing Act encouraged a
major increase in the activities of the voluntary housing movement, but this
has been completely inadequate to compensate for the continued decline in
the role of the private landlord, which has been the prime force in the reduction in the privately rented sector from 21.4 to 12.8 per cent of all households
between the last two Censuses. The proportion accounted for by the local
authority sector had risen strongly to 30.5 per cent by 1971, but over the next
10 years its increase was kept down to less than one percentage point by the
tighter public spending restrictions imposed in the later 1970s and by the
subsidized sale of council housing to sitting tenants after 1979.

By contrast, the expansion of home ownership has continued apace,
fuelled by the large subsidies provided to purchasers in the form of tax relief
on mortgage payments. Though the construction of new family dwellings has
fallen back considerably from the high levels of the early 1970s, more recently
the popularity of starter homes, the boom in building for sale for the elderly
and the sale of council houses helped to push the proportion of owner-
occupying households up from 48.1 per cent in 1971 to 55.9 per cent in 1981
and on to an estimated 62 per cent in 1985. As with the other socio-economic
measures which indicate rapid and continuing improvement in recent years, it
is unfortunate that latest data on local patterns of owner occupation
available at the time of writing (June 1986) are those provided by the 1981
Census. Even so, the latter can give us a snapshot of variations between
places and an indication of how far the changes of the previous few years
have altered the extent and pattern of these differentials.

In general, the geography of owner occupation confirms the prevailing
discussions of variability and change noted in the previous sections of this
chapter. As shown in Figure 7.5, both regional and LLMA size dimensions
are important and, once again, it is the former that is the more consistent. For

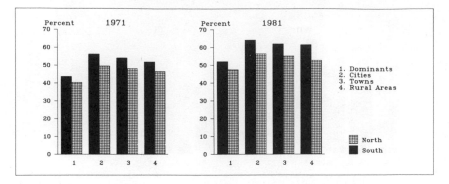

Figure 7.5 Proportion of households living in owner-occupied accommodation, by LLMA size and regional location
Source: Population Census

each of the LLMA size groups in both 1971 and 1981 the representatives of the South contain a higher proportion of owner-occupiers than those of the rest of Britain. Moreover, between the two Censuses the margin between North and South widened perceptibly, since the proportion of owner-occupiers grew by around one percentage point more in the South. The margin widened particularly sharply for the Rural LLMAs, since those in the South saw their propportion rise by 9.6 per cent compared with only 6.2 per cent for their Northern counterparts.

The LLMA size factor shows some regular features within both North and South (Figure 7.5). The Large Dominants have distinctively low proportions of owner-occupiers, because their housing stock contains well above average amounts of local authority housing and – particularly in the case of London – significant amounts of privately rented accommodation. Otherwise, however, the proportion of owner-occupiers declines along the urban–rural dimension, though because of the major increase in owner occupation in the Rural South between the two Censuses, the gradient in the South had become much shallower by 1981.

At the level of individual places, the patterns are much more difficult to interpret in relation to a single dimension than those for social class and car availability. The places with the highest levels of owner occupation in 1971 and the most rapid increase in proportion over the subsequent 10 years are presented in Table 7.4. The seaside resorts and Lancashire towns which

Table 7.4 Top 10 LLMAs for owner occupiers 1971 and increase in owner occupation 1971–81

Highest proportion	1971 %	1971–81 (% point)	Largest increase in proportion	1971–81 % point	(1971) (%)
Clacton	74.9	(+5.6)	Stevenage	+21.6	(16.3)
Accrington	71.6	(+4.4)	Newark	+17.8	(42.3)
Nelson & Colne	71.5	(+4.1)	Huntingdon	+17.4	(44.8)
Blackpool	71.4	(+4.6)	Thetford	+16.3	(43.3)
Hinckley	70.5	(+4.2)	Corby	+15.7	(18.1)
Stornoway	69.2	(−3.8)	Doncaster	+15.4	(39.6)
Southend	68.6	(+6.8)	Durham	+14.3	(45.7)
Worthing	68.7	(+6.9)	Grantham	+14.1	(43.1)
Leyland & Chorley	68.3	(+4.8)	Goole	+13.5	(50.9)
Blackburn	67.6	(+1.1)	Crawley	+13.3	(31.9)

Source: Population Census Small Area Statistics

dominate the former indicate the existence of at least two different paths towards high levels of owner occupation in the past, while Stornoway in the Western Isles suggests a third, though this case is unique in Scotland, which is generally characterized by very high proportions of publicly rented housing. Meanwhile, the largest percentage-point increases in owner occupation over the subsequent decade appear to relate either to New and Expanded Towns, where the development programmes originally laid great stress on publicly rented housing but have more recently been affected by policy changes in favour of private building, or to location in the less heavily developed parts of eastern England (Table 7.4).

Summary: socio-economic characteristics for selected LLMA categories

This chapter has examined the degrees and dimensions of differentiation within and between places with respect to three commonly used measures of social well-being – social class, car availability and housing tenure. It has also attempted to assess whether these differentials have been widening or narrowing over time. Some of the results have been remarkably clear cut, particularly the strong position of the outer parts of the London Region and central southern England and the way in which this part of Britain has been increasing its lead since the early 1970s. The relatively disadvantaged position of the Northern industrial areas and conurbations has also generally been clear, though much of their weaknesses are inherited and recent trends have been somewhat diverse.

In fact, it is not unusual for studies of social well-being to find difficulty in generalizing from a range of indicators, because each tends to measure a different aspect of wealth or deprivation. The normal way forward in these circumstances is to resort to an overall index based on the summation of each place's scores on all the indicators; and indeed this is what we do in the next chapter as we attempt to draw together the main themes of growth and decline running through the whole book. Here, by way of a summary to this chapter, we identify from the 19-fold classification of LLMAs (see Table 1.6) the five categories which began the 1970s in the most privileged position with respect to the three characteristics covered in the chapter and the five which were amongst the most disadvantaged in overall terms, and examine whether subsequent trends have brought greater divergence or some convergence.

Table 7.5 clearly confirms the importance of the regional dimension at these two extremes of social well-being. London's Subdominant Cities and Towns were both well above average on all three criteria in 1971, while in the Rest of the South so were the Service Towns (though not so high on car availability) and the Rural LLMAs (particularly strong on car availability). The change data show that both London Subdominant categories have subsequently experienced greater than average improvements, though only marginally so in respect of level of owner occupation. The Rural LLMAs have improved their position in relation to the national average particularly for owner-occupied housing, but not for higher social groups, while the Service Towns have fallen back towards the national figure on all three criteria, largely reflecting the limited degree to which the seaside resorts and retirement centres have failed to keep up with the gains made elsewhere in the South. Finally, London is included because of its relatively large proportion of the higher social groups and also because – contrary to the poor image which it has presented in terms of population change and demographic

Table 7.5   Performance on three social indicators for selected LLMA categories

LLMA category (ranked by social class 1971)	SEGs 1–5, 13		2+ Car households		Owner occupiers	
	1971	1971–81	1971	1971–81	1971	1971–81
	%	% point	%	% point	%	% point
Highest categories						
London Subdominant Cities	28.6	+5.5	12.7	+10.4	60.3	+7.9
London Subdominant Towns	26.8	+5.3	15.1	+10.8	52.7	+7.9
Southern Service Towns	26.6	+4.0	9.6	+6.5	59.4	+7.6
London	24.6	+5.5	8.9	+6.6	42.7	+8.4
Southern Rural Areas	23.5	+4.0	12.4	+7.3	51.8	+9.6
Lowest categories						
Conurbation Dominants	18.8	+4.4	6.4	+4.7	39.0	+6.9
Northern Freestanding Cities	18.7	+4.5	6.4	+5.9	49.0	+7.5
Conurbation Subdominant Cities	18.3	+4.1	7.2	+5.9	46.7	+6.1
Northern Manufacturing Towns	17.3	+4.5	6.7	+6.0	43.0	+6.0
Smaller Northern Subdominants	16.2	+4.4	6.1	+6.0	47.8	+7.5
Great Britain	21.7	+4.8	8.7	+6.8	48.1	+7.8

Source: Population Census Small Area Statistics

restructuring – it has registered significant growth in proportions of higher social groups and owner-occupying households (Table 7.5).

At the other extreme are five categories of Northern LLMAs. Amongst these, the most consistently disadvantaged in 1971 according to the three indicators were the Manufacturing Towns, the Conurbation Dominants (which score very weakly on owner-occupied housing) and the Subdominant LLMAs of the smaller Northern Metropolitan Regions (though these had close to the national average proportion of owner-occupiers). Across all these five Northern groups, there is only one instance of a higher-than-average indicator, that being for the level of owner-occupation in the Freestanding Cities, while in relation to the percentage point changes since 1971 they can boast no instance at all of an increase larger than the national shift (Table 7.5). With regard to these three social characteristics the gap between these groups of Northern LLMAs and the overall British level has been widening over the past decade.

Further reading

Two major studies examine variations in socio-economic characteristics between different parts of Britain for the 1960s, Hammond, E. 1968: *An analysis of regional and economic statistics* (Durham: Rowntree Research Unit, University of Durham), and Coates, B.E. and Rawstron, E.M. 1971: *Regional variations in Britain: studies in economic and social geography* (London: Batsford). Recent publications highlighting spatial differentials in living standards include Fothergill, S. and Vincent, J. 1985: *The state of the nation: an atlas of Britain in the eighties* (London: Pan), Osman, T. 1985: *The facts of everyday life* (London: Faber & Faber) and Champion, A.G. 1983: *England and Wales '81: A census atlas* (Sheffield: Geographical Association). Trends in car availability and housing tenure can be monitored by reference to the annual publications *Regional Trends* (London: HMSO) and *General Household Survey* (London: HMSO), while the *Labour Force Survey*, now also conducted on an annual basis, provides data on occupational composition by socio-economic groups, though in all these cases the level of spatial resolution is much broader than that provided by the Population Census. An extensive treatment of social trends in British cities, based primarily on the 1961 and 1971 Censuses, is provided by Pinch, S. and Williams, A. 1983: Social class change in British cities, in Goddard, J.B. and Champion, A.G. (eds.) *The urban and regional transformation of Britain* (London: Methuen), 135–59.

8
The geography of growth and decline

This final chapter draws on the major strands of the foregoing analysis in order to answer the types of questions posed at the beginning of the book. These questions relate to the scale and nature of differences between places in the characteristics of their residents and in the quality of opportunities and socio-economic environments which these places offer to them. They also concern the extent to which these places have been changing since the early 1970s and, in particular, whether the outcome has been a narrowing or a widening of the gap between the two extremes of most privileged and most deprived places. Most important, however, has been the attempt made in the previous chapters to identify the principal dimensions underlying the performance of places on each of the various aspects of Britain's demographic, economic and social complexion which have been examined and to assess which of these dimensions are emerging as more significant over time and which appear to be fading in their ability to explain place-to-place differentials. As outlined in Chapter 1, the debate has centred on the relative importance of the 'North–South drift' and the 'urban–rural shift', but there has also been speculation about an evolving east–west gradient of economic growth.

One message comes across very clearly from the previous six chapters. It is that, in spite of over half a century of government efforts to reduce the degree of regional economic imbalance and of 40 years of the welfare state, Britain remains an extremely diverse country. Just as in the 1930s, so also in the 1980s there are some amazing extremes between places, perhaps most strongly evidenced now, as then, by differentials in the scale of job opportunities as reflected in unemployment rates and in the level of material affluence as measured by households with two or more cars – differentials which have widened markedly within the space of the past decade. Some parts of Britain are very wealthy by national standards, have recorded substantial growth since the early 1970s and appear to have weathered the economic recession of the late 1970s and early 1980s with relative ease , while other places started the 1970s in poor shape and have subsequently seen the economic lifeblood of their communities drained away in a spate of redundancies and factory closures.

The purpose of this chapter is to identify the places in Britain which appear to have fared best in the face of changes over the past decade and those which have fared worst. Using a selection of the characteristics which previous chapters have shown to be most important in differentiating places, we have developed an index which reflects the strength and dynamism of their local economies and provides a good indication of the way in which the 'life chances' of their inhabitants have changed over this period. We rank the 280 Local Labour Market Areas (LLMAs) in Britain on the basis of this index and then examine the attributes of the places which have fared better than others in order to discover the extent to which differentials in place prosperity can be related to any particular factor or combination of circumstances. In sum, therefore, we are asking two questions; which are Britain's 'booming towns' and to what do they owe their success?

An index of local economic performance

The selection of an index with which to gauge the relative economic dynamism of places is a complicated task, because it involves decisions on the number and type of indicators to be included, the way in which individual places are scored on each indicator and, where more than one indicator is used, the way in which the scores are combined to give an aggregate index for each place. The academic literature of the last 20 years offers an embarrassingly rich variety of approaches to choose from, ranging from a single variable through the sum of rankings on several variables to multi-variate classification procedures (see, for instance, Lloyd and Dicken, 1972; Coates *et al.*, 1977). The variety of approaches is partly a reflection of the ease with which new approaches can be developed, allowing each study to adopt the system which is judged to be the most appropriate. We, too, choose to use a specially developed method which is particularly suitable for the task in hand.

In relation to the number and type of variables, our preference is to keep the number relatively small and to include measures of change since the early 1970s as well as indicators of socio-economic differentiation relating to the 1980s. The small number of variables will help us later to 'unscramble' the final scores in order to explain why particular LLMAs come out well, while the combination of change and static variables means that the index will be taking account not only of 'quantity' but also 'quality'. We opted for the five indicators shown in Table 8.1.

Among these indicators, the level of unemployment is the most obvious candidate, for this is the measure of malaise or success which is given most prominence by the media and politicians alike and which remains the dominant criterion used for the identification of areas for regional policy assistance. Given double weighting, this is balanced against two measures of employment growth, one relating to the period 1971–78 and the other tracing the ability of places to weather the recession years 1978–81. These are used to indicate long-term economic performance, which is not perfectly correlated with unemployment rates (see Chapters 5 and 6). The final third of the scoring scheme comprises population growth between 1971 and 1981 and the proportion of households with access to two more cars, the latter constituting one of the more reliable measures of material prosperity available from the Population Census.

The index is derived from these five indicators by the summation of an individual place's score on each variable. As regards the latter, we opt not for the use of ranked position but for a measure which takes account of the distribution of the scores of individual places between the maximum and minimum

Table 8.1   The composition of the index of local economies performance

Variable	Weight
1 Unemployment rate, May 1985, (%)	2.0
2 Employment change, 1971–78, (%)	1.0
3 Employment change, 1978–81, (%)	1.0
4 Population change, 1971–81, (%)	1.0
5 Households with two or more cars, 1981, (%)	1.0

values. By this method the place with the best value on an indicator is allocated the score of 1.000, that with the worst value is given 0.000, and intermediate values are calibrated on their position over the intervening range. When the scores on all indicators for each place are summed, the result is divided by the maximum possible score (6.000 in this case, given the double weighting given to unemployment rate) to give a final index on the range 0.000 to 1.000. An index of 1.000 is possible only when an LLMA is consistently the best performer on all indicators, and vice versa for an LLMA scoring 0.000 overall.

Patterns of local growth and decline

Statistical distribution of index scores

We focus initially on the statistical distribution of index scores. The highest index score achieved by any LLMA is 0.764, barely three-quarters of the maximum possible. This indicates that even the most booming of the LLMAs has a performance on at least one of the five criteria which is significantly below the highest level registered on that criterion. It also suggests that there may be more than one type of 'booming town' since the highest scoring LLMAs may have quite different combinations of characteristics. At the other extreme, the lowest index score is 0.137, considerably closer to the end of the range and suggesting a more consistent performance across all five criteria.

A fuller impression of the complexity of the patterns can be obtained from the distribution of the index scores for the full set of 280 LLMAs. If all places performed consistently on all five measures, the 280 cases would be spread evenly across the whole range, with 28 LLMAs falling in each decile along the full scale. In fact, the actual distribution (Figure 8.1) approximates to the typical bell-shape of the 'normal distribution', with the modal class being that which spans the midpoint of the scale, ie. around 0.500. On the other hand, the overall distribution pivots around a rather lower value, with the median at 0.45, confirming the previous observation that the poorer performers score more consistently across the five measures than the better performers.

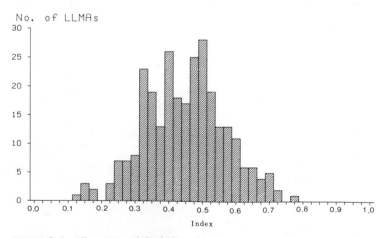

Figure 8.1   Histogram of the index of local economic performance

In this context, the statistical distribution also provides the opportunity of checking whether Britain's LLMAs divide clearly into 'Two Nations' with the better performers being largely separate from the poorer performers on the rankings for all five measures. Figure 8.1 affords some evidence of a bimodal distribution in the form of a somewhat lower than 'expected' number of cases around the median (0.454), with a subsequent rise to two secondary peaks around 0.400 and 0.325. It remains to be seen in the next section whether the LLMAs cluster in geographical terms on the basis of their Index scores.

Spatial distribution of index scores

The scores have been mapped in Figure 8.2 in such a way as to bring out two main features of the statistical distribution – the break between those above the median and those below it and the details of the patterns at the two extremes. Figure 8.2A shows parts of Britain covered by the 140 LLMAs with scores of 0.454 and over and gives a more detailed breakdown of the top quartile of the distribution. Meanwhile, in Figure 8.2B the same approach has been used for the 140 LLMAs scoring less than the median value, with the bottom quartile being further subdivided. In Table 8.2 the 10 highest and lowest scoring places are identified.

It can be seen from Table 8.2 that there is no doubt about the identity of the LLMA which has performed best on the basis of the criteria adopted for the index. Winchester's score of 0.764 is well clear of the nearest contenders. The geographical distribution of the best performing LLMAs is distinctive (Figure 8.2A). All lie within the South East where they form a virtually continous arc round the western half of the London Region, stretching from Crawley and Haywards Heath in the south to Milton Keynes and Aylesbury in the north. This zone focuses on the now legendary 'M4 Corridor', but also embraces the M3 belt of western Surrey and northern Hampshire.

Inclusion of the next 18 highest scoring LLMAs very largely serves to complete the ring round London (Figure 8.2A). Most notably, the pattern fills in on the northern side of London, extending outwards to include Bury St Edmunds, Cambridge, Newmarket and Huntingdon. The eastern half of the ring becomes better represented, with Chelmsford, Maidstone and

Table 8.2 Highest and lowest scores on the index

Highest scores			Lowest scores		
Rank	LLMA	Index	Rank	LLMA	Index
1	Winchester	0.764	280	Consett	0.137
2	Horsham	0.726	279	Mexborough	0.154
3	Bracknell	0.719	278	South Shields	0.155
4	Milton Keynes	0.702	277	Coatbridge & Airdrie	0.159
5	Maidenhead	0.697	276	Hartlepool	0.182
6	Basingstoke	0.697	275	Sunderland	0.184
7	High Wycombe	0.693	274	Bathgate	0.215
8	Aldershot & Farnborough	0.690	273	Liverpool	0.217
9	Bishops Stortford	0.677	272	Irvine	0.228
10	Aylesbury	0.675	271	Birkenhead & Wallasey	0.238
11	Hertford & Ware	0.669	270	Greenock	0.245
12	Crawley	0.668	269	Port Talbot	0.249
13	Haywards Heath	0.662	268	Peterlee	0.254
14	Woking & Weybridge	0.660	267	Middlesbrough	0.255
15	Guildford	0.644	266	Corby	0.257

Figure 8.2   Index of local economic performance, by LLMA – A: Above median; B: Below median

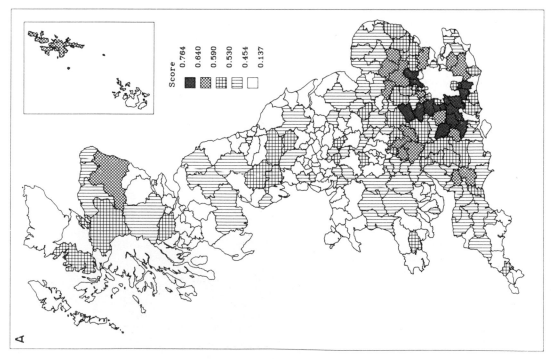

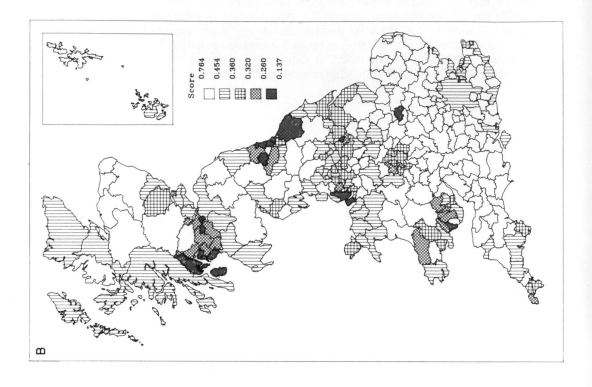

Tunbridge Wells scoring 0.590 or more, but the towns bordering on the Thames estuary do not reach this level and thus fail to complete the pattern. At this stage, too, three other parts of the country begin to feature – Aberdeen (which includes the Shetland Islands), Yeovil and Wells, and a cluster of LLMAs in the south Midlands including Cheltenham and Stratford on Avon – but these scarcely dent the dominance of the South East in the top octile of LLMAs.

At the other end of the spectrum, there is again no doubt about the identity of the poorest performance according to the index, but the geographical distribution of the bottom octile is more scattered. Consett, in north east England, scores only 0.137 and is clearly separate from the next three worst performing LLMAs: Mexborough (South Yorkshire), South Shields (Tyne & Wear) and Coatbridge & Airdrie (Strathclyde). The remaining LLMAs in the bottom 15 fill out the picture of concentrated depression in north east England and central Scotland, introduce elements of two further clusters of poor performance in South Wales and on Merseyside, and throw up the steel-closure New Town of Corby, stranded in a sea of relatively strongly performing areas in the East Midlands on the edge of the very prosperous London ring (Table 8.2 and Figure 8.2B).

The inclusion of the 20 next lowest LLMAs, with scores of 0.26–0.32, focuses the eye on the three areas that have been considered economic blackspots in Britain ever since the 1920s – central Scotland, north east England and South Wales. Besides the extra case in the North West (Wigan) and one in South Yorkshire (Rotherham), the only new additions are two representatives from Britain's newest depressed region (Smethwick and Wolverhampton in the West Midlands) and two of the most remote west coast areas (Penzance and Cardigan).

The other notable features of Figure 8.2 are as follows. The remainder of the top quartile – LLMAs with scores of between 0.53 and 0.59 – are principally located in the south-eastern corner of the country, linking up the best performing areas into a continuous zone stretching eastward from Somerset, extending round the southern and northern sides of London, and reaching into the southern parts of the Midlands and East Anglia (Figure 8.2A). The remainder of the bottom quartile – LLMAs with scores of between 0.32 and 0.36 – have, by contrast, a significantly different pattern from the more extreme cases, in particular picking out the corridor between Merseyside and Humberside – Britain's traditional Intermediate Area or 'grey area' in terms of economic blackspots and regional industrial assistance – but also featuring the remaining parts of the West Midlands conurbation (Figure 8.2B).

Key dimensions of economic performance

The index clearly confirms the existence of several important dimensions in Britain's space economy. In particular, these relate to the broad regional contrast between North and South, the urban–rural shift associated with the factor of city size, and economic structure. In this section we examine these regularities in a more systematic way in order to see how powerful an explanation they can provide for the variations in economic performance between areas and to check how consistently the possession of a favourable attribute guarantees economic success. Table 8.3 gives the distribution of LLMAs between quartiles according to index scores and explanatory criteria and shows how position in relation to a particular dimension affects the chances

Table 8.3   LLMA performance on the index, by selected characteristics

Characteristic	No. of LLMAs	Distribution by quartiles				Chances of being in	
		Bottom	3rd	2nd	Top	top quartile	top octile
Regional Location							
London Region	31	1	5	1	24	3.10	5.00
Rest of South	83	7	13	32	31	1.49	1.20
Industrial Heartland	87	29	27	22	9	0.41	0.19
Periphery	79	23	25	15	6	0.30	0.10
Population size (000s)							
Over 400	20	9	6	5	0	0.00	0.00
200–400	46	17	11	6	12	1.04	1.25
100–200	88	21	25	21	21	0.95	0.93
60–100	77	15	16	19	27	1.40	1.40
under 60	49	8	12	19	10	0.82	0.68
Manufacturing workers (% total)							
33.0 and over	69	26	16	19	6	0.35	0.00
27.0–33.0	71	22	15	10	24	1.35	1.49
20.0–27.0	74	14	15	22	23	1.24	1.67
16.0–20.0	30	1	15	7	7	0.93	1.11
under 16.0	36	5	9	12	10	1.11	0.45
Finance workers (% total)							
8.7 and over	34	1	5	4	24	2.82	4.63
7.4–8.7	35	5	9	7	14	1.60	1.16
5.4–7.4	70	16	8	24	22	1.26	0.82
4.6–5.4	60	19	23	17	7	0.42	0.38
under 4.6	75	29	25	18	3	0.16	0.00
Great Britain	280	70	70	70	70	1.00	1.00

of being represented in the top 70 and top octile of places in Britain.

As regards regional location, the advantages of the South are strongly confirmed, with 55 of the top 70 LLMAs being found there. Location within the London Metropolitan Region is particularly advantageous, with 24 of its 31 LLMAs in the top quartile. This means, in other words, that an LLMA in the London Region has over three times the chance of being in the top quartile on the index than is the case for LLMAs nationwide. The chances of these LLMAs being in the top octile are even higher, at five times the average probability. The remaining parts of the South also have a well above average chance of their LLMAs being in the top quartile, but elsewhere in Britain the chances are below half the average. The Industrial Heartland, comprising broadly LLMAs in the North West, Yorkshire and Humberside, and those parts of the Midlands which lie north of the Severn–Lincolnshire line, fare only marginally better than the Periphery, made up of the Northern Region, Wales and Scotland (Table 8.3).

For population size, the pattern is not so clear cut, but 27 out of the top 70 LLMAs had between 60,000 and 100,000 people in 1981, giving a place of this size a 40 per cent above average chance of being in the top quartile. This size group has the same degree of advantage in relation to the top octile of places, but interestingly a greater number of these very successful towns have populations of between 200,000 and 400,000, with below-average chances for towns of intermediate size. It is also clear that the smallest places recognized by the LLMA definition have relatively few representatives amongst the high fliers (Table 8.3).

As regards industrial structure, the proportion of workers employed in manufacturing also proves a relatively poor predictor, except that a very large emphasis on this sector is a clear disadvantage in terms of economic performance. On the other hand the proportion employed in finance, banking, insurance and related services is correlated strongly with economic performance, with a proportion of 8.7 per cent or more giving an LLMA 2.8 times the normal chance of inclusion in the top 70 and a massive 4.6 times the normal chance of inclusion in the top octile. Moreover, the level of benefit bestowed on a place by this characteristic declines progressively with the importance of this sector (Table 8.3).

Characteristics of Britain's booming towns

Leading naturally out of this analysis are two questions which potentially have important implications for the future, particularly for government attempts at increasing the contribution which individual places make to national economic growth and for policies aimed at keeping the degree of imbalance between places within acceptable limits. First, it is of interest to discover whether success can be explained in terms of a single type of town or whether there is no clear cut stereotype. Second is the question as to whether the type or types of towns which have been most successful can provide any lessons for less fortunate parts of the country. As a tentative first step towards answering these important but complicated questions, we examine the characteristics of the 15 places which scored highest on the index and then, because these all lie in the South and because the great divide which we have identified between the two parts of Britain may limit the degree of transferability of their benefits to the North, we go on to look at the main features of the 15 places in the North that have done best in overcoming the disadvantage of their regional location.

The top 15 LLMAs in Britain

Details of 15 LLMAs with the highest scores in the country are given in Table 8.4. It might have been expected that Winchester, so clearly the most successful town in Britain according to the index, would possess all the key ingredients in combination, but this is not the case. It is situated in the South East, but it lies beyond the zone heavily dominated by London, has not had the alternative stimulus of a planned expansion scheme, and is some distance from the 'M4 Corridor' (though it has benefited from the more recently constructed M3 motorway). On the other hand, it is in the most dynamic size range and its financial sector, while not in the same league as at Haywards Heath and Horsham, is quite strong. Moreover, other data from the 1981 Census confirm that it is a remarkable place, for more than four-fifths of its jobs are in the service sector (compared to two-thirds nationwide) and over one-fifth of its population are classed as employers, managers or professionals (half as much again as nationally). As the additional data in Table 8.4 shows, the principal features which produced such a high index score for this town were its low unemployment rate and its very strong job growth. It has had the lowest unemployment rate of all 280 LLMAs for several years and indeed was the only LLMA in Britain where, against the national trend, the rate actually fell between 1971 and 1981. Its growth in employment between 1971 and 1978 was dramatic, particularly given its low rate of population

Table 8.4   Selected characteristics of the top 15 LLMAs in Britain

LLMA	Rank in GB	Index variables					Other characteristics		
		1	2	3	4	5	6	7	8
Winchester	1	4.1	49.2	7.0	3.9	24.1	63,041	13.9	8.4
Horsham	2	6.7	24.1	9.3	19.2	27.2	75,270	22.3	14.4
Bracknell	3	7.6	32.2	−1.3	28.1	27.0	84,446	22.9	11.4
Milton Keynes	4	17.4	47.3	22.4	60.8	18.6	161,335	30.5	7.8
Maidenhead	5	6.1	10.7	1.7	9.5	33.6	92,124	28.0	11.2
Basingstoke	6	8.2	28.9	6.0	25.7	23.4	134,852	28.8	7.7
High Wycombe	7	6.1	15.1	−2.3	6.5	34.3	259,067	30.7	10.5
Aldershot	8	7.2	21.9	1.3	13.6	29.4	312,412	18.6	9.2
Bishop's Stortford	9	7.4	13.5	4.6	10.4	30.6	79,161	22.2	11.4
Aylesbury	10	6.6	24.6	−0.1	16.1	24.2	107,725	28.0	7.2
Hertford & Ware	11	4.7	24.1	−12.4	4.8	29.0	69,124	28.8	10.7
Crawley	12	4.8	18.8	−1.5	13.7	22.5	86,712	32.1	8.4
Haywards Heath	13	6.6	23.0	1.6	13.0	23.0	82,425	19.0	16.2
Woking	14	6.0	1.3	6.3	3.5	30.9	170,950	23.9	13.2
Guildford	15	5.2	−0.3	2.5	2.1	29.4	213,648	16.7	13.2
Great Britain	−	13.2	2.7	−5.1	0.6	15.5	−	27.0	7.8

Key: 1 Unemployment rate, May 1985 (%)
2 Employment change 1971–78 (%)
3 Employment change 1978–81 (%)
4 Population change 1971–81 (%)
5 Proportion of households with 2 or more cars 1981 (%)
6 Population present 1981
7 Proportion of workers in manufacturing 1981 (%)
8 Proportion of workers in finance 1981 (%)

growth, but it managed not only to sustain but build further on this achievement during the subsequent years of national recession.

Table 8.4 also shows the basis on which the other 14 top towns obtained their high scores. It is evident that by no means can they be considered to be identical 'clones' of the Winchester case in that they exhibit a wide range of values on the key criteria. Only Milton Keynes, for instance, can come close to Winchester's 1971–78 rate of employment growth, while the economies of a number of towns were far less resilient than Winchester's during the ensuing recession years. One feature which virtually all the places share is an extremely low unemployment rate by comparison with the national figure of 13.2 per cent. The exception is Milton Keynes, where apparently the exceptionally fast growth in population has outrun its rate of job growth, rapid though the latter has been. The next highest levels of unemployment in this list, found at Basingstoke and Bracknell, are also associated with rapid population growth. This suggests that there have been two routes by which a high index score has been achieved – one based on existing settlements and stimulated particularly by the growth of specialized services and the other associated with London's planned overspill and characterized by a relatively strong dependence on new manufacturing industry. This distinction is, however, subsidiary to their principal common characteristic of location in the South East.

The top 15 LLMAs in the North

This last point raises the question of how, given the importance of regional location, any places at all outside the South could manage to match the performance of these 'high-fliers'. Table 8.5 tries to provide the basis for an

Table 8.5 Selected characteristics of the top 15 LLMAs outside the South

LLMA	Rank in GB	Index variables					Other characteristics		
		1	2	3	4	5	6	7	8
Aberdeen	19	7.3	25.5	11.5	9.0	15.8	335,681	15.4	7.3
Stratford/Avon	23	9.4	11.9	4.5	6.4	28.2	57,984	22.1	10.3
Evesham	30	10.6	11.1	5.0	11.8	26.9	51,893	24.6	7.3
Kendal	37	6.3	6.5	−0.1	9.1	18.3	64,393	23.0	6.9
Macclesfield	38	8.9	13.8	−2.8	6.7	24.0	72,706	31.6	7.9
Harrogate	39	9.2	14.6	4.8	8.9	19.7	128,402	14.2	7.3
Redditch	42	16.9	25.6	2.0	46.9	19.9	85,744	44.4	5.9
Carmarthen	48	8.4	22.2	−8.9	2.8	20.6	41,916	9.6	3.5
Matlock	49	7.4	8.4	−5.0	3.7	20.9	46,196	32.1	5.6
Stafford	53	9.7	3.6	6.9	6.2	20.7	84,284	29.2	5.8
Leamington	58	10.2	6.3	1.7	4.6	21.9	113,409	35.8	7.2
Inverness	60	13.0	30.5	3.7	14.0	14.4	61,634	12.0	6.3
Penrith	65	10.5	7.8	0.3	5.5	21.1	42,223	17.3	4.9
Stirling	66	13.4	34.6	5.1	5.0	15.6	70,959	17.3	6.8
Northallerton	69	10.8	20.1	−7.8	5.1	20.5	86,038	13.3	4.7
Great Britain	—	13.2	2.7	−5.1	0.6	15.5	—	27.0	7.8

Key: as for Table 8.4

answer by listing the characteristics for the 15 LLMAs which did penetrate the South-dominated list. As noted from Figure 8.2, they are a scattered bunch and they exhibit considerable variety in certain other respects. As among the top 15, New or Expanded Town status has provided one route to a high score, as for Redditch with its New Town status. Aberdeen, Inverness and Stirling also achieved rapid employment growth during the main part of the 1970s. Aberdeen, as the dominant centre of the British oil industry, is clearly a special case, given its size; the only larger place in the top quartile nationwide is Oxford and then only at rank 50. There are, however, some common characteristics in this list of provincial boom towns, these being small size and below-average level of manufacturing, both of which seem to be associated closely with relatively low unemployment. In general, these places are service centres for largely rural areas with no strong manufacturing tradition, most of them close enough to major cities to benefit from an influx of commuters or workers nearing retirement and some of them with particular local advantages such as oil development, attraction for tourists, proximity to the dynamic South, possession of a major infrastructural investment such as a university, or designation as an administrative centre for the surrounding county or region.

Conclusion

In this final chapter a simple index based on five measures of economic standing and performance over time has been applied to the 280 LLMAs in order to provide a summary of the overall outcome of the various processes affecting places in Britain in recent years and to test the validity of alternative interpretations of recent trends in the country's evolving spatial structure. The results have revealed some very clear cut geographical patterns, most notably the overwhelmingly concentration of the most successful places in southern England, particularly within a 100 km arc to the west and north of London. Except for the oil-based growth in north-east Scotland the index finds little evidence of benefits deriving from an easterly location, but it is sensitive enough to pick out the disparity between the core of prosperity west of London and the relatively worse-off eastern part of the region. It also highlights the problems along the M62 corridor, but in provincial Britain it is the urban–rural dimension that stands out most clearly, with the industrial conurbations appearing as disaster areas in a sea of more rural areas characterized by a generally mediocre performance.

Particularly striking are the consistency with which certain places appear at the two extremes and the importance of the spatial dimension in producing local 'clusters' of LLMAs with similarly high and low scores. Though previously we have suggested that different social indicators will not reveal identical patterns of variation across the country, we have found that on virtually all the indicators, the western ring of Metropolitan Subdominant LLMAs round London and adjacent parts of the country in central southern England emerge as the most dynamic and wealthy. Meanwhile at the other end of the scale the old mining areas, steel-closure towns and port-based LLMAs in the North present the most depressed image. Moreover, the fact that static indicators and change rates both reflect these geographical patterns means that since the early 1970s the gap between the 'have' and 'have not' places has tended to get wider – a process which has accelerated in the period of recession since 1979.

For over half a century, successive British governments have been concerned about the scale of differentials between places, particularly those spanning the whole country and dividing it into a prosperous South and disadvantaged North. Despite the various levels and types of regional policies designed to keep differentials within bounds, however, Britain is more divided now than at any time since the mid 1930s. This is particularly strongly evidenced by the recent trends in house prices, which have been rising rapidly in the South East from already well-above-average levels, while remaining static or at least growing by less than the general inflation rate in many other parts of the country.

The Britain of the mid 1980s presents a depressing picture in terms of the lack of viable strategies for ameliorating this problem. Dearth of mobile international capital and lack of public sector funds severely restricts the amount of new industrial investment going into the less well-off areas; yet these places have very limited resources of their own with which to help rejuvenate their local economies. At the same time, a large number of people are locked into their local areas by the operation of the housing systems – owner-occupied as well as local authority – and cannot move to places where jobs are relatively more abundant. Indeed, employers in the Outer South East appear to find great difficulty in recruiting lower-paid staff even from inner London, let alone being able to attract people from further north, where housing costs are between a half and a third of those along the M4 Corridor.

The immediate future appears to offer more of the same. Though some success has been achieved by job creating agencies in the North, job loss is still running at a high rate and a continuation of high levels of redundancies and factory closures seems a real prospect, particularly in view of the limited progress made in these areas towards introducing new commerical products. Meanwhile, the South appears to be launched on an inflationary spiral in terms of the costs of land, housing and congestion which no politically feasible degree of relaxation in planning constraints is likely to curb and which can only be further stimulated by major infrastructural developments like the establishment of London's third airport at Stansted and the construction of the Channel Tunnel. With southerners becoming increasing reluctant to lose their toe-hold in the vibrant housing market there and with northerners facing massive housing-cost penalties for moving in the opposite direction, the divide between the two parts of Britain seems to be looming larger and larger and threatens to cleave the country into two blocks which are likely to pursue increasingly separate paths of development, thereby proving a challenge to their political unity in the longer term.

Further reading

A fuller account of this study of economic performance in Britain can be found in Champion, A.G. and Green, A.E. (1985) *In search of Britain's booming towns*, CURDS Discussion Paper 72 (Newcastle upon Tyne: Centre for Urban and Regional Development Studies, University of Newcastle upon Tyne).

Introductions to the methodology of measuring socio-economic differences between places are provided by Coates, B.E., Johnston, R.J. and Knox, P.L. 1977: *Geography and inequality* (Oxford: Oxford University Press); Lloyd, P.E. and Dicken, P. 1977: *Location in space: a theoretical approach to economic geography* (London: Harper & Row); and Smith, D.M. 1979: *Where the grass is greener: living in an unequal world* (Harmondsworth: Penguin). These studies include some examples of applications to Great Britain, but for a special study of 'levels of living' in England and Wales, see Knox, P.L. 1974: Spatial variations in level of living in England and Wales in 1961, *Transactions, Institute of British Geographers* 62, 1–24, and Knox, P.L. 1975: *Social well-being: a spatial perspective* (Oxford: Oxford University Press).

Most previous studies of socio-economic variations across Britain have used classification techniques to identify similarities between places rather than to rank them on a single index; the relative standing of each group can then be gauged from the average characteristics of places included in it. For the pioneering study in this field, see Moser, C.A. and Scott, W. 1961: *British towns: a statistical study of their social and economic differences* (London: Oliver & Boyd). The results of a classification of Districts in Britain based on 1971 Census data are described in Webber, R. and Craig, J. 1976: Which local authorities are alike? *Population Trends* 5, 13–19. Using cluster analysis, a distinction is made between 'traditional Britain' and 'new Britain' by Donnison, D. and Soto, P. 1980: *The good city: a study of urban development and policy in Britain* (London: Heinemann). The 228 Urban Regions of the CURDS Functional Region framework are classified into 13 clusters on the basis of 1981 Population Census data in Openshaw, S. and Charlton, M. 1984: The urban face of Britain, *The Geographical Magazine* 56, 421–4.

Details on regional differentials in house prices and other living costs can be obtained from Reward Regional Surveys 1986: *UK Regional Cost of Living Report* (Stone: Reward Regional Surveys). The barriers restricting migration between places are examined by Green, A.E. *et al.* 1986: What contribution can labour migration make to reducing unemployment? in Hart, P.E. (ed.) *Unemployment and labour market policies* (Aldershot: Gower), 52–81. A major empirical study of labour migration and the role of housing considerations is Johnson, J.H., Salt, J. and Wood, P.A. 1974: *Housing and the migration of labour in England and Wales* (Fanborough: Saxon House).

A useful account of government initiatives can be found in Law, C.M. 1981: *British regional development since World War I* (London: Methuen). The problems facing individual regions and the range of central and local government policies which have been designed to tackle them are described in Damesick, P. and Wood, P. (eds.) 1986: *Regional problems, problem regions and public policy in the United Kingdom* (Oxford: Oxford University Press). The implications of the government's failure to take more concerted action to deal with regional imbalances are spelt out by the Regional Studies Association (1984) *Report of an inquiry into the regional problem in the United Kingdom* (Norwich: GeoBooks).

Appendix 1
Map of the 280 Local Labour Market Areas

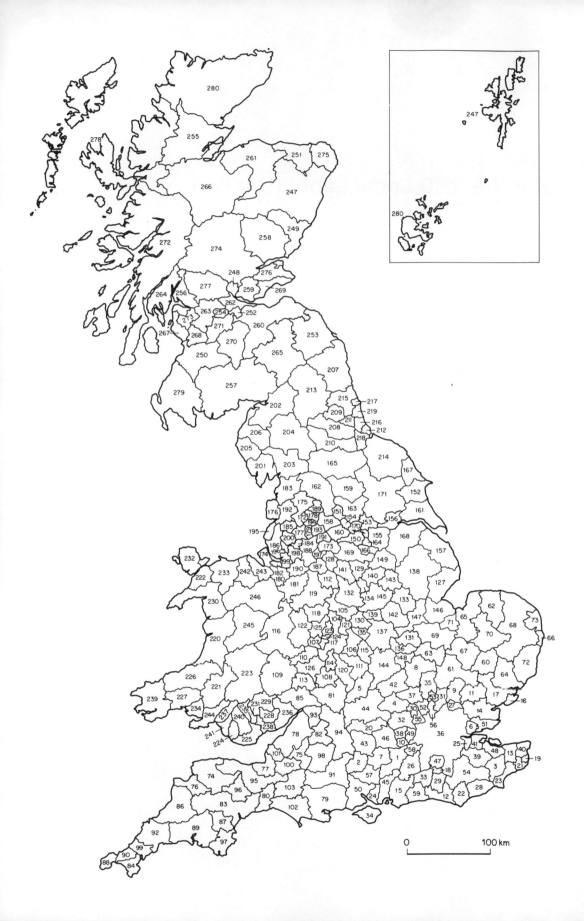

1 Aldershot & Farnborough
2 Andover
3 Ashford
4 Aylesbury
5 Banbury
6 Basildon
7 Basingstoke
8 Bedford
9 Bishop's Stortford
10 Bracknell
11 Braintree
12 Brighton
13 Canterbury
14 Chelmsford
15 Chichester & Bognor
16 Clacton
17 Colchester
18 Crawley
19 Deal
20 Didcot
21 Dover
22 Eastbourne
23 Folkestone
24 Gosport & Fareham
25 Gravesend
26 Guildford
27 Harlow
28 Hastings
29 Haywards Heath
30 Hemel Hempstead
31 Hertford & Ware
32 High Wycombe
33 Horsham
34 Isle of Wight
35 Letchworth
36 London
37 Luton
38 Maidenhead
39 Maidstone
40 Margate & Ramsgate
41 Medway Towns
42 Milton Keynes
43 Newbury
44 Oxford
45 Portsmouth
46 Reading
47 Reigate & Redhill
48 Sittingbourne
49 Slough
50 Southampton
51 Southend
52 St. Albans
53 Stevenage
54 Tunbridge Wells
55 Watford
56 Welwyn
57 Winchester
58 Woking & Weybridge
59 Worthing
60 Bury St. Edmunds
61 Cambridge
62 Dereham
63 Huntingdon
64 Ipswich
65 Kings Lynn
66 Lowestoft
67 Newmarket

68 Norwich
69 Peterborough
70 Thetford
71 Wisbech
72 Woodbridge
73 Yarmouth
74 Barnstaple
75 Bath
76 Bideford
77 Bridgwater
78 Bristol
79 Bournemouth
80 Chard
81 Cheltenham
82 Chippenham
83 Exeter
84 Falmouth
85 Gloucester
86 Launceston
87 Newton Abbot
88 Penzance
89 Plymouth
90 Redruth & Camborne
91 Salisbury
92 St. Austell
93 Stroud
94 Swindon
95 Taunton
96 Tiverton
97 Torquay
98 Trowbridge
99 Truro
100 Wells
101 Weston-Super-Mare
102 Weymouth
103 Yeovil
104 Birmingham
105 Burton on Trent
106 Coventry
107 Dudley
108 Evesham
109 Hereford
110 Kidderminster
111 Leamington
112 Leek
113 Malvern
114 Redditch
115 Rugby
116 Shrewsbury
117 Smethwick
118 Stafford
119 Stoke on Trent
120 Stratford-on-Avon
121 Tamworth
122 Telford
123 Walsall
124 West Bromwich
125 Wolverhampton
126 Worcester
127 Boston
128 Buxton
129 Chesterfield
130 Coalville
131 Corby
132 Derby
133 Grantham
134 Heanor & Ripley
135 Hinckley
136 Kettering
137 Leicester
138 Lincoln

139 Loughborough
140 Mansfield
141 Matlock
142 Melton Mowbray
143 Newark
144 Northampton
145 Nottingham
146 Spalding
147 Stamford
148 Wellingborough
149 Worksop
150 Barnsley
151 Bradford
152 Bridlington
153 Castleford
154 Dewsbury
155 Doncaster
156 Goole
157 Grimsby
158 Halifax
159 Harrogate
160 Huddersfield
161 Hull
162 Keighley
163 Leeds
164 Mexborough
165 Northallerton & Richmond
166 Rotherham
167 Scarborough
168 Scunthorpe
169 Sheffield
170 Wakefield
171 York
172 Accrington
173 Ashton & Hyde
174 Birkenhead
175 Blackburn
176 Blackpool
177 Bolton
178 Burnley
179 Bury
180 Chester
181 Crewe
182 Ellesmere Port
183 Lancaster
184 Leigh
185 Leyland & Chorley
186 Liverpool
187 Macclesfield
188 Manchester
189 Nelson & Colne
190 Northwich
191 Oldham
192 Preston
193 Rochdale
194 Rossendale
195 Southport
196 St. Helens
197 Stockport
198 Warrington
199 Widnes & Runcorn
200 Wigan
201 Barrow-in-Furness
202 Carlisle
203 Kendal
204 Penrith
205 Whitehaven
206 Workington
207 Ashington
208 Bishop Auckland

209 Consett
210 Darlington
211 Durham
212 Hartlepool
213 Hexham
214 Middlesbrough
215 Newcastle upon Tyne
216 Peterlee
217 South Shields
218 Stockton-on-Tees
219 Sunderland
220 Aberystwyth
221 Ammanford
222 Bangor
223 Brecon
224 Bridgend
225 Cardiff
226 Cardigan
227 Carmarthen
228 Cwmbran & Pontypool
229 Ebbw Vale
230 Ffestiniog
231 Gelligaer
232 Holyhead
233 Llandudno
234 Llanelli
235 Merthyr Tydfil
236 Monmouth
237 Neath
238 Newport
239 Pembroke
240 Pontypridd
241 Port Talbot
242 Rhyl & Prestatyn
243 Shotton
244 Swansea
245 Welshpool
246 Wrexham
247 Aberdeen
248 Alloa
249 Abroath
250 Ayr & Prestwick
251 Banff & Buckie
252 Bathgate
253 Berwick
254 Coatbridge/Airdrie
255 Dingwall
256 Dumbarton
257 Dumfries
258 Dundee
259 Dunfermline
260 Edinburgh
261 Elgin
262 Falkirk
263 Glasgow
264 Greenock
265 Hawick
266 Inverness
267 Irvine
268 Kilmarnock
269 Kirkcaldy
270 Lanark
271 Motherwell
272 Oban
273 Paisley
274 Perth
275 Peterhead
276 St. Andrews
277 Stirling
278 Stornoway
279 Stranraer
280 Thurso

Appendix 2

Key statistics for 280 Local Labour Market Areas

SPECIFICATION OF VARIABLES

No.	Description	Great Britain	maximum	minimum
1.	Urban Size code (see note 'a' below for categories)	N/A	N/A	N/A
2.	19-fold classification code (see note 'b' below for categories)	N/A	N/A	N/A
3.	Population Change (%), 1971-81	0.6	60.8	-12.4
4.	Population (thousands), 1981	54273.5	7836.9	35.4
5.	% aged over pensionable age, 1981	17.5	35.8	10.6
6.	Change (%) in number of households, 1971-81	7.1	68.9	-4.6
7.	Economically active per 100 economically inactive, 1981	110.4	178.3	85.2
8.	Married female economic activity rate, 1971	48.8	64.8	27.6
9.	Change (% point) in married female economic activity rate, 1971-81	8.1	17.2	1.6
10.	Employment Change (%), 1971-78	2.7	49.2	-20.9
11.	Employment Change (%), 1978-81	-5.1	22.4	-34.1
12.	Manufacturing Employment Change (%), 1971-81	-24.3	287.2	-55.7
13.	Service Employment Change (%), 1971-81	13.5	162.0	-20.4
14.	Manufacturing Rate Change (% point), 1971-81	4.6	17.2	-0.3
15.	Unemployment Rate, May 1985	13.2	26.4	4.1
16.	% economically active in managerial & professional SEGs (1-4,13), 1981	16.2	27.4	7.5
17.	% households with 2 or more cars, 1981	15.5	34.3	6.8
18.	Booming Towns Index (rank)	N/A	1	280

Note:-

'a' : Urban Size code

L - London;
D - Conurbation Dominant;
P - Provincial Dominant;
C - City;
T - Town;
R - Rural Area.

'b' : 19-fold classification code

A - London;
B - Conurbation Dominant;
C - Provincial Dominant;
D - Subregional Dominant;
E - London Subdominant City;
F - London Subdominant Town;
G - Conurbation Subdominant City;

H - Conurbation Subdominant Town;
I - Smaller Northern Subdominant;
J - Southern Freestanding City;
K - Northern Freestanding City;
L - Southern Service Town;
M - Southern Commercial Town;

N - Southern Manufacturing Town;
O - Northern Service Town;
P - Northern Commercial Town;
Q - Northern Manufacturing Town;
R - Southern Rural Area;
S - Northern Rural Area.

SOUTH EAST

LLMA Name	1	2	3	4	5	6	7	8	9	10	11	12	13	14	15	16	17	18
Aldershot	C	E	13.6	312.4	12.9	19.2	105.6	45.0	11.2	21.9	1.3	10.2	29.8	1.5	7.2	24.4	29.4	8
Andover	T	N	3.9	58.8	14.4	11.4	112.2	43.4	12.2	15.7	9.9	18.4	40.1	2.1	7.6	16.0	19.0	28
Ashford	T	H	8.7	86.0	18.0	13.6	119.1	43.0	10.7	9.0	-0.3	-5.7	16.9	2.6	12.4	20.4	19.9	86
Aylesbury	T	M	16.1	107.7	13.8	26.7	101.9	50.4	9.1	24.6	-0.1	4.7	36.4	2.6	6.6	20.4	24.2	10
Banbury	T	N	18.0	78.5	15.4	26.6	110.4	45.7	10.6	25.1	3.2	18.1	42.5	1.7	11.9	17.8	21.5	34
Basildon	T	F	17.3	168.4	11.2	26.1	107.0	48.7	4.4	12.2	11.8	-0.9	65.3	4.5	18.1	13.9	18.6	119
Basingstoke	T	F	25.7	134.9	12.4	33.0	102.1	48.8	11.4	28.9	6.0	-1.4	62.2	2.1	8.2	19.0	23.4	6
Bedford	T	M	12.1	168.3	14.3	19.4	106.7	48.8	8.9	15.7	-0.5	-8.4	30.0	3.1	9.0	18.1	20.9	35
Bishop's Stortford	T	F	10.4	79.2	15.4	17.5	106.9	44.5	9.6	13.5	4.6	0.8	27.0	1.8	7.4	26.6	30.6	3
Bracknell	T	F	28.1	84.4	12.0	44.8	93.1	50.8	9.2	32.2	-1.3	14.2	43.3	2.2	7.6	21.9	27.0	3
Braintree	T	L	14.1	80.9	16.9	17.2	118.1	45.2	7.0	7.9	-5.1	-23.4	33.9	2.9	11.1	19.0	22.7	61
Brighton	C	D	-2.9	358.7	25.3	11.9	119.6	49.0	8.4	-1.5	2.8	-22.0	8.7	2.3	12.8	19.7	13.3	165
Canterbury	T	L	6.4	117.2	11.3	11.3	133.1	46.0	9.4	10.9	2.6	0.0	18.9	1.5	13.8	20.0	23.6	124
Chelmsford	T	F	16.9	220.2	14.4	22.4	107.5	46.9	8.2	8.7	0.5	-7.8	26.4	2.0	8.6	22.0	23.6	29
Chichester & Bognor	T	L	16.1	124.0	27.9	22.2	135.1	46.2	9.8	7.7	2.9	12.9	12.2	2.0	8.6	22.2	18.9	40
Clacton	T	L	14.7	71.0	35.8	21.4	178.3	44.1	6.8	15.6	-5.2	11.1	9.6	4.4	20.3	20.0	12.8	209
Colchester	T	M	13.4	218.0	18.8	18.8	118.1	44.0	9.9	15.2	-1.5	4.2	20.8	2.3	11.6	18.6	18.0	70
Crawley	T	M	13.7	86.7	11.7	27.4	85.2	59.6	3.3	18.8	-1.5	-16.0	44.3	2.7	4.8	16.8	22.5	12
Deal	T	M	4.7	52.0	21.8	11.6	129.6	44.1	7.1	18.4	-6.8	-28.6	8.3	2.9	19.1	15.0	14.1	239
Didcot	R	R	5.7	62.7	14.3	16.2	101.9	44.9	13.6	-17.9	4.4	52.1	-19.7	2.6	9.4	20.6	22.7	73
Dover	T	M	-0.9	49.0	19.6	5.0	116.3	43.4	10.3	7.2	-6.5	-22.4	13.1	1.3	9.4	14.5	11.5	136
Eastbourne	T	L	9.5	136.3	32.8	17.1	146.2	49.7	8.4	15.8	3.4	-26.3	23.8	2.2	9.8	21.1	15.0	56
Folkestone	T	L	5.5	86.5	24.8	9.4	133.5	42.3	10.2	8.9	-0.8	-14.2	20.0	3.4	16.2	19.4	15.0	171
Gosport & Fareham	T	N	6.4	166.0	15.2	12.8	110.4	43.4	12.1	11.5	-3.7	-20.1	27.7	2.9	13.1	16.2	18.1	118
Gravesend	T	F	-0.7	107.8	14.7	6.8	111.7	40.7	10.3	-0.9	-19.3	-46.5	1.4	3.5	16.3	16.4	19.4	221
Guildford	T	F	2.1	213.6	19.8	10.6	113.5	45.9	7.9	-0.3	-2.5	-23.6	12.5	1.5	5.2	26.9	29.4	15
Harlow	T	F	2.3	98.3	11.1	16.7	91.1	54.5	5.7	-2.8	-34.1	-55.7	-20.4	4.3	9.5	15.8	20.6	167
Hastings	T	L	5.4	151.2	30.2	8.9	149.0	47.8	6.4	11.3	-1.6	-2.4	12.2	3.6	14.1	21.0	14.1	154
Haywards Heath	T	F	13.0	82.4	18.5	20.6	116.4	45.2	9.5	22.9	-2.1	16.7	35.2	3.6	6.6	25.4	23.0	13
Hemel Hempstead	T	F	7.1	115.0	13.8	18.5	96.8	55.5	4.0	13.6	-2.1	-5.2	24.6	3.6	7.8	21.1	25.1	27
Hertford & Ware	T	F	4.8	69.1	14.2	14.1	97.6	49.8	8.2	24.1	-12.4	-23.6	30.4	2.2	4.7	24.2	29.0	11
High Wycombe	T	F	6.5	259.1	14.5	12.5	104.7	47.2	8.9	15.1	-2.3	-12.1	33.4	1.7	6.1	26.4	34.3	7
Horsham	T	F	19.2	75.3	17.1	29.6	106.6	46.4	9.5	24.1	9.3	29.1	47.9	1.8	6.7	23.6	27.2	2
Isle of Wight	T	L	8.3	118.6	25.9	15.5	141.6	41.7	10.1	10.6	-3.7	-9.3	16.1	3.6	14.4	19.3	14.6	150
Letchworth	T	N	6.8	146.7	15.6	16.3	103.7	50.0	8.8	4.0	-5.4	-24.6	19.5	3.8	8.2	20.8	22.9	52
London	L	A	-8.6	7836.9	17.6	-3.7	96.8	54.0	5.0	-5.9	-3.1	-33.8	1.3	3.7	10.1	18.5	15.5	153
Luton	C	J	10.5	324.4	12.9	17.7	102.9	49.5	8.2	5.2	-8.5	-30.3	36.8	4.8	11.3	16.7	20.0	99
Maidenhead	T	F	9.5	92.1	16.3	16.3	100.6	49.5	7.5	10.7	1.7	-21.2	40.9	1.8	6.1	27.4	33.6	5
Maidstone	C	E	9.3	191.8	15.1	15.9	108.2	46.8	8.9	13.7	-3.0	-18.5	38.3	2.2	7.8	20.4	24.1	21
Margate & Ramsgate	T	L	6.0	121.7	27.4	10.4	144.5	45.9	7.6	5.0	-8.9	-7.0	-1.2	3.5	18.1	16.9	11.0	237
Medway Towns	C	E	4.9	237.2	13.7	10.1	112.2	43.4	8.7	4.2	-7.5	-31.5	25.6	4.4	16.9	14.1	15.5	203
Milton Keynes	T	N	60.8	161.5	11.7	68.9	109.2	48.7	7.4	47.3	22.4	12.7	162.0	5.9	17.4	17.6	18.6	4
Newbury	T	F	14.4	74.5	15.5	22.9	109.2	44.8	9.5	22.6	-3.4	-1.1	33.1	1.7	8.0	21.9	25.2	16
Oxford	C	J	-2.6	349.7	15.6	11.9	101.6	48.2	10.7	5.7	-0.3	-19.0	17.3	3.1	7.8	19.3	21.0	50
Portsmouth	C	D	-1.7	369.0	18.2	6.1	113.9	46.2	9.1	2.3	5.9	-0.7	15.6	3.8	13.2	16.8	16.3	141

LLMA Name	1	2	3	4	5	6	7	8	9	10	11	12	13	14	15	16	17	18
Reading	C	E	5.5	312.2	14.1	12.2	101.2	48.7	9.9	20.3	2.7	-0.5	35.0	2.1	7.9	22.3	25.5	18
Reigate & Redhill	T	F	-1.8	87.2	18.6	16.2	100.6	50.1	8.7	-0.6	-2.5	-40.9	17.1	1.9	6.2	23.8	26.1	36
Sittingbourne	T	F	8.7	109.6	16.7	13.5	120.4	43.5	6.9	10.9	-2.3	-8.3	11.3	3.1	15.5	15.9	17.2	143
Slough	C	U	-2.2	194.5	15.6	6.6	92.5	55.0	6.5	0.7	-3.8	-17.6	15.6	3.1	6.6	19.7	25.4	47
Southampton	C	J	4.9	440.2	17.3	13.6	109.6	44.9	10.4	9.8	-1.8	-4.5	20.2	2.9	10.6	16.6	19.0	71
Southend	C	E	3.4	316.4	19.6	8.1	119.0	46.1	6.5	13.1	-1.9	-6.7	18.9	3.2	15.9	19.3	18.4	147
St. Albans	T	F	3.4	125.1	15.3	11.3	100.6	51.1	8.3	13.9	-3.7	-18.8	22.8	1.6	6.8	27.2	29.2	17
Stevenage	T	N	11.4	84.4	11.8	26.8	92.5	55.4	6.8	9.9	4.4	-12.4	51.9	5.2	10.4	17.7	17.7	57
Tunbridge Wells	T	F	2.2	184.6	18.9	7.0	117.1	45.9	8.6	10.9	4.4	-10.9	22.8	1.6	7.8	23.6	23.9	31
Watford	C	E	-3.9	175.7	16.8	3.1	101.0	51.1	8.6	0.7	-2.1	-32.1	20.1	2.2	6.8	22.2	24.7	45
Welwyn	T	F	-0.2	75.5	15.4	12.7	92.1	56.7	7.2	-4.2	-0.3	-20.0	14.3	2.9	6.1	20.2	21.6	51
Winchester	T	L	3.9	63.0	19.1	11.0	108.8	49.2	10.3	49.2	7.0	-3.3	83.9	-0.3	4.1	27.0	24.1	1
Woking & Weybridge	T	F	3.5	171.0	15.5	12.0	101.7	47.3	8.7	1.3	6.3	-23.9	34.7	1.5	6.0	27.0	30.9	14
Worthing	C	L	6.8	181.2	31.9	10.0	146.6	48.2	8.4	17.1	3.6	22.8	28.9	2.2	9.6	22.1	15.0	55
EAST ANGLIA																		
Bury St. Edmunds	T	M	17.3	70.2	17.6	24.8	112.4	44.4	11.6	17.6	-1.7	17.8	33.8	1.5	8.4	19.1	22.3	20
Cambridge	C	J	9.5	245.5	16.8	16.2	106.3	49.2	9.0	19.6	-1.0	7.4	27.5	2.3	6.6	21.2	19.8	22
Dereham	R	R	14.4	53.9	21.3	20.8	128.9	39.3	10.1	8.5	-6.8	-11.5	21.3	2.4	14.4	19.9	19.1	128
Huntingdon	R	R	24.7	71.1	13.0	35.2	112.8	42.8	11.6	5.5	3.0	-3.4	25.4	3.4	10.3	19.9	23.0	33
Ipswich	C	J	5.9	258.5	18.8	13.8	115.7	43.1	10.5	10.5	-1.4	-19.3	26.8	1.9	9.3	16.3	17.2	67
Kings Lynn	T	L	10.5	110.2	20.0	16.1	124.4	42.4	9.7	13.8	1.1	2.2	35.5	4.4	15.2	16.0	17.9	122
Lowestoft	T	T	8.8	74.6	22.3	16.5	131.0	46.7	3.3	4.2	-7.3	-14.6	6.9	3.9	15.0	14.1	12.4	187
Newmarket	R	R	18.0	98.9	16.9	23.6	112.2	42.6	9.9	13.5	-2.5	-4.3	26.2	2.3	8.5	16.4	21.5	32
Norwich	C	J	9.4	401.8	20.5	16.1	118.0	45.9	8.3	12.2	-3.8	-14.8	26.8	2.6	11.0	17.3	17.1	83
Peterborough	T	M	23.4	199.2	15.3	31.1	112.6	45.0	9.3	6.2	8.1	1.2	34.8	5.3	14.9	13.9	15.6	101
Thetford	R	R	30.4	70.4	18.9	42.5	126.1	42.3	10.1	13.4	1.7	30.2	9.1	3.5	15.5	15.5	17.9	89
Wisbech	R	R	2.6	41.3	11.8	12.3	123.2	41.6	6.2	11.5	-3.5	-4.3	7.2	5.4	16.8	13.5	19.5	160
Woodbridge	R	R	2.3	52.1	21.9	6.2	130.2	38.4	9.2	7.1	-2.3	-7.1	21.1	2.0	8.9	21.6	22.0	54
Yarmouth	T	L	6.3	80.8	21.0	15.3	127.8	45.8	3.4	7.1	-6.6	-21.5	15.1	3.3	16.8	16.4	12.7	204
SOUTH WEST																		
Barnstaple	T	L	12.9	79.6	22.2	17.5	130.1	41.9	9.3	16.1	6.1	41.1	26.9	2.7	14.5	18.4	17.5	88
Bath	T	L	3.0	152.5	19.8	16.2	112.5	47.1	9.4	5.9	-2.1	-19.2	17.6	3.4	10.0	18.6	16.9	97
Bideford	R	R	7.3	38.7	22.9	15.3	132.8	40.5	7.8	12.8	-7.1	-17.1	20.8	3.4	16.7	17.9	17.1	169
Bridgwater	T	M	9.3	80.3	19.6	17.6	124.1	43.9	7.5	8.6	-5.0	-10.0	22.7	4.4	13.6	16.3	19.5	121
Bristol	P	C	0.7	740.2	17.0	8.2	107.1	47.7	9.4	3.1	-3.7	-21.9	13.3	3.6	11.1	17.0	19.1	116
Bournemouth	C	J	8.3	477.5	26.1	15.5	130.5	45.2	8.4	12.6	0.1	-2.2	21.1	2.9	12.6	20.2	19.8	79
Chard	R	R	9.7	61.7	27.7	16.8	142.5	45.9	4.6	12.4	-4.4	-2.4	17.0	2.4	10.2	20.5	18.7	68
Cheltenham	T	L	4.0	161.7	19.0	12.5	105.5	48.4	10.3	27.7	4.2	-18.8	45.0	3.4	8.7	19.9	20.0	26
Chippenham	T	N	4.8	61.6	17.9	17.9	113.7	47.5	8.5	4.7	-1.6	-18.1	27.0	2.3	8.1	15.5	20.0	59
Exeter	C	J	6.1	238.5	23.6	12.4	128.1	45.0	9.5	11.8	5.4	6.3	27.0	2.3	11.7	19.8	17.2	75
Falmouth	R	R	7.7	63.5	22.4	14.6	147.9	33.3	8.7	2.8	-10.8	-35.9	9.8	7.7	20.6	19.8	17.4	242
Gloucester	T	M	5.8	184.6	16.4	14.7	107.3	46.6	10.2	7.6	-2.1	-6.3	22.3	3.3	11.2	15.8	19.6	81
Launceston	R	R	13.7	46.5	22.8	19.5	144.0	35.4	5.0	14.7	-8.9	-8.3	19.0	4.4	15.7	20.9	21.3	126
Newton Abbot	T	L	7.4	74.9	25.7	11.3	137.4	42.6	9.7	14.3	3.6	23.3	25.9	1.9	13.3	19.7	18.1	91
Penzance	R	R	6.8	49.9	24.4	9.3	149.0	35.8	7.5	11.6	-5.5	-19.7	20.0	5.4	22.5	20.1	12.5	254

LLMA Name	1	2	3	4	5	6	7	8	9	10	11	12	13	14	15	16	17	18
Plymouth	C	J	7.5	554.5	18.9	13.6	126.2	39.8	9.7	9.2	-4.8	-5.9	11.6	4.8	14.5	14.9	13.7	159
Redruth & Camborne	R	R	12.1	57.1	19.9	15.9	140.6	37.6	7.4	7.7	-12.5	-36.6	15.6	8.4	18.8	14.6	14.5	219
Salisbury	T	M	1.5	119.8	19.6	9.7	119.4	44.7	9.1	9.9	-0.7	10.8	13.8	2.3	9.3	18.6	19.6	63
St. Austell	T	L	11.8	110.8	20.6	17.6	139.2	35.1	9.1	16.9	-3.4	-5.3	19.6	3.3	16.1	17.1	15.3	145
Stroud	T	N	10.4	69.9	19.1	15.6	118.2	47.1	8.9	16.3	-3.4	-0.1	30.9	3.4	10.6	21.4	23.2	46
Swindon	C	J	9.7	262.8	15.6	20.3	107.6	48.3	8.3	10.9	-1.2	-34.4	50.8	4.5	10.6	16.9	19.6	62
Taunton	T	M	6.6	116.9	22.7	14.3	121.6	48.9	7.6	10.5	-5.9	-24.9	16.6	2.8	10.4	17.9	17.8	87
Tiverton	R	R	10.6	40.8	20.4	18.1	129.8	41.3	9.0	8.9	-0.4	-11.6	29.2	3.3	12.7	17.9	16.7	78
Torquay	T	L	6.9	164.4	28.0	10.5	145.8	42.3	7.9	7.9	-4.9	-19.1	12.4	3.3	19.1	21.4	15.3	214
Trowbridge	T	M	12.2	126.9	17.6	21.3	115.5	47.5	8.9	12.6	1.1	-4.5	30.6	3.1	9.3	18.1	20.4	41
Truro	R	R	13.3	47.6	22.6	18.9	135.4	39.5	10.1	22.5	9.1	29.8	41.2	4.1	13.2	22.4	20.3	44
Wells	R	L	2.6	54.4	19.0	11.3	117.1	47.8	6.7	8.4	3.3	0.5	33.4	2.1	6.5	19.0	23.1	25
Weston-Super-Mare	T	L	12.4	95.5	23.5	20.3	135.5	41.1	10.3	13.0	-2.0	12.1	17.2	3.5	16.2	21.2	19.6	134
Weymouth	T	L	5.6	113.6	22.5	13.4	127.4	42.1	10.2	11.8	-4.1	-5.3	14.0	2.1	10.2	19.1	16.7	84
Yeovil	T	M	13.7	125.4	20.6	19.3	123.9	43.9	8.4	10.5	7.4	1.1	40.3	2.4	8.0	18.3	21.1	24
WEST MIDLANDS																		
Birmingham	D	B	-4.2	1447.3	15.9	2.7	106.3	52.6	6.4	-3.1	-8.9	-29.6	7.8	7.6	15.2	14.5	15.2	215
Burton on Trent	T	P	10.0	152.1	16.0	17.4	111.3	45.8	6.7	5.8	-5.6	-17.6	12.0	4.0	11.5	13.9	17.5	109
Coventry	C	D	-3.2	496.8	15.6	5.2	106.9	49.8	9.0	-3.4	-14.4	-39.0	20.3	8.3	15.0	13.3	14.3	228
Dudley	C	G	1.6	232.7	15.6	8.7	102.6	52.1	6.5	2.3	3.7	-15.3	28.3	7.8	21.0	14.6	17.1	223
Evesham	R	S	11.8	51.9	19.8	18.4	114.9	47.6	7.9	11.1	4.9	29.4	26.5	1.8	10.6	22.4	26.9	30
Hereford	T	P	6.6	110.7	18.6	16.1	116.4	44.3	9.1	7.1	-3.5	-6.2	13.9	3.3	12.3	17.1	21.6	95
Kidderminster	T	P	7.9	106.7	16.0	12.9	109.2	52.4	4.8	-1.4	-8.8	-26.0	10.0	6.3	14.2	18.5	24.4	139
Leamington	T	I	4.6	113.4	15.0	13.7	100.9	49.8	11.0	6.3	-1.6	0.4	15.4	3.0	10.4	15.7	21.9	58
Leek	R	S	0.5	35.4	18.0	3.1	128.4	53.2	5.9	2.4	4.6	-30.0	42.4	3.0	10.4	15.7	19.4	93
Malvern	R	S	5.7	46.2	20.5	16.5	128.4	50.1	6.3	9.6	3.0	12.0	19.8	3.8	12.7	21.4	23.2	72
Redditch	T	H	46.9	85.7	11.6	53.8	101.1	57.0	3.7	25.6	2.0	0.4	82.2	6.1	16.9	15.6	19.9	42
Rugby	T	I	3.4	80.2	15.8	9.8	108.3	48.0	10.6	2.8	2.3	-11.8	24.5	3.8	12.6	18.6	19.3	113
Shrewsbury	T	P	5.9	134.1	18.5	12.0	116.2	44.4	8.8	15.1	9.4	-22.2	16.8	9.3	12.5	18.6	20.9	105
Smethwick	C	G	-3.5	210.0	17.8	2.8	108.7	54.9	4.6	-4.8	-22.2	-36.7	-0.6	9.2	14.4	10.8	10.9	255
Stafford	T	P	6.2	84.3	14.4	14.6	102.1	49.5	10.8	3.6	6.9	-8.5	25.4	2.2	9.7	18.5	20.7	53
Stoke on Trent	C	K	0.2	531.0	16.6	7.9	103.7	55.3	6.4	-1.4	-9.1	-24.3	8.3	5.4	12.1	12.8	15.0	170
Stratford-upon-Avon	T	H	6.4	58.0	19.8	13.1	109.4	47.0	9.5	11.9	4.5	5.4	25.1	7.0	9.4	25.0	28.1	23
Tamworth	T	Q	37.4	94.6	10.6	45.1	111.4	44.4	8.2	24.1	-12.5	-33.0	44.6	8.7	26.0	13.7	18.7	218
Telford	T	Q	22.5	163.0	13.8	30.8	118.5	45.0	7.1	18.8	-9.8	-16.8	32.9	9.2	20.9	14.6	17.7	185
Walsall	C	G	-0.7	278.6	14.3	7.0	108.6	49.7	6.8	1.0	-13.2	-35.1	27.4	9.2	16.9	11.8	14.4	234
West Bromwich	T	H	-5.4	128.9	17.0	4.6	108.5	55.4	1.6	-1.9	-11.7	-41.6	42.9	12.8	12.9	7.9	7.6	230
Wolverhampton	T	G	-0.1	421.8	14.9	7.2	108.3	48.3	7.5	-0.8	-17.0	-32.3	1.2	8.5	17.3	13.2	15.8	247
Worcester	T	O	5.0	137.8	17.7	13.4	107.5	51.5	6.3	1.9	-1.1	-18.5	13.9	5.0	12.9	18.5	23.6	103
EAST MIDLANDS																		
Boston	T	L	9.6	91.6	21.5	16.0	124.3	45.0	6.5	7.0	-2.8	-3.3	13.6	4.1	17.4	15.7	16.2	160
Buxton	T	K	2.9	53.9	17.9	9.3	107.9	51.1	8.5	8.1	-9.6	-10.5	17.2	3.5	10.2	18.4	17.2	114
Chesterfield	C	K	0.6	170.3	17.6	8.6	115.2	44.4	9.1	10.7	-8.6	-22.1	24.0	3.7	13.6	11.9	11.8	177
Coalville	T	Q	7.9	59.6	16.8	15.0	112.2	47.4	5.9	10.2	-21.8	-26.7	18.6	3.3	10.1	12.7	13.1	131
Corby	T	N	-0.1	60.8	12.7	14.9	110.5	52.2	5.8	-5.1	-29.5	-50.1	16.5	16.1	16.5	9.8	11.7	266

LLMA Name	1	2	3	4	5	6	7	8	9	10	11	12	13	14	15	16	17
Derby	C	K	-0.9	313.1	16.9	4.9	109.0	46.8	10.5	4.6	-5.1	-13.4	16.1	3.1	11.6	14.3	14.1
Grantham	T	N	11.6	55.4	17.0	18.2	115.1	44.7	9.9	21.5	-2.7	8.9	31.5	3.4	12.6	16.0	17.2
Heanor	T	H	6.5	114.2	17.5	13.6	113.3	44.9	9.7	0.6	12.6	5.9	23.1	3.5	16.4	16.0	13.1
Hinckley	T	I	15.6	66.6	15.0	21.1	97.6	58.5	5.3	0.1	-2.9	-19.6	24.7	4.3	11.1	14.7	18.9
Kettering	T	N	9.6	79.3	18.6	13.7	115.7	53.2	5.9	5.6	-7.3	-21.4	21.9	6.8	11.1	15.2	16.5
Leicester	C	J	2.8	554.2	15.9	8.1	101.3	56.6	7.0	8.2	-2.5	-14.4	28.2	5.6	10.9	14.9	15.7
Lincoln	T	M	6.6	210.7	17.1	14.0	116.4	41.6	11.4	10.7	-4.0	-13.2	22.2	3.7	13.5	15.5	15.9
Loughborough	T	P	7.1	69.9	16.4	15.3	104.1	55.1	6.4	13.1	-15.1	-19.6	26.9	3.6	7.8	16.9	16.6
Mansfield	C	I	2.7	234.6	16.0	10.5	117.2	44.8	8.5	4.6	-4.5	-2.2	25.8	3.2	12.3	10.0	11.5
Matlock	R	S	3.7	46.2	19.4	11.1	109.9	45.4	11.1	8.4	-5.0	-27.9	31.6	1.6	7.4	20.0	20.9
Melton Mowbray	R	R	12.0	56.0	15.3	18.2	110.8	45.0	9.4	7.0	5.6	15.5	18.3	2.9	12.0	18.0	20.3
Newark	T	U	5.0	59.3	17.2	13.4	115.9	43.0	11.7	5.5	18.8	3.1	35.4	3.9	16.6	18.2	18.5
Northampton	C	J	18.0	241.9	15.8	24.4	103.6	53.1	7.9	25.0	-2.3	-1.2	43.3	3.9	10.9	16.0	17.7
Nottingham	P	C	-1.1	672.0	16.8	6.0	105.9	52.6	7.8	6.6	-7.8	-25.5	23.4	4.4	13.2	14.3	12.7
Spalding	R	R	9.1	62.0	19.2	15.5	112.9	49.2	4.5	4.8	-3.0	5.2	7.3	3.9	12.0	16.2	19.6
Stamford	R	R	7.4	54.4	17.4	16.5	116.0	42.5	10.3	7.2	-0.2	-3.5	28.1	2.9	12.8	20.1	21.4
Wellingborough	T	N	12.8	104.7	16.8	16.8	112.5	54.5	4.5	11.1	-8.7	-18.5	31.4	5.0	11.2	14.2	16.4
Worksop	T	P	4.4	108.5	15.6	11.4	118.1	42.9	8.7	21.7	-8.5	-5.7	16.1	3.5	12.7	13.3	14.5
YORKSHIRE & HUMBERSIDE																	
Barnsley	C	I	-0.3	201.5	16.3	6.9	119.0	42.3	12.2	13.6	-6.4	-16.3	27.8	3.8	16.9	10.2	9.4
Bradford	C	K	-4.1	358.2	16.0	-0.8	113.6	57.1	2.6	-0.2	-10.1	-38.8	14.7	6.8	15.3	12.7	9.8
Bridlington	R	S	-10.5	56.5	24.4	13.6	133.4	39.2	11.3	18.8	-11.9	18.3	19.1	8.7	16.9	18.7	13.1
Castleford	T	I	-1.4	109.3	15.3	6.7	114.5	43.7	10.8	15.4	-3.2	2.6	21.5	4.6	13.6	9.8	9.9
Dewsbury	T	I	1.2	162.2	15.9	5.0	112.9	51.7	8.3	0.6	-5.7	-21.7	19.3	6.4	15.3	14.3	12.3
Doncaster	C	K	4.1	258.6	14.8	12.9	116.7	41.7	10.2	9.9	-9.9	-18.7	13.5	5.4	17.5	12.0	9.8
Goole	R	S	8.3	43.6	16.5	14.1	112.7	42.6	9.4	21.9	-18.1	8.1	4.3	3.6	16.1	14.5	14.5
Grimsby	C	K	2.5	218.6	16.6	9.4	116.1	41.1	11.9	6.5	-8.7	-0.1	5.5	4.4	16.6	14.3	13.2
Halifax	T	Q	-2.1	191.1	18.6	1.1	108.6	58.1	7.0	1.5	-10.7	-24.4	18.1	5.9	12.2	13.5	11.8
Harrogate	T	O	8.9	128.4	20.2	13.4	114.9	47.3	10.0	14.6	4.8	-1.5	25.5	1.9	9.2	22.6	19.7
Huddersfield	C	K	0.4	209.8	17.9	4.9	114.0	52.4	6.5	-4.0	-15.8	-40.8	11.9	6.6	12.0	15.3	12.6
Hull	C	K	-0.9	428.2	17.0	10.5	116.9	44.8	7.9	2.7	-7.5	-25.3	27.6	5.9	16.6	13.9	11.3
Keighley	T	P	-7.3	111.9	19.2	10.5	111.7	57.1	4.5	4.4	-5.0	-23.6	32.3	3.2	11.5	15.8	14.4
Leeds	P	C	-3.6	743.6	17.8	2.8	109.0	54.3	7.0	-0.3	-6.4	-32.8	10.9	4.7	12.6	15.6	12.4
Mexborough	T	I	-4.0	86.4	16.3	4.6	128.7	42.8	7.0	-17.6	-6.3	-36.7	13.6	6.6	23.4	7.5	6.8
Northallerton	R	S	5.1	86.0	16.9	13.7	115.8	40.3	12.0	20.1	-7.8	17.2	12.7	3.0	10.8	20.5	20.4
Rotherham	C	I	1.1	169.8	15.4	8.8	117.6	44.0	10.2	7.7	-9.0	-22.7	27.6	7.7	20.4	10.2	9.3
Scarborough	T	O	3.6	77.1	15.9	9.8	134.6	44.0	9.6	16.4	-8.5	-3.0	9.3	2.6	13.9	17.8	9.9
Scunthorpe	T	Q	4.5	186.5	25.9	13.0	123.1	38.7	9.0	8.0	-22.4	-31.6	10.4	8.8	15.1	13.3	14.8
Sheffield	P	C	-2.7	642.4	18.6	3.4	109.7	50.4	9.4	-1.7	-9.1	-34.6	15.8	5.6	14.8	13.3	10.6
Wakefield	C	I	6.3	212.1	15.6	15.1	111.3	46.8	10.9	11.1	-6.0	-9.5	22.7	2.8	13.1	13.1	12.1
York	C	K	6.9	257.0	18.0	13.3	107.4	47.9	10.4	4.5	2.4	-6.8	15.9	1.7	10.2	17.0	14.7

LLMA Name	1	2	3	4	5	6	7	8	9	10	11	12	13	14	15	16	17	18
NORTH WEST																		
Accrington	T	I	-2.6	67.1	18.8	-0.2	109.4	63.6	3.3	-5.9	-7.6	-23.4	1.0	5.2	14.4	11.3	9.4	233
Ashton & Hyde	C	G	-0.2	212.2	16.8	3.0	104.6	59.0	5.4	-1.2	-11.0	-33.5	32.2	6.4	16.0	12.2	11.6	232
Birkenhead	C	G	-4.0	355.7	18.2	3.4	104.8	44.5	11.4	-1.3	-4.1	-29.4	32.9	6.9	24.0	17.5	14.6	271
Blackburn	C	D	-0.3	195.6	17.2	2.1	113.5	59.8	3.5	6.2	-12.4	-27.4	18.6	5.8	24.5	13.4	12.9	279
Blackpool	C	K	0.1	295.9	25.5	6.0	122.1	50.6	9.5	8.4	-3.1	-6.7	12.3	3.3	16.3	16.4	12.9	199
Bolton	C	G	0.6	264.1	16.8	4.2	110.4	56.8	5.8	-1.8	-9.8	-31.3	9.9	6.4	16.0	14.2	12.5	227
Burnley	T	O	-2.6	94.1	18.0	0.3	107.7	64.8	2.9	0.3	-10.9	-29.0	16.2	5.4	12.7	11.4	9.3	210
Bury	T	H	-0.3	136.1	15.6	3.4	105.3	55.5	7.9	10.2	-15.4	-25.3	20.7	5.5	13.5	15.3	14.9	181
Chester	T	H	0.8	110.9	17.3	8.4	110.6	43.7	12.9	3.1	-3.0	-43.4	22.7	5.5	11.7	19.2	17.5	115
Crewe	T	P	2.8	129.7	17.8	9.1	110.4	46.4	10.7	11.6	-7.6	-7.5	15.7	3.9	10.1	15.1	17.7	96
Ellesmere Port	T	O	8.0	77.9	11.9	19.7	105.5	45.4	10.2	-5.6	-15.6	-30.1	7.8	7.4	11.2	12.8	16.2	162
Lancaster	T	O	-1.8	127.8	10.1	4.7	123.5	49.7	6.4	-0.3	-10.3	-14.1	8.6	5.1	15.1	17.0	13.1	191
Leigh	T	H	-0.7	118.6	15.7	4.7	110.1	54.6	7.6	8.3	-15.4	-35.4	16.1	5.6	16.7	11.1	11.4	240
Leyland & Chorley	T	H	16.6	117.6	14.8	20.9	107.7	53.7	6.3	9.0	-11.7	-16.4	22.0	3.8	13.2	15.2	17.8	125
Liverpool	D	B	-12.4	944.5	16.3	-2.9	109.7	49.6	9.9	-9.2	-12.7	-38.3	-10.1	8.8	19.0	11.3	9.3	273
Macclesfield	T	H	6.7	72.7	16.7	12.2	101.8	53.9	9.9	13.8	-2.8	-9.7	30.5	2.6	8.9	21.5	24.0	38
Manchester	D	B	-11.1	1167.9	17.8	-4.6	108.6	53.1	7.6	-2.9	-8.1	-35.1	4.2	5.8	13.6	14.3	12.3	220
Nelson & Colne	T	I	0.3	85.7	19.8	2.0	112.0	62.9	1.6	7.7	-13.7	-14.1	8.9	4.4	13.4	11.8	11.6	197
Northwich	T	G	6.1	108.7	15.0	12.5	113.2	45.3	7.9	7.9	-14.0	-14.6	39.1	6.1	15.3	18.9	21.4	133
Oldham	C	G	-1.8	220.0	17.0	1.6	102.9	62.5	4.8	-5.8	-14.5	-37.8	4.8	6.3	14.3	11.6	10.4	245
Preston	C	D	1.2	223.5	17.0	6.4	109.3	55.2	6.9	1.4	5.4	-2.1	11.9	4.4	12.4	15.4	15.9	130
Rochdale	T	I	6.0	152.9	15.8	7.6	108.7	61.0	3.1	-4.9	-4.5	-40.8	41.7	7.4	17.9	13.8	12.3	236
Rossendale	T	I	4.0	53.5	22.9	5.6	107.4	64.3	2.7	-7.5	-0.7	-40.0	20.4	6.0	12.9	22.8	13.1	206
Southport	T	I	4.0	104.0	15.0	7.5	120.6	43.2	10.0	-8.4	-0.7	-18.1	13.7	3.8	18.3	17.6	17.6	186
St. Helens	T	H	-1.2	156.9	15.0	6.0	115.5	49.9	6.6	11.6	-10.8	-33.1	51.2	6.7	17.1	10.9	11.6	224
Stockport	C	G	3.1	254.1	16.6	8.6	105.1	51.9	9.3	10.1	-1.4	-14.6	25.0	3.9	13.7	20.8	19.0	123
Warrington	T	I	2.8	192.1	15.5	9.2	107.7	49.1	10.5	1.8	-4.9	-33.4	28.9	5.8	14.2	14.6	16.6	166
Widnes & Runcorn	T	I	23.6	139.4	13.3	31.6	118.7	46.4	6.1	1.1	1.9	-9.4	35.8	7.4	21.1	12.7	12.3	213
Wigan	C	G	13.3	244.7	14.6	19.4	114.8	49.7	8.5	1.1	-10.7	-26.4	13.7	6.4	22.7	11.5	11.7	263
NORTH																		
Barrow-in-Furness	T	P	-0.3	117.4	19.5	5.2	114.8	46.1	9.7	-1.5	-1.1	-14.9	12.4	4.0	10.4	12.3	12.1	146
Carlisle	T	P	0.6	134.5	13.2	8.5	109.1	49.3	7.9	0.4	-5.1	-21.8	2.5	4.5	11.6	14.1	14.7	151
Kendal	T	S	9.1	64.4	22.3	13.1	118.2	50.8	7.0	6.5	-0.1	-4.0	17.4	1.8	6.3	18.6	18.1	37
Penrith	R	S	5.5	42.2	18.6	11.1	119.0	37.2	10.2	7.8	0.3	-1.5	21.5	2.6	10.5	18.6	21.1	65
Whitehaven	T	Q	2.0	62.8	15.0	10.2	109.7	43.9	10.1	10.6	7.4	-29.2	7.5	2.5	13.4	12.3	12.2	137
Workington	T	P	2.2	74.7	18.1	9.4	116.7	46.1	7.4	-0.2	-16.3	-37.5	11.4	6.3	15.8	13.0	12.6	235
Ashington	T	I	1.9	126.8	16.5	7.3	120.4	42.6	11.8	0.9	-10.3	-5.8	17.2	1.9	14.0	10.5	10.9	189
Bishop Auckland	T	Q	2.1	154.0	18.5	10.9	113.1	47.4	8.2	6.1	-13.0	-16.5	11.4	7.4	18.7	10.5	10.0	256
Consett	T	O	-5.1	48.5	18.5	2.5	123.9	42.8	10.7	6.2	-33.6	-53.8	-0.3	17.2	24.5	12.0	11.1	280
Darlington	T	O	0.5	114.1	18.1	8.0	111.2	47.4	9.3	5.9	-9.8	-19.7	5.4	4.9	13.8	14.0	12.9	192
Durham	T	I	4.9	85.6	15.5	11.4	111.1	47.9	10.9	26.4	-1.6	9.9	35.2	1.6	12.4	15.2	12.0	107
Hartlepool	T	I	-4.6	94.9	15.1	3.6	112.0	44.8	9.3	-9.0	-8.4	-35.2	16.2	8.3	23.9	16.0	12.9	276
Hexham	R	S	2.1	37.3	22.1	6.3	121.7	43.2	9.5	9.0	-3.7	-8.5	18.0	3.0	10.5	18.7	17.9	98
Middlesbrough	D	B	0.0	362.3	15.0	8.0	121.1	41.8	8.4	5.9	-16.6	-34.3	7.1	9.2	21.4	13.0	12.8	267
Newcastle upon Tyne	D	B	-0.9	944.7	17.0	7.1	110.1	47.4	11.1	3.5	-11.4	-25.1	7.9	5.9	16.5	13.1	8.4	252

LLMA Name	1	2	3	4	5	6	7	8	9	10	11	12	13	14	15	16	17	18
Peterlee	T	I	-6.5	70.0	15.6	0.6	125.0	40.2	10.9	-3.5	-5.1	29.9	17.1	5.7	18.9	7.9	7.1	268
South Shields	C	G	-9.4	160.4	17.6	-1.1	113.3	45.5	8.2	-2.5	-15.1	-40.8	5.8	7.0	23.2	10.3	6.8	278
Stockton-on-Tees	C	I	5.3	186.4	13.3	15.3	110.2	44.1	10.6	8.3	-8.0	-31.1	47.9	7.4	18.4	13.1	12.9	222
Sunderland	C	K	-8.8	274.2	16.6	0.2	119.0	44.4	8.2	-6.2	-11.7	-39.6	9.0	8.0	21.5	9.6	7.0	275
WALES																		
Aberystwyth	R	S	3.7	44.3	23.1	11.1	132.2	40.7	11.2	11.9	2.4	-30.5	28.4	3.5	12.9	21.8	18.5	100
Ammanford	R	S	10.5	45.5	21.8	17.0	138.7	37.7	12.5	-0.9	5.2	29.6	26.9	5.6	23.1	12.4	16.2	243
Bangor	R	S	3.0	68.0	19.2	9.1	136.2	37.8	11.7	30.1	-6.5	-32.1	30.6	2.3	18.3	15.6	17.7	158
Brecon	R	S	9.3	39.4	20.4	16.8	122.0	43.8	9.1	8.0	-1.8	16.3	14.5	4.6	12.1	13.9	20.9	80
Bridgend	T	I	9.8	82.7	14.9	18.4	118.7	38.0	17.2	22.5	-15.8	23.7	13.3	4.6	10.9	13.9	15.9	102
Cardiff	C	D	-0.8	441.3	16.6	6.9	115.6	45.3	10.5	-3.5	-4.7	-36.8	4.4	5.7	14.9	16.9	15.2	200
Cardigan	R	S	11.6	43.9	21.6	15.7	145.4	33.3	9.8	0.8	1.2	12.6	25.2	4.5	25.9	19.0	22.6	249
Carmarthen	R	S	2.8	41.9	19.5	11.6	126.6	40.4	10.2	22.1	-8.9	36.4	15.9	6.0	8.4	12.1	20.6	48
Cwmbran & Pontypool	R	I	1.7	99.3	15.7	10.3	118.9	44.7	11.6	-13.1	-8.9	-16.7	28.0	6.0	14.8	12.1	14.0	184
Ebbw Vale	T	Q	-0.0	101.0	18.9	7.4	133.5	38.9	11.6	-11.0	-7.5	-48.9	15.7	8.9	19.0	10.6	11.3	261
Ffestiniog	R	S	-0.7	49.5	22.7	3.3	146.0	34.4	8.7	4.4	-9.3	-5.9	-3.4	3.9	15.8	19.9	19.6	183
Gelligaer	T	I	10.2	74.7	15.2	7.6	133.6	38.8	10.2	7.2	-14.3	-13.0	20.7	5.3	20.3	10.0	9.5	265
Holyhead	R	S	10.5	52.2	17.4	17.6	148.4	30.2	9.9	11.0	-3.6	25.8	11.5	2.6	23.0	16.7	18.3	225
Llandudno	T	O	3.5	92.1	28.1	9.1	145.7	43.0	11.2	11.0	-1.9	-3.5	13.6	3.6	15.3	21.3	15.5	157
Llanelli	T	Q	-2.0	75.4	20.5	5.9	129.9	41.6	11.5	0.9	-17.7	-35.4	19.8	9.5	14.7	10.8	10.6	244
Merthyr Tydfil	T	Q	-3.9	60.7	17.8	3.0	128.9	43.3	11.7	14.6	-20.7	-24.6	1.3	6.9	15.1	9.7	7.8	246
Monmouth	R	S	12.4	63.7	17.9	18.7	121.2	43.3	8.3	5.7	-1.9	-7.8	29.8	3.6	17.2	18.8	23.5	129
Neath	T	I	-1.8	67.2	19.9	7.1	126.3	39.4	12.1	-1.3	-12.7	-47.5	20.8	7.3	15.8	10.3	15.0	250
Newport	C	D	-1.5	193.2	15.9	6.0	118.5	42.6	11.4	-1.0	-14.0	-31.1	0.8	7.9	15.0	13.3	14.1	217
Pembroke	R	S	9.9	100.3	16.9	16.5	130.4	33.3	11.4	11.8	0.1	12.8	23.5	2.6	21.2	17.5	18.5	198
Pontypridd	C	I	-1.6	233.9	17.1	5.0	129.6	42.2	10.3	5.6	-10.5	-24.1	24.7	7.4	17.3	10.4	9.6	251
Port Talbot	T	P	-3.0	108.5	17.5	17.8	130.7	38.5	12.3	-20.9	-7.9	-38.3	25.8	10.5	17.8	10.4	10.4	269
Rhyl & Prestatyn	T	P	11.1	88.8	24.6	17.2	146.2	41.1	8.8	-10.5	-0.2	-2.7	18.6	5.6	19.8	19.7	17.4	188
Shotton	T	H	9.8	122.6	15.2	16.8	123.7	36.7	13.1	25.8	-21.6	-39.2	75.2	10.4	17.2	13.8	18.5	173
Swansea	C	D	-1.4	247.5	18.4	5.8	121.2	42.0	13.3	17.0	-8.1	-26.6	35.2	7.0	16.4	13.9	13.9	195
Welshpool	R	S	12.3	43.6	18.6	19.2	120.0	38.8	9.6	12.6	0.9	52.1	10.3	3.4	14.1	15.4	23.6	74
Wrexham	T	Q	4.9	166.1	17.8	11.6	124.8	41.1	9.4	8.7	-7.5	-21.8	27.1	6.0	16.3	13.8	16.9	178
SCOTLAND																		
Aberdeen	C	K	9.0	335.7	16.9	15.3	101.8	45.8	12.3	25.4	11.5	-14.2	47.1	0.4	7.3	15.4	15.8	19
Alloa	T	Q	4.7	51.9	14.0	11.6	113.1	46.0	10.3	-3.7	-7.9	-15.6	-10.3	5.2	17.8	12.7	12.0	248
Arbroath	R	S	7.6	64.3	18.4	13.1	120.0	42.0	10.9	9.2	-6.3	4.9	4.2	2.5	15.9	15.5	12.0	194
Ayr & Prestwick	T	P	-0.7	152.6	17.4	8.4	120.1	40.5	11.5	6.1	-3.3	-11.5	23.8	7.2	16.6	15.9	12.4	208
Banff & Buckie	R	S	1.7	40.4	19.6	6.6	135.2	30.3	11.9	8.5	2.1	-0.5	25.9	0.9	11.7	14.7	16.1	111
Bathgate	T	I	-3.0	63.1	13.3	6.4	105.6	49.0	11.3	-0.4	-14.8	-24.1	6.7	6.2	21.2	9.3	8.5	274
Berwick	R	S	4.3	50.8	21.5	8.9	119.6	42.3	10.0	1.6	-3.1	-4.3	12.0	3.0	11.6	16.8	15.4	138
Coatbridge & Airdrie	T	H	0.6	110.7	12.8	9.7	114.7	43.6	9.9	-12.7	-9.1	-51.8	23.5	9.7	24.4	16.9	7.6	277
Dingwall	T	H	34.0	50.2	15.1	37.5	130.5	32.9	9.6	40.1	-12.9	-287.2	24.7	0.8	26.4	13.0	15.7	144
Dumbarton	T	H	-0.9	78.3	14.9	9.3	111.6	42.3	12.6	-0.8	-11.6	-46.7	15.2	6.7	20.0	13.1	11.2	264

LLMA Name	1	2	3	4	5	6	7	8	9	10	11	12	13	14	15	16	17	18
Dumfries	T	O	1.1	98.4	18.5	9.7	112.9	44.6	11.6	8.2	7.1	-8.0	30.9	4.4	12.2	16.0	15.7	108
Dundee	C	K	-4.6	243.3	18.2	2.9	105.0	56.5	6.9	1.3	-7.4	-39.4	23.6	5.6	15.9	13.3	10.1	238
Dunfermline	T	Q	-3.4	126.0	15.4	12.3	112.7	45.1	10.5	0.4	-1.6	-10.3	3.3	3.3	15.2	13.7	11.2	201
Edinburgh	P	C	-0.6	684.1	17.3	7.1	99.3	49.7	13.3	5.5	-0.6	-10.6	14.0	2.7	12.0	15.8	10.6	156
Elgin	R	S	11.6	80.9	16.3	20.8	122.0	34.8	13.1	12.0	3.4	2.6	30.0	3.6	15.0	17.3	14.9	132
Falkirk	T	Q	2.1	149.3	15.3	12.8	106.4	46.0	10.9	-3.3	-7.3	-21.3	-0.3	5.5	18.1	11.7	10.7	253
Glasgow	D	B	-12.1	1206.9	16.1	-4.2	107.6	46.8	11.4	-4.7	-8.9	-38.0	1.2	6.3	16.8	12.7	8.3	262
Greenock	T	P	-7.2	125.2	17.6	1.9	116.7	41.6	12.7	-3.6	-9.7	-29.2	9.0	6.5	19.1	12.6	8.6	270
Hawick	R	S	1.5	58.4	20.7	7.9	102.9	53.8	11.4	10.6	-4.7	-13.6	24.4	2.9	7.9	15.3	13.5	82
Inverness	T	O	14.0	61.6	15.9	22.8	108.9	43.2	11.6	30.4	3.7	99.0	35.1	1.6	13.0	16.0	14.4	60
Irvine	T	Q	6.1	116.2	15.6	13.9	126.4	39.5	10.9	8.1	-15.9	-31.1	17.3	9.1	23.0	13.4	8.7	272
Kilmarnock	T	P	1.4	82.2	16.0	8.8	112.0	47.3	9.2	-9.4	-12.5	-40.7	9.7	7.1	17.3	11.5	11.0	258
Kirkcaldy	T	P	-2.2	156.9	17.3	6.9	113.6	47.4	10.5	16.7	-9.8	-9.5	24.6	4.3	15.6	11.9	10.2	205
Lanark	R	S	-1.9	40.3	16.9	5.5	121.8	40.1	10.2	17.9	-12.3	-34.7	42.3	6.4	19.2	14.9	14.9	172
Motherwell	C	G	-0.4	285.0	13.8	8.2	114.6	43.9	9.9	-1.5	-10.4	-33.6	16.4	8.5	19.1	11.3	9.7	260
Oban	R	S	7.7	63.3	17.1	12.4	123.1	36.6	10.5	8.4	-4.0	-13.9	15.8	4.2	15.9	17.1	13.7	175
Paisley	C	G	-3.6	163.7	15.1	5.4	103.0	48.7	12.6	3.0	-18.1	-47.6	16.2	6.7	16.5	12.1	10.1	257
Perth	T	O	1.5	95.7	20.8	8.1	113.7	48.5	9.6	6.6	-0.4	-7.4	14.1	2.9	10.4	17.8	15.1	110
Peterhead	R	S	17.1	54.9	14.9	23.2	116.9	38.2	10.3	21.6	-5.0	-10.5	28.5	1.2	12.3	12.4	13.2	92
St. Andrews	R	S	-0.8	39.9	22.3	5.3	126.4	43.2	12.6	-18.0	10.0	-39.3	5.4	3.1	11.8	21.6	14.8	155
Stirling	T	O	4.9	71.0	15.8	10.8	111.6	45.0	13.6	34.6	5.1	-12.9	74.9	4.7	13.4	16.9	15.6	66
Stornoway	R	S	11.2	47.3	21.1	12.1	148.5	27.6	15.5	27.9	19.6	-38.8	69.3	0.4	21.1	12.8	12.8	142
Stranraer	R	S	2.7	42.6	18.4	11.3	128.0	36.6	10.4	9.5	-1.2	-3.5	29.8	4.9	17.8	17.3	14.8	196
Thurso	R	S	3.1	48.7	17.3	10.3	122.6	35.7	10.6	13.7	-3.5	16.0	18.0	1.7	14.2	16.4	14.7	148

Appendix 3
The 19-fold classification of Local Labour Market Areas

London

London

Conurbation dominants

Birmingham, Glasgow, Liverpool, Manchester, Newcastle upon Tyne

Provincial dominants

Bristol, Edinburgh, Leeds, Nottingham, Sheffield

Sub-regional dominants

Blackburn, Brighton, Cardiff, Coventry, Middlesbrough, Newport, Portsmouth, Preston, Swansea

London subdominant cities

Aldershot & Farnborough, Maidstone, Medway Towns, Reading, Slough, Southend, Watford

London subdominant towns

Basildon, Basingstoke, Bishop's Stortford, Bracknell, Braintree, Chelmsford, Crawley, Gravesend, Guildford, Harlow, Haywards Heath, Hemel Hempstead, Hertford & Ware, High Wycombe, Horsham, Maidenhead, Newbury, Reigate & Redhill, Sittingbourne & Milton Regis, St Albans, Tunbridge Wells, Welwyn, Woking & Weybridge

Conurbation subdominant cities

Ashton & Hyde, Birkenhead & Wallasey, Bolton, Dudley, Motherwell, Oldham, Paisley, Smethwick, South Shields, Stockport, Walsall, Wigan, Wolverhampton

Conurbation subdominant towns

Ashington, Bury, Buxton, Chester, Coatbridge & Airdrie, Consett, Dumbarton, Durham, Ellesmere Port, Leigh, Macclesfield, Northwich, Redditch, Rochdale, Shotton, Southport, St Helens, Stratford-on-Avon, Tamworth, Warrington, West Bromwich, Widnes & Runcorn

Smaller northern subdominants

Accrington, Barnsley, Bathgate, Bridgend, Castleford & Pontefract, Cwmbran & Pontypool, Dewsbury, Gelligaer, Hartlepool, Heanor, Hinckley, Leamington, Leyland & Chorley, Mansfield, Mexborough, Neath, Newark, Peterlee, Pontypridd, Port Talbot, Rotherham, Rugby, Stockton-on-Tees, Wakefield

Southern freestanding cities

Accrington, Barnsley, Bathgate, Bridgend, Castleford & Pontefract, Cwmbran & Pontypool, Dewsbury, Gelligaer, Hartlepool, Heanor & Ripley, Hinckley, Leamington, Leyland & Chorley, Mansfield, Mexborough, Neath, Newark, Peterlee, Pontypridd, Port Talbot, Rotherham, Rugby, Stockton-on-Tees, Wakefield

Southern freestanding cities

Bournemouth, Cambridge, Exeter, Ipswich, Leicester, Luton, Northampton, Norwich, Oxford, Plymouth, Southampton, Swindon

Northern freestanding cities

Aberdeen, Blackpool, Bradford, Chesterfield, Derby, Doncaster, Dundee, Grimsby, Huddersfield, Hull, Stoke on Trent, Sunderland, York

Southern service towns

Barnstaple, Bath, Boston, Canterbury, Cheltenham, Chichester & Bognor, Clacton, Eastbourne, Folkestone, Hastings, Isle of Wight, Kings Lynn, Lowestoft, Margate & Ramsgate, Newton Abbot, St Austell, Torquay, Weston-Super-Mare, Weymouth, Winchester, Worthing, Yarmouth

Southern commercial towns

Aylesbury, Bedford, Bridgwater, Bury St Edmunds, Colchester, Deal, Dover, Gloucester, Lincoln, Peterborough, Salisbury, Taunton, Trowbridge, Yeovil

Southern manufacturing towns

Andover, Ashford, Banbury, Chippenham, Corby, Gosport & Fareham, Grantham, Kettering, Letchworth, Milton Keynes, Stevenage, Stroud, Wellingborough

Northern service towns

Burnley, Darlington, Dumfries, Harrogate, Inverness, Kendal, Lancaster, Llandudno, Perth, Scarborough, Stirling, Worcester

Northern commercial towns

Ayr & Prestwick, Barrow-in-Furness, Burton on Trent, Carlisle, Crewe, Greenock, Hereford, Keighley, Kidderminster, Kilmarnock, Kirkcaldy,

Loughborough, Nelson & Colne, Rhyl & Prestatyn, Rossendale, Shrewsbury, Stafford, Workington, Worksop

Northern manufacturing towns

Alloa, Bishop Auckland & Aycliffe, Coalville, Dunfermline, Ebbw Vale, Falkirk, Halifax, Irvine, Llanelli, Merthyr Tydfil, Scunthorpe, Telford, Whitehaven, Wrexham.

Southern rural areas

Bideford, Chard, Dereham, Didcot, Falmouth, Huntingdon, Launceston, Melton Mowbray, Newmarket, Penzance, Redruth & Cambourne, Spalding, Stamford, Thetford, Tiverton, Truro, Wells, Wisbech, Woodbridge.

Northern rural areas

Aberystwyth, Ammanford, Arbroath, Banff & Buckie, Bangor, Berwick, Brecon, Bridlington, Cardigan, Carmarthen, Dingwall, Elgin, Evesham, Ffestiniog, Goole, Hawick, Hexham, Holyhead, Lanark, Leek, Malvern, Matlock, Monmouth, Northallerton & Richmond, Oban, Pembroke, Penrith, Peterhead, St Andrews, Stornoway, Stranraer, Thurso, Welshpool

Bibliography

Bibliography

Allon-Smith, R.D. 1982: The evolving geography of the elderly in England and Wales. In Warnes, A.M. (ed.) *Geographical perspectives on the elderly* (Chichester: Wiley), 35–52.

Armstrong, H. and Taylor, J. 1985: *Regional economics and policy.* Oxford: Philip Allan.

Beacham, R. 1984: Economic activity: Britain's workforce 1971–81. *Population Trends* **37**, 6–14.

Berg, L. van den, Drewett, R., Klaassen, L.H., Rossi, A. and Vijverberg, C.H.T. 1982: *Urban Europe: a study of growth and decline* Oxford: Pergamon.

Blackaby, F. (ed.) 1979: *De-Industrialisation.* NIESR Policy Papers 2. London: Heinemann.

Cambridge Economic Policy Group 1980: Urban and regional policy with provisional regional accounts 1966–78. *Cambridge Economic Policy Review* **6**.

Champion, A.G. 1976: Evolving patterns of population distribution in England and Wales 1951–71. *Transactions, Institute of British Geographers New Series* **1**, 401–20.

——1981: Population trends in rural Britain. *Population Trends* **26**, 20–3.

——1983a: *England and Wales '81: a census atlas.* Sheffield: Geographical Association.

——1983b: Population trends in the 1970s. In Goddard and Champion 1983, 187–214.

Champion, A.G., Coombes, M.G. and Openshaw, S. 1983: A new definition of cities. *Town and Country Planning* **52**, 305–7.

Champion, A.G. and Green, A.E. 1985: *In search of Britain's booming towns.* CURDS Discussion Paper 72 (Newcastle upon Tyne: Centre for Urban and Regional Development Studies, University of Newcastle upon Tyne.)

Coates, B.E., Johnston, R.J. and Knox, P.L. 1977: *Geography and inequality.* Oxford: Oxford University Press.

Coates, B.E. and Rawstron, E.M. 1971: *Regional variations in Britain: studies in economic and social geography.* London: Batsford.

Compton, P.A. 1982: The changing population. In Johnston and Doornkamp 1982, 37–73.

Coombes, M.G. (ed.) 1987: *British cities: a tale of two nations.* Oxford: Oxford University Press.

Coombes, M.G., Dixon, J.S., Goddard, J.B., Openshaw, S. and Taylor, P.J. 1982: Functional Regions for the Population Census of Great Britain. In Herbert D.T. and Johnston, R.J. (eds.) *Geography and the urban environment: progress in research and applications* **5** (Chichester: John Wiley), 63–112.

Craig, J. 1983: The growth of the elderly population. *Population Trends* **32**, 28–33.

Damesick, P. 1986: Service industries, employment and regional development in Britain: a review of recent trends and issues. *Transactions, Institute of British Geographers, New Series* **11**, 212–26.

Damesick, P. and Wood, P. (eds.) 1986: *Regional problems, problem regions and public policy in the United Kingdom.* Oxford: Oxford University Press.

Davis, N. 1976: Britain's changing age structure 1931–2011. *Population Trends* **3**, 14–17.

Department of Employment 1984: Regional labour force outlook for Great Britain. *Employment Gazette* **92**, 56–64.

Drewett, R., Goddard, J. and Spence, N. 1976: *British cities: urban population and employment trends 1951–71.* London: Department of the Enviroment.

Ermisch, J. 1980: Women's economic position and demographic changes. *Occasional paper* 19/1. London: Office of Population Censuses and Surveys, 36–63.

——1983: *The political economy of demographic change.* London: Heinemann.

Fothergill, S. and Gudgin, G. 1982: *Unequal growth: urban and regional change in the UK.* London: Heinemann.

——1983: Trends in regional manufacturing employment: the main influences. In Goddard and Champion 1983, 27–50.

Fothergill, S., Kitson, M. and Monk, S. 1985: Urban industrial change: the causes of the urban-rural contrast in manufacturing employment trends. *Inner Cities Research Programme research report* 11. London: HMSO.

Fothergill, S. and Vincent, J. 1985: *The state of the nation: an atlas of Britain in the eighties.* London: Pan.

Frost, M.E. and Spence, N.A. 1983: Unemployment change. In Goddard and Champion 1983, 239–59.

Goddard, J.B. 1983: Structural change in the British space economy. In Goddard and Champion 1983, 1–26

Goddard, J.B. and Champion, A.G. (eds.) 1983: *The urban and regional transformation of Britain.* London: Methuen.

Goddard, J.B. and Coombes, M.G. 1983: Local employment and unemployment data. In Healey, M. (ed.) *Urban and regional industrial research; the changing UK data base.* Norwich: GeoBooks.

Greenhalgh, C. 1979: Male labour force participation in Great Britain. *Scottish Journal of Political Economy* **26**, 275–86.

Green, A.E. 1985: Unemployment duration in the recession: the Local Labour Market Area scale. *Regional Studies* **19**, 111–29.

——1986: The likelihood of becoming and remaining unemployed in Great Britain 1984. *Transactions, Institute of British Geographers New Series* **11**, 37–56.

Green, A.E. and Owen, D.W. 1984: Where have all the jobs gone? *The Geographical Magazine* 56, 346–51.

Green, A.E., Owen, D.W., Champion, A.G., Goddard, J.B. and Coombes, M.G. 1986: What contribution can labour migration make to reducing unemployment? In Hart, P.E. (ed.) *Unemployment and labour market policies* (Aldershot: Gower), 52–81.

Hall, P., 1971: Spatial structure of metropolitan England and Wales. In Chisholm, M., and Manners, G. (eds.), *Spatial policy problems of the*

British economy (Cambridge: Cambridge University Press), 96–125.

Hall, P. and Hay, D., 1980: *Growth centres in the European urban system*. London: Heinemann.

Hall, P., Thomas, R., Gracey, H. and Drewett, R., 1973: *The containment of urban England: 1. Urban and metropolitan growth processes or Megalopolis denied*. London: Allen & Unwin.

Hammond, E. 1968: *An analysis of regional and economic statistics*. Durham: Rowntree Research Unit, University of Durham.

Hawkins, K. 1984: *Unemployment*. Harmondsworth: Penguin, 2nd edn.

House, J.W. (ed.) 1982: *The UK space: resources, environment and the future*. London: Weidenfeld & Nicholson, 3rd edn.

Johnson, J.H., Salt, J. and Wood, P.A. 1974: *Housing and the migration of labour in England and Wales*. Farnborough: Saxon House.

Johnston, R.J. and Doornkamp, J.C. (eds.) 1982: *The changing geography of the United Kingdom*. London: Methuen.

Joshi, H., Layard, R. and Owen, S.J. 1985: Why are more women working in Britain? *Journal of Labour Economics* **3**, 147–77.

Keeble, D. 1976: *Industrial location and planning in the United Kingdom*. London: Methuen.

——1980: Industrial decline, regional policy and the urban–rural manufacturing shift in the United Kingdom. *Environment and Planning A* **12**, 945–62.

Kelsall, R.K. 1979: *Population*. London: Longman, 4th edn.

Kennett, S. and Spence, N. 1979: British population trends in the 1970s. *Town and Country Planning* **48**, 221–4.

Knox, P.L. 1974: Spatial variations in level of living in England and Wales in 1961. *Transactions, Institute of British Geographers* **62**, 1–24.

——1975: *Social well-being: a spatial perspective*. Oxford: Oxford University Press.

Law, C.M. 1981: *British regional development since World War I*. London: Methuen.

Law, C.M. and Warnes, A.M. 1976: The changing geography of the elderly in England and Wales. *Transactions, Institute of British Geographers, New Series* **1**, 453–71.

Lawton, R. 1982: People and work. In House 1982, 103–203.

Lee, T.R. 1977: *Race and residence*. Oxford: Clarendon Press.

Lloyd, P.E. and Dicken, P. 1972: *Location in space: a theoretical approach to economic geography*. London: Harper & Row.

Marquand, J. 1983: The changing distribution of service employment. In Goddard and Champion 1983, 99–134.

Martin, R.L. 1985: Monetarism masquerading as regional policy? The government's new system of regional aid. *Regional Studies* **19**, 379–88.

Martin, T. 1985: *Employment change in the South East Region*. London: The London and South East Regional Planning Conference, Regional Monitoring Group, Employment and Economy Working Party.

Massey, D. 1983: Industrial restructuring and class restructuring: production decentralization and local uniqueness. *Regional Studies* **17**, 73–90.

——1984: *Spatial divisions of labour: social structures and the geography of production*. London: Methuen.

Massey, D. and Meegan, R. 1982: *The anatomy of job loss: the how, why and where of employment decline*. London: Methuen.

Metcalf, D. and Richardson, R. 1984: Labour. In Prest, A.R. and Coppock, D.J. (eds.), *The UK economy: a manual of applied economics*. (London:

Weidenfeld & Nicolson, 10th ed), 243–302.

Moser, C.A. and Scott, W. 1961: *British towns: a statistical study of their social and economic differences*. London: Oliver & Boyd.

Office of Population Censuses and Surveys 1978: *Demographic review 1977: a report on the population in Great Britain*. London: HMSO.

——1979: Population of New Commonwealth and Pakistani ethnic origin: new projections. *Population Trends* **16**, 22–7.

Openshaw, S. and Charlton, M. 1984: The urban face of Britain. *The Geographical Magazine* **56**, 421–4.

Osman, T., 1985: *The facts of everyday life*. London: Faber & Faber.

Owen, D.W., Coombes, M.G. and Gillespie, A.E. 1986: The rural-urban shift and employment change in Britain 1971–81. In Danson, M. (ed.) *Redundancy and Recession: Restructuring the Regions?* (Norwich: GeoBooks).

Owen, D.W., Gillespie, A.E. and Coombes, M.G. 1984: 'Job shortfalls' in British Local Labour Market Areas: a classification of labour supply and demand trends 1971–81. *Regional Studies* **18**, 469–88.

Peach, C. 1968: *West Indian migration to Britain: a social survey*. Oxford: Clarendon Press.

Pinch, S. and Williams, A. 1983: Social class change in British cities. In Goddard and Champion 1983, 135–59.

Regional Studies Association 1984: *Report of an inquiry into the regional problem in the United Kingdom*. Norwich: GeoBooks.

Reward Regional Surveys 1986: *UK regional cost of living report*. Stone: Reward Regional Surveys.

Robert, S. and Randolph, W.G. 1983: Beyond decentralization: the evolution of population distribution in England and Wales, 1961–81. *Geoforum* **14**, 75–102.

Roberston, J.A.S., Briggs, J.M. and Goodchild, A. 1982: *Structure and employment prospects of the service industries*. London: Department of Employment Research Paper 30.

Robinson, O. and Wallace, J. 1984: Growth and utilization of part-time labour in Britain. *Employment Gazette*, September 1984, 391–7.

Runnymede Trust 1980: *Britain's black population*. London: The Runnymede Trust and the Radical Statistics Race Group.

Short, J.R. and Kirby, A.M. (eds.) 1984: *The human geography of contemporary Britain*. Basingstoke: Macmillan.

Smart, M.W. 1974: Labour market areas: uses and definitions. *Progress in Planning* **2**, 239–55.

Smith, D.M. 1979: *Where the grass is greener: living in an unequal world*. Harmondsworth: Penguin.

Spence, N., Gillespie, A., Goddard, J., Kennett, S., Pinch, S. and Williams, A. 1982: *British cities: analysis of urban change*. Oxford: Pergamon.

Townsend, A.R. 1983: *The impact of recession: on industry, employment and the regions, 1976–81*. London: Croom Helm.

——1986: The location of employment growth after 1978: the surprising significance of dispersed centres. *Environment and Planning A* **18**, 529–45.

Vining, D.R. and Pallone, R. 1982: Migration between core and peripheral regions: a description and tentative explanation of the patterns in 22 countries. *Geoforum* **13**, 339–410.

Warnes, A.M. and Law, C.M. 1984: The elderly population of Great Britain: locational trends and policy implications. *Transactions, Institute of*

British Geographers New Series **9**, 37–59.

Webber, R. and Craig, J. 1976: Which local authorities are alike? *Population trends* **5**, 13–19.

White, D. 1985: Tilting Britain onto its side. *New Society*, 14 June, 383–5.

White, M. 1983: Long-term unemployment – labour market aspects. *Employment Gazette*, **9**, 437–43.

Woods, R.I. 1977: A note on the future demographic structure of the coloured population of Birmingham, England. *Journal of Biosocial Science* **9**, 239–50.

Worswick, G.D.N. 1984: Two great recessions: the 1980s and the 1930s in Britain. *Scottish Journal of Political Economy* **31**, 209–28.

Index

Index

Aberdeen, 20, 21, 22, 49, 55, 57, 63, 65, 67, 80, 82, 87, 95, 107, 111
Aberystwyth, 55, 93
Accrington, 38, 40, 44, 49, 52, 98
age structure, 33–8; Great Britain, 33; individual LLMAs, 33–5; *see also* elderly
Airdrie, *see* Coatbridge & Airdrie
Aldershot & Farnborough, 20, 21, 34, 49, 65, 73, 79, 80, 87, 91, 94, 105, 110
Andover, 73, 87
Assisted Areas, 2, 4, 69; *see also* regional policy
Aylesbury, 79, 105, 110

Banbury, 18, 20
Banff & Buckie, 57, 80, 82
Bangor, 55, 79, 82
Basildon, 37, 41
Basingstoke, 18, 20, 21, 37, 40, 41, 49, 63, 65, 73, 105, 110
Bathgate, 40, 41, 91, 94, 105
Birkenhead & Wallasey, 20, 21, 105
Birmingham, 11, 20, 23, 37, 38, 41, 43, 44, 49, 65, 67, 87
Bishops Stortford, 79, 87, 91, 94, 105, 110
Blackburn, 38, 40, 44, 98
Blackpool, 98
Bognor, *see* Chichester & Bognor
Bolton, 44
Borders, 41, 52
Bournemouth, 20, 21, 37, 38, 65
Bracknell, 20, 21, 37, 38, 40, 49, 94, 105, 110
Bradford, 20, 21, 40, 41, 43, 44, 49, 52, 95
Braintree, 40
Bridgend, 52
Brighton, 20, 21, 41, 49, 69
Bristol, 11, 24, 37
Buckie, *see* Banff & Buckie
Burnley, 38, 40, 44, 52
Bury, 40
Bury St Edmunds, 18, 80, 87, 105

Camborne, *see* Redruth & Camborne

Cambridge, 4, 55, 65, 105
Canterbury, 55
car availability, 94–7; Great Britain, 90; Zones, 90–1; individual LLMAs, 94–6; regional divisions, 95, 97; LLMA classes, 99–100
Cardigan, 107
Carmarthen, 111
Castleford & Pontefract, 91
central Scotland, 4, 63, 67, 93, 95, 107
central southern England, 57, 73, 99
Chard, 37
Chelmsford, 20, 21, 34, 105
Cheltenham, 65, 107
Chester, 52, 69, 93
Chichester & Bognor, 37
Chippenham, 79
Chorley, *see* Leyland & Chorley
Cities, *see* LLMA size groups
Clacton, 33, 34, 37, 38, 41, 98
Clydeside, 41, 52, 83; *see also* Glasgow; west central Scotland
Coatbridge & Airdrie, 41, 65, 79, 80, 94, 105, 107
Colchester, 20
Colne, *see* Nelson & Colne
Consett, 20, 21, 49, 55, 65, 69, 79, 80, 82, 105, 107
Conurbation Dominants, *see* LLMA classes; LLMA size groups
Conurbation Subdominants, *see* LLMA classes
Corby, 37, 38, 40, 49, 65, 69, 79, 80, 82, 91, 93, 98, 105, 107
Cores, *see* Zones
Cornwall, 55
Cotswolds, 69
counterurbanization, 3; *see also* decentralization; urban–rural shift
County Durham, 93
Coventry, 20, 37, 65, 69
Crawley, 37, 40, 44, 52, 79, 87, 98, 105, 110
Cumbria, 67, 73, 93

daily urban system, 7
decentralization, 3, 17, 18, 93; *see also*

139